YO-AVB-151

Sport Diving
The Instructional Guide to Skin & Scuba

Mort Walker

Henry Regnery Company · Chicago

Library of Congress Cataloging in Publication Data

Walker, Morton.
  Sport diving.

  Bibliography: p.
  Includes index.
  1. Skin diving.   I. Title.
GV840.S78W34   1977   797.2'3   76-6289
ISBN 0-8092-8176-7
ISBN 0-8092-7855-3 pbk.

Copyright© 1977 by Morton Walker
All rights reserved
Published by Henry Regnery Company
180 North Michigan Avenue, Chicago, Illinois 60601
Manufactured in the United States of America
Library of Congress Catalog Card Number: 76-6289
International Standard Book Number: 0-8092-8176-7 (cloth)
                                 0-8092-7855-3 (paper)

Published simultaneously in Canada by
Beaverbooks
953 Dillingham Road
Pickering, Ontario L1W 1Z7
Canada

To Joan Walker, my land-based buddy,
who enjoys sport diving vicariously

Contents

Acknowledgments   ix
Foreword   xi
Preface   xv

1   Underwater Sport for Everyone   1
2   Underwater Swimming Requirements   13
3   Skin-Diving Equipment   35
4   Scuba-Diving Gear   66
5   Preparing to Use Scuba   114
6   How to Operate Underwater   129
7   Underwater Physiology   146
8   Physical Law Demands Underwater   159
9   Diving Know-how   173
10   Averting the Hazards of Scuba Diving   203
11   Particular Diving Precautions   218
12   Putting Your Diving Skill into Action   239
Appendix 1: Glossary   251
Appendix 2: Aquadoc Listings for All Regions   255
Appendix 3: International Listing of Recompression
          Chambers   262
Appendix 4: Self-Grading System for Scuba   283
Appendix 5: Equipment Suppliers   285
Appendix 6: Scuba Certification Programs   292
Appendix 7: Questions Diving Instructors Often Ask
          and Answer   293
Appendix 8: Bibliography   299
Index   302

The Sage of the Deep (a song of scuba divers)

Arcadio (Cai-Cai) Cicilia
Bonaire, Netherlands Antilles

All who would dive for pleasure
Swim the reefs or search for treasure
Enjoy the life beneath the sea
Like the fishes swimming free

Hear the jumble of your bubbles
Leaving all your surface troubles
Watch the reefs and don't destroy them
Feed the fish and don't annoy them

Make your diving safe and fun
Learn to walk before you run
Go below and have no fear
There's a presence always near

Follow the rules wherever you roam
And underwater you'll be at home
In ocean deep or river broad
You'll know that you have found—Sod.*

* Sod is the mythical god of Bonairian divers, a kind of
  King Neptune who keeps them protected against harm.

Published with permission of Arcadio (Cai-Cai) Cicilia

Photograph by Jo Furman.

Acknowledgments

The idea for this book has been germinating for years. One day I brought it to Richard Curtis, my literary representative; he said, "Fine, write an outline and I'll see if a publisher is interested." With acceptance by the Henry Regnery Company, I followed the outline and began to contact participants in the sport and industry of diving for information and photographs. The result of our joint efforts is reflected here. I owe a lot of people a thank you!

First, I am grateful to a pioneer in the industry: Ed Brawley, President of the Professional Diving Instructor College and Ed Brawley's Skin Diving School, Monterey, California. Ed read my manuscript for accuracy. Then he sent me quantities of photographs to illustrate it.

Next I thank the two photographer stars who adorn these pages with their pictures, Jo Furman and Bruce "Teacher" Bowker, for their graphic accompaniment to my attempt to express with words. Their underwater photography technique is unsurpassed.

Gayle Anspack, diving instructor of Cayman Kai Resort Ltd., a diving resort at Grand Cayman, B.W.I., also sent photographs, and led me to underwater scenes of unsurpassed beauty.

I thank Ginny Casey and Manny Berlinrut of the Bonaire Tourist Information Office, whose lively interest in my project stimulated my travel to Bonaire, Netherlands Antilles, where many of the photographs reproduced here were taken. It was there that I met Jo Furman, Bruce "Teacher" Bowker, and that swashbuckling character and expert diver, Captain Don Stewart.

Outstandingly helpful was Ron Ribaudo of Ribaudo and Schaefer, Inc., the advertising agency for Frank Sanger's two companies, Parkway Fabricators and Poseidon Systems, U.S.A. Both of these diving industry people deserve recognition.

Of the various equipment manufacturers participating in this project for the welfare of the sport diver, C. Ed Pemberton, Jr., formerly of Dacor Corporation, was most conspicuously cooperative. Also assisting with photographs and catalogues were U.S. Nemrod, Inc., U.S. Divers Company, Healthways, Scubapro, Sportsways, Aquadive, Inflatable Systems, Inc., Helle Engineering, Inc., Scuba Spec., Inc., Royak, Inc., Aqua Bell Corporation, and others.

I acknowledge such underwater sport information sources as *Oceans* magazine, *Sea Frontiers*, the U.S. Navy Experimental Diving Unit, and *Skin Diver* magazine. Jack McKenney, *Skin Diver*'s former editor, was kind enough to allow reproduction of a rare photograph taken on the decks of the sunken *Andrea Doria*. Especially, I give acknowledgment to Jon Hardy, General Manager of the National Association of Underwater Instructors (NAUI), who filled my material need for more and better instruction for the new sport diver. Dennis Graver, National Training Director of the Professional Association of Diving Instructors, Inc., lent me a load of informational material too. John Gaffney, Executive Director of the National Association of Skin Diving Schools, contributed information that filled a need. Medical facts for Chapter 11 come from *Emergency Medicine* and William L. Orris, M.D.

Most of all I appreciate my wife, Joan Walker, who found me isolated during the writing of this book. With the utmost of understanding, she did all that she could to sustain me. Although she is not a diver, Joan travels to diving sites with me. She enjoys the sport secondhand and expresses a delightful enthusiasm for it.

—Morton Walker, D.P.M.

Foreword

Every diver knows that scuba diving is the most spectacular sport available to the public today. Fortunately, such books as Dr. Morton Walker's *Sport Diving: The Instructional Guide to Skin and Scuba* provide a preview of the excitement and rewards inherent in it.

I know that the thousands of readers exposed to this guidebook will feel the same enthusiasm that comes through in its writing. People's imaginations are bound to be stimulated by the vast amount of information packed into its contents. I have read the instructional sections thoroughly—twice, in fact—and I affirm that the diving information offered here is accurate and useful. Now I hope that readers who become infected with Dr. Walker's lively interest in the subject will apply their new knowledge. Expectantly, they will act on the desire to take the next step and go to a professional instructor for the proper training.

Over the past few years diving has been changing and evolving so fast that one finds it almost impossible to keep up with what has been happening. New items of equipment and new and better diving techniques have been developed and introduced. They make diving safe for almost anyone. Today we understand that safe use of scuba is a matter of proper training, not of brute strength. With instructors simulating every possible emergency

situation that could arise underwater and teaching how to con-
front it, each student is able to handle himself properly.

Everyone who has been involved with the teaching of diving or
has worked at being a diver originally dived as a hobby. There
simply was not enough money in the sport for people to become
full-time instructors or to make a living as professional scuba
divers. Now the circumstances are all changed. The modern
professional diving instructor is more skilled than any instructor of
the past and positions are open to professional scuba divers all
over the world. Equipment specialists are trained as counselors to
handle any questions on the subject—a tremendous improvement
over clerks who used to hand people a box and say that the
instructions were inside. Dive shops, which are now specialty
stores, direct their efforts to assist the aspiring diver from his
training period all the way through the buying process for suitable
equipment. Dive shops also act as the center of diving activities,
and even provide information on travel to diving areas around the
world.

From my position in the industry, I can see the direction diving
and its enthusiasts are taking. The social side of diving is
beginning to appear and new resorts are catering to that special
type of clientele. Resorts are coming to realize that it is
advantageous to keep divers warm and comfortable and let them
mingle with other divers in surroundings reminiscent of the
atmosphere around a ski lodge. Boat trips have been arranged
that accommodate only divers and their companions. The
managers of resorts and trips are getting training on how to take
care of almost all the needs of a diver, including on-the-spot
equipment service.

As travel becomes easier and less expensive, more and more
people will travel to exotic diving spots around the world to
sample different areas for underwater sport. Surely, this sort of
recreational activity must eventually become an important part of
the diving industry.

Every indication points to the prediction that soon new equipment will be marketed to sport divers to open up the great depths
of the oceans—the continental shelf, as an illustration. Thus the

future of the diving industry, and the future of underwater sport as well, is limited only by imagination.

Moving sport diving ahead and providing for its future is now a big business, employing thousands of dedicated men and women throughout the world. This informative and exciting book will establish a valuable link among the diving industry professionals, the nondiving public, and the advanced amateur sport divers already indoctrinated in the glories of the sport. Primarily, though, it is on behalf of diving professionals that I wish to thank Dr. Morton Walker for this fascinating, very readable, and worthwhile undertaking.

—Ed Brawley
President, Professional Diving Instructor College

Preface

Overhead, cotton-candy clouds were pink in a pale blue sky; under the water's surface great fish cruised by. The diver hovered, neutrally buoyant, waiting for the decompression minutes to tick by. Just below him was the subsea drop-off with its cobalt-blue abyss falling to 6,000 feet. Near the cliff edge were beautiful underwater gardens: massive coral hummocks, narrow coral canyons, long coral tunnels; great tangles of brightly decorated sea fans, rubbery-fingered sponges of purple, green, and orange, willowy sea plumes and flowering gorgonians. "Magnificent," he thought. "I'm lucky to see it—too bad more people can't."

I was that diver, and the place was the picturesque North Wall at Grand Cayman Island, British West Indies. The experience left me determined to bring the beautiful deep to landlocked people.

The best way to do it, I believed, was with an all-inclusive instructional book. I decided to report everything I could about sport diving for use and enjoyment by both sexes, all ages, the physically and emotionally fit and those who wish to be, adventurers, the science-minded, recreationalists, explorers, admirers of natural artistry, and those many individuals seeking more fulfillment out of life.

Much of myself is in this book—places I've dived and experiences I've had. My intent is to educate people about proper diving technique with graphic examples from real life. Hopefully, too, this method makes reading entertaining and animates a potentially dry subject. Stories of diver danger and escape are put there too, in order to emphasize the lesson to be learned: diving is easy and pleasant, when you feel secure in your knowledge.

No one is likely to master the intricacies of scuba diving merely from reading a book. Rather, direct training is needed, training in open water by a professional instructor—skin diving begins with instruction, and a certified professional instructor is the only one who should teach you how to use scuba equipment. But this book is a ready informational reference, and will answer most diving questions when the professional instructor is not around. It includes all of the currently correct procedures taught by the major diving instructor organizations. I am convinced that enjoyable sport diving begins with education, with self-confidence in the subject. I have tried to supply that education in print and pictures.

A reader-diver should also have the opportunity to independently make adjustments to his own equipment without having to pay a tradesman to do it. Anyone can punch a hole in a strap or shave lead slivers from a weight. Where I have found some alteration in gear easy and useful, I explain how to accomplish it. The option then lies with you—make the repair yourself or turn it over to a craftsman. Diving may or may not be a do-it-yourself sport, depending on your handiness and know-how. At the least, you should have the liberty to choose.

Scuba diving offers you a sense of freedom not found in any other sport—even in skydiving. This is actual physical freedom, with zero gravity. Diving lets you fly through the underwater depths in three dimensions. By itself, this ease of movement brings peace of mind, a freedom from restriction with no limitation and no attachments. Combined with the vastness of area and enrapturing beauty of the underwater world, this feeling fills the mind with a kind of grave exaltation; it leaves one awestruck by some metaphysical fourth dimension.

The people who take part in sport diving are genuine, marvelously open, friendly, and helpful. Actually, they have to be that way, because they depend on each other. But this camaraderie is inherent in the sport's environment, for underwater everyone is made to be democratic. How much wealth you have, what job you work, or who you know is far less important than the submarine adventure you face at the moment. Don an exposure suit and suddenly you're just another one of the divers. Skin diving is the great equalizer, and the only inconstants are your personal judgment, diving skill, and physical and emotional fitness.

This book is written for the novice diver who needs the theory before he tries the experience, for the advanced amateur seeking new vistas for exploration, and finally for the professional diving instructor who prefers to supplement teaching with text readings. All the staples are here, and there are garnishments for the serious diving buff who wants to put diving skills to work.

My original goal has been achieved; I believe I've written the book I first envisioned. When I hover now over the cliff edge of that Cayman Island Wall and peer into the indigo depths of its unfathomable void, I know that I am not alone: you are with me, and so are divers everywhere. The book is here; the rest is up to you.

—Morton Walker, D.P.M.
October 1, 1976

1

Underwater Sport
for Everyone

Diving, for pleasure, profit, and excitement, is growing more popular each year. I predict that by the year 2000 it will equal or surpass golf and tennis as a recreational pastime. Four million scuba enthusiasts were counted in 1975, and the number of snorkel divers, while uncountable, has been projected in the tens of millions. Increasing numbers of skin divers want to explore, photograph, and move as they please without surface attachment in the underwater world of innerspace, the area of unexplored beauty and vast natural resources that lies underwater.

Earth's innerspace is becoming increasingly accessible to the average person who dons self-contained underwater breathing apparatus, scuba. Innerspace gives us water for parched countries, harvests of many edible varieties of marine life, almost half of the world's oil, submerged mountains of ores and minerals. Yet engineers know less of this region than they do about outer space.

Sport divers are helping to change all that. The National Association of Underwater Instructors has, each year for the past five years, reported an increase of almost 35 percent in new certified scuba diver enrollment. Other certifying agencies report

The underwater world is becoming increasingly accessible to the average sportsperson—male and female—who dons self-contained underwater breathing apparatus (scuba).

Photograph courtesy of Dacor Corporation.

similar interest in new certifications. Skin diving, in fact, is expanding faster than any other water sport in the United States, with 3,800 certified active scuba instructors in the nation. About 5,000 skin-diving equipment retailers sell diving masks, fins, and snorkels, and 2,500 scuba equipment retailers sell a full line of diving equipment and supplies. This does not include the extra snorkel gear sold incidentally in toy stores, pharmacies, variety stores, and other outlets.

Outside of the United States, about 150 sport diving resorts in the Bahamas, the Caribbean, Mexico, and the Pacific cater to the diver's needs; there are at least another fifty in the Mediterranean, the Red Sea, and the Indian Ocean. The current trend in diving is toward resort travel and vacation diving. There's a heavy accent on the social aspects of this activity—39.3 percent of all skin diving participants travel outside the continental United States on dive trips and diving vacations. Another 67.7 percent of diving enthusiasts are journeying outside their resident states on dive trips and vacations within this country. The average distance these divers travel each year is 2,155 miles.

Who Is a Diver?

Who are all these underwater sport enthusiasts? The median age of the active diver is twenty-six and a half years, with 57.2 percent of them in the eighteen-to-thirty-four age bracket. However, some divers are already collecting social security. In Barbados, one of the Windward Islands of the British West Indies, I spoke with an American woman, a grandmother, diving with her grandchildren. Her own two sons were unable to dive; one had lung disease from cigarette smoking and the other had rapid heart palpitations. She was making three dives a day.

Many middle-aged people are turning to skin diving as a way to lend excitement to their lives. More and more they are making an appreciable entry into this greatest and most thrilling of sports. They are well educated, too, with 67.8 percent having attended college or graduate school.

According to the sport's leading magazine, *Skin Diver,* the diver's median household income in 1974 was $19,455. At least 89.6 percent of underwater sports people own one camera or more; 50.5 percent own one or more boats, at an average cost of $3,229. Their average investment in diving equipment is $703, and they spend an estimated total of $150,000,000 annually on retail diving equipment, dive trips, air refills, repairs, etc. Approximately one-third of this amount is paid out for travel and vacation diving.

All these figures are verified by an annual reported growth rate in diving industry sales of 20 percent. Thus, in answer to the question of who is a diver, the reply is, everyone who wants to dive.

Types of Diving

Skin diving technically refers to swimming on the surface and under the surface of the water while making use of certain advantageous swimming equipment. It is a catchall term that takes in the employment of scuba as well as the simple use of snorkel gear.

Snorkel diving is swimming with the use of a rubber or plastic breathing tube. The big advantage of snorkeling is that it's easier and less tiring to swim with your head down and your face in the water than it is to lift your face above the surface to breathe.

Snorkel divers wear face masks for clear underwater vision. Human eyes have lentil-shaped lenses, unlike the spherical eyes of

Skin Diving is a catchall term that takes in the employment of scuba as well as the simple use of snorkeling gear. Technically, it refers to swimming on the surface and under the surface while making use of certain advantageous swimming equipment. *Photograph courtesy of Bonaire, in the Dutch Caribbean.*

fish; they cannot focus when they are in direct contact with water, and cannot compensate for light refraction, which is seen as a sparkling blue haze. The tempered glass faceplate of the face mask lets you see the tiny details of a lake, river, or sea bottom by keeping out the water. It also enlarges objects by one-third, making them seem one-third closer than they actually are, but this can be adjusted to.

The free breathing of the snorkel tube lets you keep a constant watch on the scenery below. That's the great fun of snorkeling —eavesdropping on the activities of interesting fish, mollusks, polyps, or water worms. When a snorkeler wants a closer look he can keep a sea creature in sight as he surface dives.

Snorkelers also wear fins or flippers on their feet. These propulsive devices, usually made of firm rubber, provide you with more efficient use of energy and faster transport through the water.

To give yourself negative buoyancy after a surface dive and prevent an unwanted ascent, you can attach a weight belt to your waist. This extra weight allows you to steady yourself on the bottom without holding on to an underwater object. But over-weighing is inadvisable because it makes you expend too much energy; it can make you become exhausted in a short time.

Ed Brawley, President of the Professional Diving Instructor College, Monterey, California, suggests that positive buoyancy is lost for a breath-holding diver at ten or twelve feet because his lungs compress. He will be at neutral buoyancy below that depth. If you want to skin dive wearing a wet suit, find your neutral buoyancy at ten feet. Then you will be positively buoyant by only five pounds at the surface.

Free diving takes in both the breath-holding snorkel diver and the scuba diver with a tank on his back and a regulator in his mouth to deliver air on demand. The term conveys the feeling that an underwater swimmer has the freedom of a fish. You can maneuver how and where you like underwater. Free diving does not include the natural diver who uses no diving aids. *Skin diving* and *free diving* are often used interchangeably, but the descriptive term of "breath-holding" or "compressed-air-breathing" should go with the form of free diving you are speaking of.

The most primitively equipped breath-holding free divers are the Japanese Ama, who descend seventy-five feet or more for 100 dives a day in their search for seafood.   The only diving

Free diving indicates that an underwater swimmer has the freedom of a fish. It's your option to maneuver how and where you want. But the term is used interchangeably with *skin diving* and applies to the breath-holding snorkel diver as well as the scuba diver with a tank on her back and a regulator in her mouth that delivers air on demand. Shown is a scuba diver swimming free!

Photograph courtesy of Bonaire Tourist Information Office.

accessories these women may use are wet suits, weights, and underwater goggles. The goggles fit over their eye sockets, with a small pear-shaped rubber bulb projecting from the side of each eyecup. As the diver descends, mounting water pressure forces air from the bulb into the eyecup, relieving presure on the eye socket. To prevent fogging, the divers rub their goggles with mugwort, whose juices form a protective film on the glass. Wet suits are a newly introduced innovation for these divers; their weights are still heavy rocks, carried down in their arms.

Opening Innerspace to Youngsters

There's no greater pleasure than teaching a youngster to snorkel for his first time out. A child enjoys being introduced to this secret wonder world where every observer becomes an immediate, enthusiastic amateur scientist. Snorkeling gives children and adults the opportunity to explore innerspace together.

The wonder-filled watery world is opened to the eyes of surface skimmers with the face mask. Beautiful plants, colorful sponges, odd-shaped corals, and weird and handsome animals of all sizes and forms make this domain a child's natural habitat. Your youngsters—even as young as four years—can share with you the fun and excitement of exploring it after you teach them how to snorkel.

Beautiful plants, colorful sponges, odd-shaped corals, weird and handsome animals of all sizes and forms make this domain a child's natural habitat. Here is a sea anemone nestled in a tube sponge in the waters of Bonaire, Netherlands Antilles. *Photograph by Aaron Furman, Jr.*

Teenage Sport Divers

Of course, teenagers newly participating in this most educational
of sports gain the most from scuba diving. Nothing matures a
person faster than scuba certification. Here the teen must learn to
work in a group, follow orders, and keep a cool head. Early in the
instruction, he learns that drugs, alcohol, and cigarette smoking
will prevent him from being a good diver. In fact, these
temporary stimulants used underwater may even endanger his
life.

Education about our universe is one of the outstanding benefits
of diving. Since 70 percent of the Earth is covered by water, the
teen discovers that much of the future lies in the oceans. It is a
place in which virtually all fields of human endeavor must come
together—engineering, botany, biology, archaeology, medicine,
geology, other areas of science, and even economics.

To pursue this endeavor further, a knowledge of scuba diving
and underwater techniques is needed. It's a skill that is valuable
for youngsters to acquire early. Although the YMCA requirement
is fifteen years of age or older for scuba certification, some
certifying agencies give junior instruction at age twelve. When I
ask my own young son Jules what he's going to be when he grows
up, he unhesitatingly answers: "I'm going to be an oceanographer!"

Women Make the Best Divers

Since diving is uninteresting for mere spectators, many otherwise
uninvolved people have been forced into participation. Women
of all ages and occupations have found skin diving comfortable
and enjoyable. The secret for diving success is to avoid diving
while wearing misfit gear. Properly fitted diving dress and the
right type of equipment make a world of difference—maximum
enjoyment or miserable cold and fright.

Women are becoming even more enthusiastic about diving than
are men because watermanship doesn't demand great physical
strength. Instead, it's necessary to use correct and comfortable
equipment with a background of excellent training. And training

course openings are being reserved for women more and more. For example, at the University of California, Santa Cruz, in each year's quarter, the basic and the ocean diving sections are divided, with half the vacant spaces reserved for women and half for men. The University has a supply of fifty-cubic-foot tanks for smaller people (both male and female) so that the sheer weight and bulk of scuba gear are diminished.

It may be a form of reverse sexism, but throughout the sport women are being encouraged to become teaching assistants and instructors. The result is inevitable—when nondiving women see other women in positions of authority in this traditionally men's sport, they will find the enthusiasm to participate themselves.

It has been proved that women make the best divers and swimmers. Two scientists, Dr. David R. Pendergast and Dr. Donald W. Rennie, physiologists at the State University of New York, Buffalo, have found after a three-year study of swimming efficiency that women are more efficient in the water than men.

The scientists performed their studies in a sixty-meter circular swimming tank, hooking up swimmers to energy-measuring devices that were monitored during the tests. They learned that humans are fairly inefficient in the water, men even more than women: "Females are about 5 percent efficient," says Dr. Pendergast, "and males are only 3 percent efficient." This is because the greater amount of fatty tissues in women's chests and legs makes them more buoyant than men. While a male uses energy just to stay horizontal, a female can use her energy to propel herself. Because of this, a woman expends 30 percent less energy swimming the same distance at the same velocity as a man.

Scuba Diving After Forty

The diving grandmother who accompanies her grandchildren underwater and leaves her sick sons on the beach is not uncommon. Scuba diving after the age of forty is more and more being adopted as part of a lifestyle.

There is *no maximum age* for diving. The Underwater Explorers Club, the headquarters for the International Underwater Explorers Society, Ltd., Freeport, Grand Bahamas, has proved that three hours is enough time to adequately train novices, forty years old and older, so they can experience an exciting open-water dive. John Englander, the Society's president, explains, "We conduct a daily three-hour instruction, which is designed around the resort vacationer. It consists of several hours of instruction in our pool and deep tank, describing basic skills. The following day the participant goes out to the coral reef with an instructor on a scuba dive."

Wally Schirra, one of the United States' original astronauts and a scuba diver, says: "A person doesn't have to be a daredevil or an adventurer to take up scuba diving. If you can breathe, you can dive!"

Business and industry are establishing a growing interest in the fitness of their employees. This makes good sense from a management viewpoint. Company-sponsored fitness programs and weight-control programs tend to reduce absenteeism, accidents, and sick pay. What's more, employees in good physical condition are more alert and more productive, and their morale is higher. Fitness for scuba diving fits into the scheme of things. It promotes enthusiasm in a healthy hobby and provides camaraderie among fellow workers who join together in scuba diving clubs. Not the least of these employee participants in diving are people over the ages of fifty and sixty.

Underwater swimming offers you a variety of therapeutic effects to lengthen life. It strengthens the muscles of the respiratory system and tends to reduce the resistance to air flow. As a consequence, more air is taken into the lungs and more oxygen pumped into the blood stream. This, in turn, causes a strengthening of the heart and a greater pumping efficiency to send this cell-rejuvenating blood around the body.

Scuba and skin diving help to tone up muscles throughout the body, thereby improving the general circulation, lowering blood pressure, and reducing work on the heart. Thus, the final effect won't be to burden the heart muscle with more work but to relax its work load. The blood circulating through the body carries with it a higher ratio of oxygen bonded in hemoglobin in its red cells. A greater amount of oxygen is carried to every body cell—something anyone over forty can use.

Diving with Disabilities

Through the three-hour scuba diving course mentioned earlier, the Underwater Explorers Club has taught, among others, paraplegics, amputees, asthmatics, and at least one blind person. Diving holds no limitation for people with disabilities. That's true primarily because underwater they are weightless, equal to people with full physical abilities. There is no gravitational pull to overcome.

For example, two men from different areas, despite being completely incapacitated in their legs because of accidents, have learned to enjoy the thrill of sport diving to its fullest, with most of the skills of able-bodied divers. Having been confined to a wheelchair for more than two years after a mountain climbing fall, Mike Leiser took instructions at Midwest Divers Supply, Fort Collins, Colorado. He now enjoys the undersea sport as fully as any other diver. Denny R. Wood of Miami, Florida, although he is paralyzed from the mid-chest level down, has done a lot of activities underwater: night dives, spearfishing, underwater photography, shelling, lobstering, and even some very cautious cave diving.

Mental Outlook

No matter what your life's work may be, you can't help but acquire a different perspective when you've traveled beneath the sea. Take a look at the most desolate wasteland beach and realize that under the surface of the water beyond it, there is a fantastic world of color and beauty that pales anything on land. Diving gets you to a place of quiet, too, which will be a respite from traffic, people, noise, telephones, and newspapers. You are weightless—you can glide or soar, leap, swim, or float. There is no other experience like it. You feel carefree and relaxed.

Scuba diving offers a very important emotional experience, one

Under the surface of the water there is a fantastic world of color, and shapes, and beauty that pales anything on land.   *Photograph by Jo Furman.*

that is needed in today's hectic, trouble-filled living. As human beings, we are born with a nervous system geared for flight and hunting. But sitting in an office all day or standing at an assembly line or watching television in the evening gives virtually no vent to this nervous energy. All that nervousness changes under water.

Facing the unknown with its pleasures and precautions beneath ocean, river, or lake can give anyone enough excitement, thrill, and challenge to last from dive to dive. Your ability to cope in unusual circumstances is tested, and that is a physically healthy and mentally beneficial circumstance. It forces you to rely on your personal ability and to come to terms with life as it actually is—cold water, poor visibility, the equipment you must rely upon, the need to make sure your body is in perfect working order. This is a far cry from turning the key to start the motor of a 300-horsepower automobile—and you won't get mugged or run over by a car underwater, either.

2

Underwater Swimming Requirements

Your Need for Watermanship

Sport diving demands some advanced knowledge to ensure that you'll be safe and happy underwater. It will give you fun and adventure if you learn its essentials and practice its skills.

Anyone who decides to invest time, energy, and money in a course of instruction does it with an expectation of some good result. But seldom will you or I invest in the educational process itself. We sign up, instead, to get the results of that process—something we can use to improve the quality of life. Underwater sport diving does just that. It supplies stirring experiences, great fun, and thrilling adventure.

Before any of this can come about, however, you are going to have to learn diving's requirements and apply your new training. If you have yet to take a skin diving course but are considering doing it, you should be aware of one underlying aptitude that first you must possess. That is watermanship.

Watermanship is self-confidence in floatability, physical coordination, health in body and mind, and ability to swim. These psychological and physiological components allow you the sense

13

of security that's needed for scuba and skin diving. The fear and anxiety associated with venturing into a foreign environment are normal, but watermanship helps set them aside. It lets you find yourself at home on the surface of the water and under it.

Ed Brawley tells me that sometimes one never realizes watermanship: "I think there is no one particular skill that a person will have to make him a good diver. Even expert swimmers sometimes have a lot of trouble and can't feel at home *under* the water. The danger is that they revert to swimming training. Their urge is to return to the surface and safety, which is not the best practice in most cases. The best procedure, we find, is for new divers to learn proper technique during the diver training program. The only way to gain a sense of security is to repeat the scuba training exercises over and over again. That's the way to feel secure."

How can you finally manage watermanship? The task takes some personal conditioning of your body. You are going to have to set a few goals and pass certain fitness self-tests.

Swimming Requirements
The Council for National Cooperation in Aquatics, where official representatives from national aquatic organizations come together to help advance the field, have suggested the minimum standards for a diving course candidate. He/she must be able to—

1. Tread water for three minutes with feet only.
2. Swim 300 yards without fins.
3. Tow an inert swimmer forty yards without fins.
4. Stay afloat for fifteen minutes without any type of accessories or aids.
5. Swim underwater for fifteen yards without fins and without a pushoff.

The ability to accomplish these requirements indicates some degree of watermanship for self-preservation. You must be able to fill these requirements just to enroll in a basic scuba course. Because skin and scuba diving are definitely physical sports, participants must be in good physical condition, with knowledge of the basic swimming skills, and must feel confidence in their own watermanship so that panic won't strike under emergency conditions. Some professional instructors have told me that they have made excellent divers even out of nonswimmers. Having swimmers in the class, though, is a lot easier on the instructor. And swimming skill is important for secure watermanship.

Watermanship Guidelines

For training in basic scuba skills, the instructor associations of this country have established some guidelines. The basic minimum requirement for training and certification in the National YMCA Scuba Program, for example, is a 300- to 400-yard swim exercise. This requirement is part of every course, along with a long list of other water skills. The Professional Association of Diving Instructors (PADI) basic scuba course insists on a 400-yard swim with all scuba gear on. And the National Association of Underwater Instructors (NAUI) diver certification program requires a 440-yard swim with snorkel gear in ten minutes or less. As indicated, most of the instructor associations clearly define the skills and tests for watermanship.

This kind of watermanship can't be considered a one-shot fitness test of swimming skill, either. While scuba diving with all gear worn, it's not uncommon for the ascended diver to perform a quarter-mile (440 yards) swim on the surface—against currents and wave action, too. With an air tank on his back, a surface swimmer is forced to assume an angle in the water that increases his cross-sectional area, thus slowing his progress.

Laboring against surface currents calls for swimming skills, but instincts for swimming actually interfere with diving techniques. A person who learns to dive must use intelligence and suitable equipment, and one of the watermanship alterations he must make is to train away the human survival instinct to swim. Training in watermanship includes the ability to willfully desist from dog-paddling out of the unnatural water environment. It is not easy to set aside the urge to hold your head high and out of the water to breathe through your nose. Pulling in air through the snorkel in an emergency situation takes practice and exertion of the will. It encompasses a basic reconditioning of the instinct to escape.

Ed Brawley's instructors admit, for example, that a person who gets totally tired in the ocean feels compelled to escape it. He or she heads for shore or for a distant rock to hold on to, but that's taking a wrong action. It actually increases the danger by making the swimmer work harder and get more tired. The proper action to overcome fatigue is to float face-down in the water and rest, using the snorkel to breathe. That's watermanship!

"Underwater with scuba," says Brawley's teaching manual, "if a person feels uncomfortable, the escape instinct would be to head for the surface as fast as possible. Again—the completely wrong response." Knowing what to do is having scuba diving skill, but having the confidence to carry out proper procedure even in the face of your survival instinct—that is watermanship.

An incident I was involved in may point up how important watermanship is. Diving in a group off Andros Island, Bahamas, my diving companion was a sixteen-year-old boy. We had just ascended from a current-tossed dive of thirty minutes at 50 feet. Our approach to shore was against the wind, with choppy swells that had begun while we were underwater. Salt spray was splashing against our face masks.

My young companion's complexion had turned as blue as the water. I noticed that he shivered with cold. Raw chills made his teeth rattle around his regulator mouthpiece. The thin wet-suit top he wore was insufficient for the unusual refrigerated currents we had met on the bottom, and I guessed that the neoprene of his wet suit had lost much of its insulating effect from its compression at depth.

Also, down there the air we breathed from our cylinders was cooled under pressure and then expanded through an orifice when we inhaled it. This expansion cooled the air even more. Any diver taking in compressed air has to heat each breath to 98.6° F. for use internally. That was an added chilling effect for my sixteen-year-old buddy, already overexposed to cold currents and wearing reduced insulation. He was being chilled inside and out. At that moment he needed all the watermanship he possessed.

As we flippered together toward shore, I observed an obvious example of poor prior training and what you must safeguard against. He seemed unable to make any progress. Twice I stopped my surface advance and swam back ten yards to fetch him. The second time I pulled the safety buckle on his weight belt and carried his leads with me to relieve him of the burden.

He grabbed hold of me and stuttered that he felt the cold fingers of panic snatching at him. "I feel like I'm going to sink," the boy said. "I can hardly breathe!" He was still inhaling dehydrated compressed air through his regulator. My troubled buddy persisted in humidifying each breath from his own vapors. I forced him to substitute the snorkel for his regulator. I knew that inhaling atmospheric air would let him breathe more easily. He resumed swimming toward the shore.

Fatigue and water pressure had made the boy feel as if he could not inhale deeply, and the animal survival instinct had taken over his thinking. He wanted only to escape, and thus attempted to get his body higher up and out of the water. But he refused to heed my shout to inflate his personal flotation device. I decided that whoever had certified this fellow for ocean diving was an accessory to potential manslaughter.

As minutes passed, the bottom rose steadily, but my young buddy never noticed. In continuing apparent panic he dropped his equipment piece by piece. First he unfastened and let sink his air cylinder, with regulator and submersible pressure gauge attached. I surface dived and picked them off the bottom in twelve feet of water. At intervals I gathered up other items— diver's knife, depth gauge, underwater camera, and more.

I shouted again, "Inflate your life vest." The weight of his equipment and mine kept me from catching up to him as he struggled in terror toward shore. As a final desperate act he grabbed off his face mask with the snorkel attached, flailed at the wave crests, and kicked. Yet I knew that the spot where he dog-paddled was just about chest deep. The swimming instinct of any animal made him flop on the surface with big splashes even as I yelled, "Put your feet down—stand up!" He heard nothing and saw nothing in his total panic. If he had put down his feet, he would have been able to stand on a solid bottom, but terror and screaming fatigue had made him blind and deaf in his struggle to survive. All watermanship had long since left him.

Breath Holding

Recreational diving need not be like some Marine Corps-style training. Skin diving is for sport, but personal physical fitness will ensure your fullest enjoyment and relaxation. Among the physical capabilities you should develop is an ability for holding your breath.

An increased lung capacity requires continual conditioning. If you don't want to work on body buildup, then don't, but the lungs and diaphragm must be used and kept conditioned. Constant expansion by deep inhalation exercises will hold them in tone. These are best performed each time you swim, perhaps three times a week. Do at least a quarter-mile per session in a pool or other water facility. Unquestionably, this is the best way to stay in shape for scuba and skin diving. How you are conditioned is directly proportional to how long you can remain immersed during diving.

Breath-holding capacity varies from person to person. The difference in ability results from two factors. Variable sensitivity can produce a lesser desire for one person to breathe than for another. This may be the case even though both persons' oxygen and carbon dioxide tensions have reached the same level. And the amount of willpower you muster can influence the amount of respiratory stimulation you will tolerate before you must inhale. The power of will to prevent the break to breathe depends on experience, practice, and self-confidence.

Rising carbon dioxide tension from breath holding directly stimulates the respiratory center. Falling oxygen tension stimulates the need for air to go through chemoreceptors in your body. As the two chemical components, CO_2 and O_2, approach each other in volume and tension, a breathing stimulation results that becomes difficult to restrain. At some point (up to two minutes in the average free diver who is well experienced) you will be forced to break the holding pattern and resume breathing.

Full lungs provide a larger reservoir of oxygen and a larger space for carbon dioxide. Therefore, you can hold your breath longer if the lungs are really full than if you merely inhale and hold it at the normal inspiration position. A skin diver descending to depth can hold his breath longer underwater than he can at the surface. This is because an increased number of oxygen molecules are compressed into the air in his lungs. The deeper one dives, the longer breath can be held. And when combined with hyperventilation, the breath-holding time can be increased sometimes by half.

Hyperventilation

Hyperventilation is the result of breathing more than is necessary to keep the body's carbon dioxide tensions at the proper level. If you hyperventilate and then dive to forty or fifty feet, you will be able to hold your breath comfortably for quite a period of time. That's because your CO_2 tension is reduced and the partial pressure of oxygen in the lungs is maintained to some degree by the depth pressure.

During ascent the partial pressure of oxygen in the lungs will drop suddenly. Then you'll want air fast even before you can reach the surface. That's when danger can strike from a lack of experience with diving. You can lose consciousness from oxygen starvation as you rise to the surface.

In the incident I cited with the sixteen-year-old diver who found it difficult to breathe while experiencing panic, his unintentional hyperventilation probably was a contributing cause. In a stress situation, unintentional hyperventilation can be triggered by nervous tension. It reduces carbon dioxide tensions to the point of producing serious symptoms—lightheadedness, tingling sensations, weakness, headache, numbness, faintness, and blurring of vision. These can strike a diver underwater or on the surface. A nervous sensation of suffocation often starts the panic process and brings on hyperventilation. To preclude this sort of unsuspected hyperventilation or low carbon dioxide tension, physical fitness preparation is necessary. Before attempting extensive diving after a long layoff, get yourself into good physical shape.

Floatability

Early in your first splashes around the old swimming hole you will become aware of your floatability. Did you know that your personal buoyancy is based on nature's physical laws of flotation? These laws can be summarized as follows:

- A body sinks in fluid if the weight of fluid it displaces is less than the weight of the body.
- A submerged body remains in equilibrium, neither rising nor sinking, if the weight of the fluid it displaces is exactly equal to its own weight.
- If a submerged body weighs less than the volume of liquid it displaces, it will rise and float with part of its volume above the surface. A floating body displaces its own weight of a liquid.

The laws in nature that govern floatability are based on Archimedes' principle: *any object wholly or partially immersed in a liquid is buoyed up by a force equal to the weight of the liquid displaced.*

For example, a 180-pound, six-foot-tall person submerged in the ocean would displace approximately 2.89 cubic feet of salt water. At 64 pounds per cubic foot (the weight of sea water), the amount of salt water displaced would weigh 185 pounds (fresh water weighs 62.4 pounds per cubic foot). The displacement is five pounds more than this person's weight: he would be positively buoyant. He could not sink unless he took on five more pounds to make him less floatable.

Divers overcome positive buoyancy by donning lead weights strung on a webbed belt. Some folks have an average body density that is greater than that of the water. Their bodies thus weigh more than the water they displace, and they are naturally negatively buoyant.

Why are some people more floatable than others? Positive or negative buoyancy is determined by how much fat you have and how much lung capacity you've developed. Since fat is lighter than muscle and bone, it weighs less in water. A fat person, therefore, generally floats more easily than a lean one. A greater lung capacity also buoys up a person, as would an inflated life vest. An individual who surface dives with a full inhalation of air won't find himself negatively buoyant until he's descended fifteen to twenty feet. Below that he may be forced to swim and kick vigorously to manage an ascent because the air in his lungs gets so compressed he becomes overly "heavy" at depth.

Knowledge of your floatability is part of watermanship. Neutral buoyancy underwater has you completely weightless. Yet, upon descending, air trapped in a neoprene wet suit will cause you to grow heavier and more negatively buoyant. Be conscious of this fact and inflate your buoyancy compensator (BC) as required on the way down to maintain neutral buoyancy at depth.

Photograph by Morton Walker.

In addition, a scuba diver wearing an exposure suit carries air trapped within the suit material. This gives him still more buoyancy. To overcome his wet-suit buoyancy along with his body's natural buoyancy, a diver may have to don more lead for greater poundage. Yet, upon descending, the suit's trapped air will compress. A diver will thus find himself getting heavier the deeper he descends. As a safety measure, be alert to the fact that you may have to drop a costly machined lead weight to return to the surface from a very deep dive. An excellent practice is to inflate your buoyancy compensator as required on the way down to maintain neutral buoyancy at depth. Knowledge of your floatability is part of watermanship.

Water Confidence and Scuba Certification

Anyone with watermanship—ages twelve to eighty, men and women, boys and girls, even the handicapped—can dive with scuba. All it takes is confidence in your ability to handle yourself in the water.

This is a self-confidence that grows as you acquire more skill. Insecurities you may begin with will be eliminated as you provide yourself with adequate training. From a scuba course of instruction you will learn techniques that make diving truly safe, easy, and natural. From such a course you should learn simple, effective procedures to handle any conceivable emergency.

In a scuba certification course of instruction, techniques are taught which make diving truly safe, easy and natural. Here, an instructor from Ed Brawley's Skin Diving School, Monterey, California demonstrates to a class the most efficient way to tuck a regulator under the backpack to avoid getting it in the sand while he puts on the rest of his gear.

Photograph courtesy of Ed Brawley's Skin Diving School, Ed Brawley, Inc.

A scuba certification course, for instance, could consist of at least thirty-six hours, about eleven meetings, with the final lesson in open water. The YMCA-certified scuba course requires two open-water scuba dives. In my opinion, all scuba courses should be taught in open water. Yet that is not often the way they are given today.

Here is a sample schedule of a scuba certification course as presented for scholastic course credit at an undergraduate college:

Lesson 1 *Classroom:* Diving requirements and snorkeling equipment, orientation, introduction of instructors, welcome.
In water: Swimming evaluation.

Lesson 2 *Classroom:* Scuba and accessory equipment.
In water: Basic lifesaving.

Lesson 3 *Classroom:* Diving physics.
In water: Introduction to snorkel diving.

Lesson 4 *Classroom:* Diving physiology.
In water: Snorkel diving.

Lesson 5 *Classroom:* Diving maladies.
In water: Introduction to scuba.

Lesson 6 Midterm Test.
Classroom: 25 questions combining true-and-false and short-answer questions and essay questions. Correction and discussion of answers.
In water: Skin diving—entry, surface dives, clear mask, don scuba and entry, up and down maneuvering.

Lesson 7 *Classroom:* First aid and treatment of diving maladies.
In water: Buddy breathing.

Lesson 8 *Classroom:* Bends and decompression tables.
In water: Ditch and don equipment (ditch and don are being eliminated from many courses because ditching in open water has turned out to be unnecessary and dangerous).

Lesson 9 *Classroom:* Tank and regulator.
In water: Complete ditch and don.

Lesson 10 *Classroom:* Underwater environment.
In water: Advanced scuba.

Lesson 11 Final Examination.
Classroom: Written test of 50, 75, or 100 questions, including some essay.
In water: All of the foregoing water work performed to perfection in open water.

Professional diving instructors connected with dive shops and diving resorts perform superb jobs of instructing and certifying divers. Their period of instruction is often shorter and involves water work done not in pools but in open water.

Professional diving instructors connected with dive shops and resorts perform superb jobs of instructing and certifying divers. Here, an instructor prepares to demonstrate to a pool class how to take a tank off underwater.

Photograph courtesy of Ed Brawley's Skin Diving School, Ed Brawley, Inc.

Physical Capacity

Before taking up scuba diving you should undergo a physical examination by a licensed physician, preferably one who is aware of the demands of the sport. As a help to him, ask him to read the following passage before he signs any application and release form for you to enroll in a skin and scuba diving course.

To the physician:

Scuba diving can require exertion.   The diver must be free of cardiovascular and respiratory diseases.   An absolute requirement is the ability of the middle ear and sinuses to equalize pressure.   Any condition that risks the loss of consciousness under water may disqualify the applicant for diving.   Sedentary people (especially over age forty) deserve special scrutiny.   Emotional instability is a contraindication for scuba diving.

Having read and understood the above, I

_____ M.D.

certify that _____

(name of diving participant)

is physically and emotionally able to participate in a scuba certification course of instruction.

_____

(Signature of physican)

_____

(Date)

Physicians are often asked to conduct a physical examination for patients applying for jobs, joining football teams, or getting married.   Skin diving and scuba diving should also require this exam.   Actually, though, there is just one main reason for automatic disqualification from participating in the sport of underwater diving—epilepsy, a hazard that could cause the death of a diver underwater.   The peculiar factors involved with scuba diving make epilepsy an absolute and automatic cause for rejection of a person as a scuba participant.

Even a ruptured eardrum can be repaired, and the patient may dive again.   Other problems, such as heart involvements or respiratory ailments, vary greatly from one person to the next. Physicians suggest, in fact, that the weightlessness of scuba diving eases heart strain, for the underwater environment even rests the cardiovascular system.   Heart and respiratory patients should have themselves checked thoroughly by their physicians, therefore, before categorically excluding themselves from the sport.

Health problems that should be investigated as possible contraindications to scuba diving are:

- Frequent colds or sore throat
- Hay fever or sinus trouble
- Trouble breathing through the nose (other than during colds)
- Painful or running ear, mastoid trouble, broken eardrum
- Asthma or shortness of breath after moderate exercise
- Chest pain or persistent cough
- Spells of fast, irregular, or pounding heartbeat
- High or low blood pressure
- Any kind of "heart trouble"
- Frequent upset stomach, heartburn, or indigestion; peptic ulcer
- Frequent diarrhea or blood in stools
- Stomach pain or backache lasting more than a day or two
- Kidney or bladder disease; blood, sugar, or albumin in urine
- Syphilis or gonorrhea
- Broken bone, serious sprain or strain, dislocated joint
- Rheumatism, arthritis, or other joint trouble
- Severe or frequent headaches
- Head injury causing unconsciousness
- Dizzy spells, fainting spells, or fits
- Trouble sleeping, frequent nightmares, or sleepwalking
- Nervous breakdown or periods of marked depression
- Phobia for closed-in spaces, large open places, or high places
- Any neurological condition
- Train, sea, or air sickness
- Alcoholism or any drug or narcotic habit (including regular use of sleeping pills, stimulants, etc.)
- Recent gain or loss of weight or appetite
- Jaundice or hepatitis
- Tuberculosis
- Diabetes
- Rheumatic fever
- Any serious accident, injury, or illness not already mentioned on this list

A Diver's Swim Strokes

Snorkel diving and scuba diving make use of equipment that provides the diver with increased efficiency on the water's surface and at depth. Rubber foot fins furnish speeds up to three times normal for even the fastest kicks. Arm strokes are almost unnecessary for a free diver. His hands should be left free for holding objects, and, in fact, arm strokes may even hinder the diver's progress underwater. However, a few of the more adaptable strokes may sometimes be needed.

Snorkel diving and scuba diving make use of rubber fins worn on the skin diver's feet which furnish propulsive speed up to three times normal for even the fastest barefoot kicks. Arm strokes are almost unnecessary, and the hands may be left free for holding objects.   *Photograph by Bruce "Teacher" Bowker.*

The *breast stroke* permits the smoothest forward motion. With arms outstretched in front of you, fingers together, and palms slightly cupped, sweep the arms backward and slightly downward and raise the head to breathe, if on the surface. At the same time carry on the flutter kick or the dolphin kick. Recover from the stroke when the hands reach shoulder level and move them toward the center of your chest to repeat the stroke.

The *underwater dog paddle* is less efficient. With arms extended or slightly bent at the elbows, pull downward toward your chest, alternating arms.

The *elementary back stroke* is most useful for its resting effect on the legs. While wearing an air tank, this stroke is useful only if your life vest is inflated and holding your head out of the water. Otherwise you'll be carried backward and downward by the tank's weight. Extend your arms to the sides just above shoulder level and sweep toward your hips to hold them for a moment in a glide; carry on the flutter kick or the dolphin kick. Then repeat the motion.

The Diver's Fin Kick

Wearing fins for snorkel or scuba diving reduces the need for arm strokes with the steady use of fin kicks. Stroking with the arms causes more drag than the progress is worth for the energy expended. Hold your arms next to your body or behind your back as you move through the water. This will cut down resistance. Underwater, the hands and arms are for grasping objects, for pushing yourself away from coral heads, or for shooting a speargun.

Fin kick with a slow, steady flutter, knees quite straight. Don't beat the surface; that will frighten away the wildlife you are anxious to see. Also, the fin blade flopping on the water's surface dissipates some of the muscle power you need for forward propulsion. A habitually bad kick can be corrected by raising your head slightly. This lowers your feet to keep them in the water.

Each kick should be paced so as to accomplish the maximum

Kick with a slow, steady flutter, and knees quite straight. Pace yourself so as to accomplish the maximum glide. Watch a bigger fish swim and notice that every swish of his tail fin takes him in a maximum glide before he flips into the next.

Photograph by Morton Walker.

glide before beginning the next one. As you skin dive during practice, say to yourself: "Take it easy, easy, easy, relax, go slow and steady." Then follow your own advice. Watch a bigger fish swim and notice that every swish of its tail fin takes it in a maximum glide before it flips into the next.

As your leg muscles develop and get conditioned to the new demands you are putting on them, the fin kick will become more natural for you. But before that conditioning happens, the first few times out, you'll be feeling tired, and you'll have a stiff and fatigued sensation in your muscles afterward. Keep up the practice anyway, using your diving accessories. Try them out in deeper water in a few surface dives. Even well-established scuba divers, after they've experienced a long layoff between dive trips, recondition themselves with some practice snorkel diving first.

The two best kicks performed while wearing fins are the flutter kick and the dolphin kick. The *flutter kick* is the well-known up-and-down beat of the crawl stroke. This kick uses the resistance and flexibility of the fin blade to its maximum and produces the best forward motion. With legs horizontal, knees straight, and toes pointed, move one leg toward the bottom. Upon completion of the downward thrust, draw the leg back up to the body positioned in a comfortable curve so that the fins don't come out of the water. The same kick can be accomplished on the left or right side or on the back. Do not bend the knees; this bending is called "bicycling" and is poor technique. It won't support you well or move you effectively. With each leg kicking, alternate the flutter.

Do not bend the knees. This bending is called "bicycling" and is poor technique. Bicycling won't support you well or move you effectively. The diver in this photograph is making very little headway although he is working hard.

Photograph by Morton Walker.

The *dolphin kick* is performed as if your two feet were tied together like the caudal fin of the big water mammal it is named after. A dolphin kick gives strong forward motion. Carry it through by thrusting downward, straightening the knees and bending slightly at the waist. Then point the toes and straighten your legs until about halfway up and bend the knees again. Don't overbend your waist or knees. Just kick easily so as to cause a slight flip of the fins at the peak of the upward and downward motions.

Treading water while wearing fins is performed with very little effort to hold you in a vertical position. Slowly alternate leg kicks.

Add *sculling* motions of the arms if an excess of weight causes too much negative buoyancy. For sculling, move the hands in a figure-eight pattern with the palms cupped slightly and the fingers together.

Surface Dives

The uninformed might think that diving from the water's surface to the bottom of a lake or river takes little skill. The result is that many unknowing snorkelers trying to take an in-depth look at some handiwork of nature underwater expend unnecessary energy. They use only a sprinkling of seconds to gain an insufficient pleasure from their experience. If they would practice the proper way to achieve slick, efficient surface dives, they could enjoy deeper dives, maintain longer bottom time, feel less fatigue, and generally benefit from the skill. If you know a few secrets of correct surface diving, you can make your skin diving experience really great.

The amount of time you might anticipate on the bottom is determined in large measure by the kind of start you manage at the top. Wearing snorkeling gear, it's logical to consider that if you are forced to fight to submerge, you will have dissipated much of your inhaled air and energy before you get very far beneath the surface.

To become familiar with the sensations of skin diving and increase the ability to hold your breath, practice the exercise of bobbing. *Bob-dive* by inhaling deeply at the surface; slightly raise your body out of the water, exhale some air, descend feetfirst to a depth of about fifteen feet, and stay there. When you feel the compulsion, rise to the surface. Then repeat the maneuver. Each time you bob you'll find yourself comfortably able to stay down longer, even with the loss of a little air from the lungs.

THE CANNONBALL TUCK SURFACE DIVE

Slick surface dives are performed through three standard techniques: the cannonball tuck, the jackknife pike, and feetfirst. For the *cannonball tuck,* lie flat on the surface, inhale a deep breath through the snorkel, quickly tuck your knees up to your chest, and roll your body forward and down like a cannonball so that your head and shoulders turn toward the bottom. Then forcefully straighten your legs to lift them high and shoot them up and out of the water. The weight of your legs above the water will propel you deep. Don't begin to kick until your flippers have entirely submerged to avoid splashing and churning the surface.

The second surface dive, the *jackknife pike,* is performed similarly, but after inhaling, bend sharply at the waist and lift only your hips while holding your legs straight. Kick both legs up and out of the water, arch your back, and stroke with spread arms to

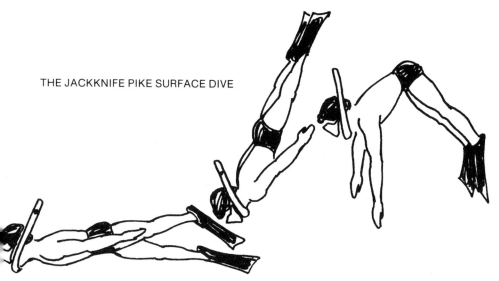

THE JACKKNIFE PIKE SURFACE DIVE

pull you down. The weight of hips and legs will push from above
to glide you gracefully deep. As soon as you've stroked and are
plummeting bottomward, bring your hands to your sides for
torpedolike momentum and continue the downward course. Hold
your foot fins directly above your head in a vertical position to use
minimum oxygen, keep complete dive control, and gain maximum
thrust.

The *feetfirst dive* is less effective than the previous two, but it

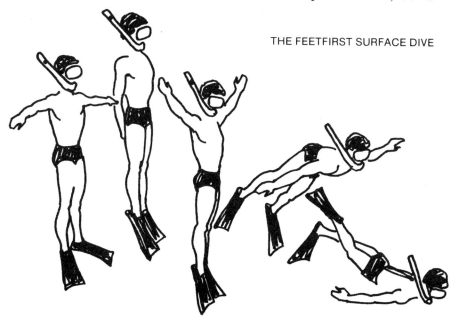

THE FEETFIRST SURFACE DIVE

lets you start from a floating, "standing" position and prevents disturbance at the surface when you are stalking a fish. Execute the dive by bobbing the head and shoulders up and as far out of the water as possible. Do this by grabbing a lungful of air and throwing your arms high above your head. This action will first lift you and then cause the weight of your arms and shoulders to drive you under feet first. Once under the surface, perform the cannonball tuck to turn headfirst. Make more headway by pulling against the water with straight arms and cupped hands. This dive technique tends to consume an inordinate amount of time and wastes an excess of energy—so use it sparingly.

3

Skin-Diving Equipment

Since it was invented during World War II, an estimated ten million people worldwide have used open-circuit self-contained underwater breathing apparatus, scuba. Many millions of other people have used snorkeling or other forms of skin-diving equipment. They have reaped pleasure and profit from employing diving matériel well adapted to requirements without sinking their pocketbooks or setting budgets adrift.

How to Buy Skin-Diving Equipment
Changes and refinements in the vast selection of skin-diving equipment are constantly taking place. The consequence is that even veteran divers have to reapprise themselves of what is current in diving products. Novice divers should most certainly become informed before they make equipment investments.

The diving professionals who can help you with information about the necessary diving gear to match your requirements are dive shop sales personnel, who themselves dive often, and the working scuba instructor, who will take the opportunity to discuss different types and brands of diving gear with you. But ideally, your purchase procedure should first involve a personal investigation to pinpoint the kinds of equipment you need. Then take that need to a dive shop equipment counselor. To acquire equipment that's proper, it is necessary to give that counselor several pieces of pertinent information. For example, you might explain the conditions under which you will usually dive, the extent of your skills, or the amount of diving time you've had underwater. This knowledge should help the counselor offer correct diving equipment recommendations.

The only limitation then is the depth of your pocketbook. And diving gear can be expensive! Innovations and modifications of gear require research and sometimes risk. Research and risk are built into the cost of manufacturing and marketing the variety of dive products.

A more important consideration than the extent of your financial investment is that the equipment you acquire must be comfortable in use. A buoyancy compensator, for instance, that chafes your neck into a fiery red when you are descended to 120 feet or a pair of fins that rubs your toes raw as you're attempting to swim on the surface against choppy waves, are unpleasant even to contemplate.

Your aim in acquiring diving gear should always be to choose functional, well-designed, correctly fitted, and proved safe equipment of excellent quality. It is true that products with these attributes are not initially inexpensive. But when the cost is divided by the time you'll be using the gear, and considering that your diving enjoyment and even your life is dependent upon it, price should be no obstacle in your purchase decisions.

To net the greatest return from investing your diving equipment dollars, follow this procedure:

1. Seek expert advice.
2. Come as close as you can to matching your needs.
3. Check the new gear for quality.
4. Try it on for fit.

There is no substitute for slipping into the equipment before you buy it and use it underwater.

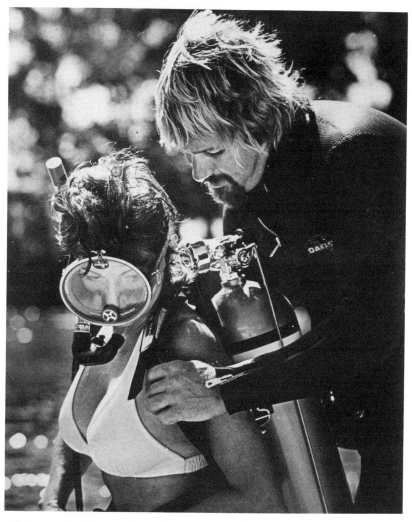

Seek expert advice, and check the gear for quality and fit before investing in new equipment.

Photograph courtesy of Dacor Corporation.

Skin diving begins with acquisition of the proper equipment. The absolute basics include those free-diving items that let the swimmer see and move underwater without much effort and help him breathe surface air. Something probably surprising to some people is that personal flotation gear is included in this category. Thus, the diver's mask, the snorkel, a pair of fins, a life vest or buoyancy compensator, and a surface float make up the equipment required by the snorkeling skin diver. Note that the surface float is being phased out in favor of the buoyancy compensator alone, which does the jobs of both a life vest and a surface float.

An instructor helps a student diver adjust his buoyancy compensator (BC). Note that the BC is currently taking the place of the surface float and even the life vest. The BC alone does the jobs of both of these formerly necessary pieces of equipment.

Photograph courtesy of Ed Brawley's Skin Diving School, Ed Brawley, Inc.

Surface Air Supply Diving

A form of diving akin to snorkeling is *surface air supply* or *hookah* diving. A compressor pump floating on the surface gathers fresh air, filters it, and pushes it through a length of hose up to 100 feet long into the diver's face mask. The diver can breathe purified air easily underwater without having to ascend to the surface. Instead of carrying compressed air in a tank strapped to his back, the diver can maneuver underwater for as long as the gasoline-driven compressor's fuel-tank capacity holds out—about one hour for two divers at twenty-five feet. This system has been used extensively for gold diving in wilderness streams.

The surface air supply compressor is known as a hookah unit. It simply unites the regulator with the surface air supply by means of a hookah adapter. A unit retails in the vicinity of $300. Free air is delivered to the diver at 30 psi to 50 psi from a 3-horsepower to 5-horsepower engine. The regulator should have a one-way valve.

The surface air supply compressor unit requires daily washing in fresh water to remove dirt and salt. The flotation collar should be deflated between uses and the masks and hoses that go with the unit should be cleaned and cleared. Storage should be in a cool, dry, well-ventilated place, as with any diving gear.

Between diving seasons, drain the fuel from the compressor's tank and consume any left-over gasoline in the engine by running it until it dies. Maintain the compressor motor as you would an outboard engine. In addition, seal any opening with masking tape to keep out dirt and moisture. Since your safety is determined by the compressor's condition, make sure that before you operate it the following season, a dealer has serviced it.

Another form of surface air supply diving is the oldest recorded diving system. It is a surface-supplied-air technique used in antiquity by the Phoenicians to recover treasure from sunken ships. It is as simple as an empty glass thrust upside down into water. Air in the glass stops water from rising inside it. Supply a continuous flow of fresh air and you have a miniature diving helmet.

That is the principle of the *Aqua Bell® diving helmet.* The helmet has four clear faceplates permitting almost unlimited vision. You don't hold a regulator in your mouth or wear a face mask covering your nose and eyes; breathable air is held inside the helmet by water pressure. A ballasted collar, holding up to forty pounds of iron ore or sand and gravel, rests on the diver's shoulders to keep the helmet on. The diver can descend to 35 feet and walk along the bottom. This unusual helmet is useful for gold diving, scraping boat hulls, and collecting tropical fish from blue waters. It costs $50; it is available with an $11 hand pump or a heavy-duty air supply compressor at $110 or with a standard 110-volt AC air supply compressor at $70.

The Aqua Bell Diving Helmet has a ballast weight collar that sits on the diver's shoulders. Air is supplied by a hand pump or by the standard or heavy-duty air supply compressor as in hookah diving. Descents are readily made to 35 feet.
Photograph courtesy of Aqua Bell Corporation.

Snorkel Diving Gear

To assist with the use of scuba gear and to enhance the enjoyment of diving, a variety of skin-diving accessories is employed. Among these accessories is the *snorkel*, a short tube for breathing at the surface. Snorkel diving or snorkeling includes the use in combination of the snorkel tube, a diver's face mask, and a pair of fins. The diver breathes through the snorkel tube and swims face-down.

Combining these three pieces of equipment lets you inspect the bottom from the surface for an unlimited time, traveling at swimming speeds almost triple your barefooted rate. When you want to submerge for closer looks at underwater objects, you inhale sharply, hold your breath, and surface dive.

Submergence lasts for as long as a lungful of air will hold out. Breath-held dives usually let you descend from ten to sixty feet. The average American male who does not dive as an occupation can ordinarily sustain himself at 25 feet for about forty-five seconds. Spearfishing experts, however, are known to be able to hunt their prey even at depths of 90 feet, breath-holding for periods up to two minutes.

Divers' Face Masks

The air space between the diver's face and the window of his mask lets him see the underwater world. In modern diving masks, rubber walls surround tempered glass and cover the nose and eyes; the mouth is not covered. Suction inside these sealed walls, and a rubber head strap, hold the whole face mask close against the diver's forehead, temples, and side cheeks and under his nose. In this way a submerged person can equalize pressure buildup within the mask by exhaling through his nose. The tempered-glass window, of one layer with a minimum thickness of five millimeters, allows for very little distortion. Since man is an air-adapted creature, when he skin dives he must carry his air environment with him. The specially designed face mask helps to do that.

For diving innerspace, vision is the most important sense.

Although the other senses are essential, we obtain 80 percent of our environmental information through seeing. Man is a visually sensitive animal, just as the dog is olfactorily sensitive and the dolphin is auditorily sensitive. Seeing clearly and efficiently underwater is important to your welfare and safety as well as to your enjoyment.

Man is a visually sensitive animal. Seeing clearly and efficiently underwater is important to your diving welfare and safety as well as to your enjoyment. A diver's mask allows him to see within innerspace.

Photography by Gayle Anspach, courtesy Cayman Kai Resort Ltd.

But different properties of water affect the transmission of light through that medium. For example, sediment, plankton, debris, weather conditions above the surface, the position of the sun, surface turbulence, and other factors affect the range of visibility underwater. The deeper you descend, the less light is available and the less you can see. Different colors, owing to the wavelengths of light, are absorbed at varying levels of depth. This also affects your vision.

Optical effects are produced between the water and the air lens in the mask faceplate. Underwater, everything you look at appears at least 25 percent larger because of natural magnification of image size. This creates a considerable disturbance in your depth perception in that medium. The consequence is that the mask you wear to see underwater is probably your most important piece of skin-diving equipment.

Manufacturers offer many different styles of face masks, ranging in price from $2.50 to $25. Certain features are a must. The window should be shatterproof glass. Some masks do feature plastic faceplates, but these scratch easily and tend to fog with vapor more quickly than those of tempered glass. The best masks fit the contours of a diver's face, are made with soft rubber cushion around the periphery of their walls, are comprised of

The window to the diver's world is the water tight mask. It should have rims, buckles and bolts made of a noncorrosive metal such as chrome-plated brass. Its sealing parts of rubber should have a stiff body, soft watertight skirt and a flexible, split strap such as this mask supplied by U. S. Nemrod, Inc. *Photograph courtesy of U. S. Nemrod, Inc.*

noncorrosive hardware, and allow easy access to the fingers for clearing pressure from ears and sinuses.

Heed this word of caution: *goggles have no place as a substitute for the single-lens face mask.* The two separated lenses of goggles cause double vision and distortion unless they are aligned just right—a rare occurrence. In addition, goggles offer you no way to equalize pressure within the separate eyepieces, so eye squeeze and subsequent injury can result.

Heed this word of caution: goggles have no place as a substitute for the single-lens face mask in free diving. For example, the Nereida Goggles shown, distributed by U.S. Nemrod, Inc. are exclusively designed to fit close to the eyes for maximum visibility and offer complete protection for swimming long distances in chlorinated pools or salt water. But they are not suitable for scuba diving. The two separate lenses will not allow you to equalize pressure within the separate eyepieces. Eye squeeze can result.

Photograph courtesy of U.S. Nemrod, Inc.

Eye squeeze is a constant hazard, even with a face mask. One forty-four-year-old Indiana woman with whom I dived in Curacao, Netherlands Antilles, was new to scuba diving and unacquainted with the bulging pressure symptoms of eye squeeze. She ended up with ruptured blood vessels around her eyeballs and a spoiled diving vacation. Simply blowing air from her nose into her mask would have equalized the pressure enough to prevent the problem, but she had probably not been warned about this hazard during her certification training. People who are trained properly won't ever have eye squeeze.

Purge valves built into the faceplate are useful for the easy clearing of any water that might leak into the mask. But a mask of the best quality that fits correctly should not leak water in any case. Some masks have ear and sinus pressure-equalizing pads or nose grabbers of the Pinocchio type. These are effective substitutes for purge valves. Besides, some purge valves do leak.

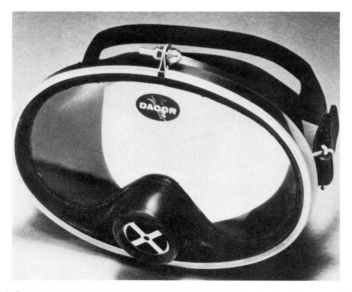

This Dacor mask has a purge valve built into the faceplate for the easy clearing of water that might leak into the mask.   *Photograph courtesy of Dacor Corporation.*

The only way to enter the water when you are wearing a face mask is feetfirst. Never dive into the water from a height headfirst while wearing a mask or step off with your face turned downward. If you did this your mask would be forced sharply against your face, and you could be injured. The mask could break your occipital bone or nose or cause such strong suction that you couldn't pull the mask off your face without help. Enter the water instead feetfirst, protecting the faceplate with your hand over the mask and with your chin up.

This Scubapro Close-up Mask brings the lens closer to the eyes to provide a larger field of vision and less displacement than the large volume masks. Some masks, such as this one, have a nose grabber of the Pinnochio type for clearing the ears and sinus cavities conveniently. *Photograph courtesy of Scubapro.*

The Snorkel Tube

Named for the device on a German submarine called the *schnorkel,* which let engines breathe, the skin diver's snorkel tube lets air into his mouth as he swims on the surface. A molded rubber mouthpiece with bite tabs inside carries air to the windpipe. Use of the snorkel for breathing is excellent because it precludes the use of a full face mask. *Avoid any type of mask that covers your mouth. Use a snorkel instead.* Most full face masks leak water.

A proper snorkel tube is made of flexible material that will stand erect and out of the water. It should not be so pliable that it will bend or be squeezed together by the pressure of swimming. Snorkels of the corrugated extension variety that curve into a J

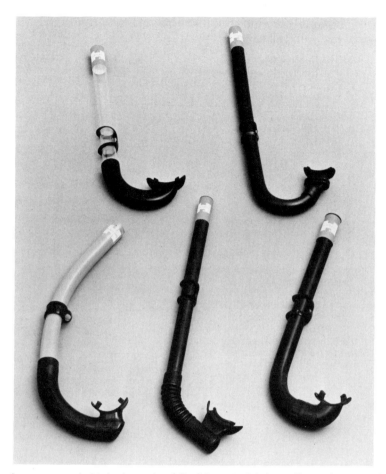

A proper snorkel tube is made of flexible material that will stand erect and out of the water, and possesses a comfortable mouthpiece attached at the J-shaped oral end. These are examples of the many types manufactured by Healthways. *Photograph courtesy of Healthways.*

when inserted in your mouth are suitable only if the bending rubber is not overly soft. Some have a fancy clearing valve as an added feature, but more often than not that special addition breaks down and chokes you with water leakage.

The most important feature of a good plastic or rubber snorkel tube is its comfortable mouthpiece, attached at the J-shaped oral end. The mouthpiece must not wobble when you skin dive on the water's surface; otherwise the result is likely to be irritated gums from constant friction.

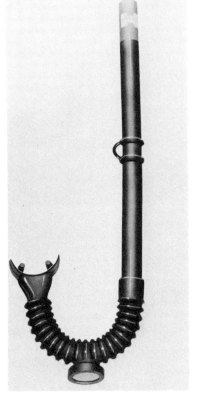

Snorkels of the corrugated extension variety that curve into a J when inserted into your mouth are suitable only if the bending rubber is not overly soft. Some, such as the model shown, have a fancy clearing valve as an added feature, but more often than not that special addition breaks down and chokes the diver with water leakage. This type is not recommended.
Photograph courtesy of Healthways.

I have seen women and children attempting to use wide-diameter, long snorkels made for men. The problem with an oversized snorkel is the difficulty involved with blowing water from the tube. An overly large tube is easy to inhale through, but it lets water linger in the J and so tends to choke the snorkeler, an experience that could turn a person away from the sport. Get the right size snorkel tube to make sure your snorkeling is pleasant.

Tubes that come apart or are made in sections are less desirable than the one-piece varieties: the more parts that are movable, the more chance they may separate. Snorkels can cost anywhere from $2.50 to $7.50, depending on their features.

Without question, your tube for surface breathing should be devoid of Ping-Pong-ball attachments at the top. The theoretical plan of an air-filled plastic ball shutting out water when you submerge is only a sales pitch. When you attempt to expel water from the tube, the ball causes extra water resistance and a feeling of pressure; on the surface, it bumps the tube in a rat-a-tat vibration. The laws of physics are on your side to keep water back and prevent it from coming down the tube to drip into your throat. As you submerge, first hold your breath. This counterforce prevents water within the upper portion of the snorkel tube from sliding the rest of the way down the tube, and water will not reach your mouth. Trapped air acts as a pressure resistance and prevents oral flooding.

Storage of snorkel tubes is the simplest of tasks. The entire process consists of rinsing the tube in fresh water and drying in air out of the sun. A good added idea, though, is to leave it lying straight or hanging down from a hook.

Swim Fins

Swim fins or flippers, usually made of rubber, can double or triple your underwater swimming speed. Combined with the knee-leg kick, added impetus from the fins pushes against water resistance and acts as an aid to conserve your muscle strength and caloric energy. Fins allow you more time for in-water activity, to accomplish more work or have more fun.

What is the action of fins as they push you through the water? Surprisingly, the most effective part of the fin kick occurs during leg extension on the downward stroke. Your power comes not from bending the leg but from straightening it. You feel the strain in your ankles.

Since foot comfort through proper fit is the most important aspect of buying a pair of fins, try on several styles before making your purchase. The whole idea is to prevent friction and foot chafe. You will feel mighty miserable from a skin burn or a blister being rubbed on toes or heel bones if your swim fins don't fit just right. Swimming with fin-caused foot abrasions in salt water can be a particularly acute form of agony.

Since foot comfort through proper fit is the most important aspect of buying a pair of fins, you will be wise to try on several styles before making your purchase. Shown at the top of the photo is the "Scubafin" and below is the "Whaler"—both fin types made by Healthways. The rubber crossed bands are fin retainer straps.   *Photograph courtesy of Healthways.*

Be aware of this, too—oversized fins or too-rigid plasticized fins tire out a beginner's legs much too quickly. It's better to start into the sport of skin diving with a pair of semiflexible flippers. Also act cautiously in buying a bargain at end-of-season sales. Rubber goods could have become dried out and brittle in summer display windows, and rubber fins can crack and crumble.

Before attempting to don your fins, wet your feet and wet the fins. You will find it easier to slip into them that way. The fin style with an adjustable fin seems to protect the entire bottom of the foot against sharp rocks and coral. The open heel can be made safer by wearing diving boots. Another option is the nonadjustable fin with an open heel. The choice is a matter of personal taste and not as significant as it may sound.

The newest development in fins is the Farallon Fara-Fin. This swim fin design is a radical departure from any other fin ever manufactured. It has two half-inch stainless steel tubes, secured one on each side of the foot pocket. They extend back about three inches. Connected to these tubes by an elbow that locks into

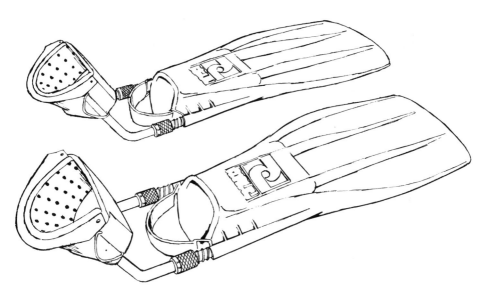

The Farallon Fara-Fin rigidizes the ankle in the "neutral" position by locking it with a stainless steel flex frame. It offers immediate heelstrap adjustment to maintain a firm fit as your wet-suit boots compress with depth.

position at 35 degrees back from the vertical are two more stainless steel tubes, one on each side. These are fastened to an orange Lexan leg cuff that fits around the back of the leg just below the calf. A neoprene pad is cemented to the inside of the cuff for comfort and to prevent slippage. In addition, a two-inch wide Velcro strap opens to a length of thirteen inches to fasten around the front of the leg and to hold the leg firmly in position against the cuff. The elbow can bend forward 30 degrees from the vertical to allow walking and standing in the fin.

The Fara-Fin is $59.95, the most expensive pair of fins on the market. Other types can be purchased in a range from $15 to $30.

Personal Flotation Devices

A safety aid for in-water face-up positioning for a diver in trouble is mandatory. Consequently, wearing a personal flotation device is necessary as part of the skin diver's usual equipment. Not uncommonly snorkelers disdain use of a life vest or buoyancy compensator, but the personal flotation device has saved the life of many a skin diver. If the face mask is the skin diver's most important piece of equipment, the personal flotation device certainly comes a close second.

A personal flotation device keeps you buoyant in case you are hit by crippling cramps or become overfatigued. It can float you through a rip current or over the waves of a striking squall or carry you to the surface if a piece of diving equipment fails. The personal flotation device is a true lifesaver. Not only does it act as

Personal flotation devices come in many sizes and forms. Some are strictly of the emergency life vest type as shown. They are made self-inflating by means of a carbon dioxide cartridge or an oral inflator. *Photograph courtesy of Dacor Corporation.*

an essential emergency rescue aid, it can help the scuba diver adjust his underwater buoyancy. It works also as a lifter of heavy objects from the sea floor in treasure hunting or archaeological research.

The most commonly used personal flotation device from the war surplus market was the Mae West life vest. This has been replaced by the buoyancy compensator that slips over the head and rests on the shoulders. Some safety vests are comprised only of one front panel, which has sufficient buoyancy power to hold the diver's head out of the water. Others are of the double-pillow type, with front and back panels. Panels are fastened around the waist by a strap. Another strap passes under the crotch and fastens to prevent the vest from riding up when it is inflated. These harness straps should attach to the vest so as not to put stress on its inflatable portions.

Personal flotation devices have been made self-inflating by

1. Small and compact, folded in wearing position.

2. Inflator is pulled and vest inflates and opens automatically

3. Vest is fully inflated to standard size.

The self-inflating personal flotation device works quickly and effectively merely from pulling the detonator cord. However, it has been looked upon with disfavor lately because an emergency pull at depth can cause too quick an ascent. Consequently, this type of carbon dioxide cartridge device should be looked upon only as a means of staying afloat on the surface. *Photograph courtesy of Dacor Corporation.*

means of a carbon dioxide cartridge. In a predive checkup, remove the CO_2 cartridge, lubricate the cartridge chamber with silicone spray, operate the detonator, and reinstall the cartridge. The vest with oral inflator alone has been looked upon lately with more favor because emergency pulls on the CO_2 cord have caused too-quick ascents with resultant deaths from air embolism. The air in self-inflating vests cannot be valved off fast enough to adjust the rate of ascent. A spring-loaded nozzle should make up the shutoff of the oral inflator where the tip opens the inflation tube merely by being depressed.

Postdive care of life vests, buoyancy compensators (BC), and other life-preserving tools made of nylon, Hypalon, or neoprene includes rinsing in fresh water and drying well after each use. To make sure they hold their shape through prolonged nonuse, it's a good idea to inflate the pillow portion with a half-charge of air. Avoid placing personal flotation devices near heat or in the sun.

Topside care of personal flotation gear includes thorough inspection before each dive. You should inflate your life vest and BC and submerge them in a filled bathtub to check for leaks. Disassemble your carbon dioxide mechanism and clean the cartridges. Occasional application of an acrylic spray will prevent corrosion of the CO_2 mechanism. Always make sure the O-rings are clean, and always replace them if necessary. The puncture pin for activating the CO_2 cartridge should retain its sharpness and be easy to pull into action; sharpen it if necessary.

A buoyancy compensator with its own inflator system must function properly. To check this, disassemble the inflator mechanism, look closely at its O-rings to spot wear, and lubricate them or replace them if need be.

Incidentally, any personal flotation device that lacks a crotch strap can be modified with an added homemade one. Attach the strap from the front bottom of the vest or the BC, around the back and up to the neck. This will hold the device down better and stop its choking effect when inflated.

Emergency diving vests are priced above $50 by most manufacturers. The number of deluxe features and the lifting capacity decide cost. Some possess pockets or push-button automatic inflators. Others are made of more durable material or contain oversized carbon dioxide cartridges similar to the scuba diver's buoyancy compensator.

Although the buoyancy compensator is becoming a popular part of the deeper diver's outfit, it is useful also for personal flotation during snorkel diving. Consequently, it is described here rather than in the next chapter.

Buoyancy Compensator

The most recent development in the evolution of underwater personal safety is the buoyancy compensator (BC). It is a working tool that makes your diving safer and more enjoyable. BC evolution came about through advanced diving instruction methods. With this tool long swims with full equipment have become safer because surface swim exhaustion has been eliminated. In addition, during a dive automatic features let you adjust your buoyancy so that you need never be inadvertently negatively buoyant.

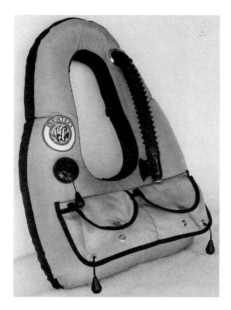

The buoyancy compensator (BC) is a working tool that makes diving safer and more enjoyable. Automatic features let you adjust personal buoyancy to eliminate negative buoyancy quickly and easily. The BC shown, made by Seatec, features a large hose with purge type mouthpiece, automatic overpressure valve with manual air dump, twin CO_2 cartridges mounted under protective pockets, a urethane inner bladder, a spine strap, waist strap, and adjustable buckle. *Photograph courtesy of Seatec.*

Buoyancy compensator vests are available with an oral inflator or with an oral inflator and mechanical inflator. They serve for personal flotation or are attached to the scuba assembly; the At-Pac brand is an example of the latter. The At-Pac is an integrated scuba/weight buoyancy system marketed in the United States by Watergill. It consists of a backpack attached to a fiberglass shroud, which encloses single or twin cylinders, a weight compartment, and a bag that can be filled with air from the cylinders to provide buoyancy. The BC portion of the apparatus includes a horseshoe-shaped nylon bag with an internal bladder laced to the backpack. When connected to a single-hose demand valve outlet, it can be inflated to adjust buoyancy or provide emergency lift.

Before water entry, the buoyancy compensator is inflated. Once in the water on the surface, you valve off air to allow for descent. The BC vest is a diver's elevator to the bottom. To descend, hold hose over your head to let air escape. Increasing water pressure as you descend will force more air out of the vest to allow an effortless and slow drop to your level of neutral buoyancy.

Once underwater, you can compensate for your loss of buoy-

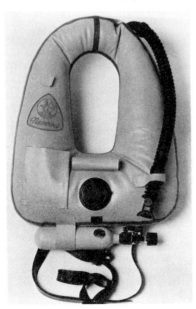

Some types of Buoyancy Compensators feature their own self-contained high-pressure air bottle that instantly inflates by means of pushing a large button. The Nemrod Scuba Vest shown delivers 36 pounds of surface buoyancy and has a large diameter corrugated oral inflator with a buoyancy control valve. The large-diameter automatic purge valve protects the vest when interior pressure exceeds 2-psi ambient water pressure. The air bottle can be used as an auxilliary emergency breathing device and is refilled from your scuba tank. *Photograph courtesy of U.S. Nemrod, Inc.*

ancy by simply exhaling the equivalent of a breath or two of air into the vest.   Do it orally or mechanically—some types of compensators accept air through a low-pressure port on the first stage of a single-hose regulator.   By pushing a button you can inflate the vest from air in your tank.   This lets you go up and down like a yo-yo, at your pleasure.   With application of the BC device you can maintain neutral buoyancy with almost no effort. Inflate a little to go up; raise the oral inflator to deflate a little and go down.

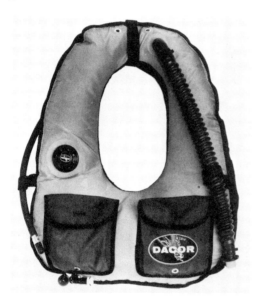

Some BCs accept air through a low-pressure port on the first stage of a single-hose regulator. By pushing a button you can inflate the vest from air in your tank. This lets you go up and down like a yo-yo, at your pleasure. The Dacor Seachute Vest is such a BC. Shown here, the Seachute allows inflation (1) from the diver's air tank through the air inflation hose, (2) orally into the air or CO_2 bladder, (3) from the 25-gram CO_2 cartridge. The CO_2 bladder is a completely independent component with its own over-pressure relief valve, drain, and inflate-deflate hose.
Photograph courtesy of Dacor Corporation.

A word of caution must accompany this explanation of the BC. Because of the large volume of air the BC holds, it is possible for you to ascend too fast.   You could accelerate out of control if the expanding air is not valved off fast enough.   Use your underwater watch to count seconds and compare them with the rate of ascent in feet as recorded on your depth gauge.   Your maximum speed of ascent must not be more than sixty feet per minute.

Buoyancy control pack conversion kits are made to convert regular backpacks to buoyancy control packs.   Such a conversion unit costs about $130. A lower-priced personal flotation BC unit is in the $80-$85 range. A fully assembled, deluxe At-Pac-type BC, the kind with an oral and mechanical inflator in combination with the weight belt and backpack, costs in the vicinity of $165.

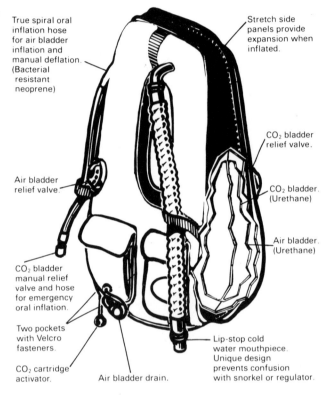

True spiral oral inflation hose for air bladder inflation and manual deflation. (Bacterial resistant neoprene)

Stretch side panels provide expansion when inflated.

Air bladder relief valve.

CO_2 bladder relief valve.

CO_2 bladder. (Urethane)

Air bladder. (Urethane)

CO_2 bladder manual relief valve and hose for emergency oral inflation.

Two pockets with Velcro fasteners.

CO_2 cartridge activator.

Air bladder drain.

Lip-stop cold water mouthpiece. Unique design prevents confusion with snorkel or regulator.

BUOYANCY COMPENSATOR

Other Personal Flotation Equipment

Floats, buoys, inflated rubber inner tubes, surf mats, paddleboards, and boats are other flotation equipment that should be employed by skin divers. Any of these can be useful for helping you to carry game or equipment, to act as an emergency life preserver, to serve as a resting platform, and to float the "diver down" flag. *Skin dive only where an effective float flying a "diver down" flag is anchored close by you.* The flag wards off boats from

Ball-like bladders are popular low-cost floats for flying the diver's flag. Shown is the Dacor Inflatable Buoy with Diver's Flag which has a unique water compartment in the base to keep the flag in an upright position even in rough water.

Photograph courtesy of Dacor Corporation.

your swimming line and acts as the bearing point for your dive direction and time period.

Ball-like bladders and tire inner tubes make up the most inexpensive and popular of floats. Use only undamaged inner tubes. To the bottom and into the center of the inner tube, you can tie a gunnysack net of extra-long length. This is convenient for holding game from spearfishing and shelling. To keep blood from seeping into the water from speared fish, line the gunnysack with a large plastic bag of the kind used for garbage containers.

General Care for Diving Gear

Not only for long-term storage but after any dive, certain maintenance procedures should be followed for your face mask and other diving equipment.   Here are general procedural steps to take:

- Make sure any metal frame that's part of a piece of gear is not misshapen or bent.
- Keep equipment, especially rubber products, away from any form of heat, such as stoves or radiators. And don't ever leave them lying exposed to the sun.
- After use in salt water, rinse diving accessories in fresh water; rinse off chlorinated water after snorkel practice in a swimming pool.
- Dry the material thoroughly by wiping it with a soft cloth.
- For equipment storage over extended periods between dive trips, sprinkle any rubber parts with talcum powder, hydrous silicate of magnesia, or cornstarch. This prevents the rubber from cracking as a result of dry brittleness.

Water Transportation

I was scheduled to skin dive during a Central American marine archaeological research venture. I knew that I had to backpack all my equipment during forced marches through the vine-tangled, bug-biting, malaria-infested jungle of Panama. The long, narrow channel where I had to search was choked with turtle grass and water lily pads. It lay far inland, and the sturdy boat I needed for diving to uncover ancient Indian relics also had to be carried in on my back. Only the most portable and dependable equipment would suffice. What kind of boat did I choose?

Inflatable Craft

Without question, my selection was one of the many varieties of *inflatable craft* manufactured. These craft are durable, portable, seaworthy, virtually unsinkable, and ideal for sport diving, water exploration, and underwater research. Good inflatables are constructed of heavy nylon cloth, usually coated with synthetic rubber. They stow in a duffel bag; the floorboards pack in a valise about the size of a suitcase. Assembly and inflation can be accomplished in less than ten minutes.

Inflatable boats are advantageous for skin divers because they are stable. The wide beam and low center of gravity allow you to walk on the buoyancy tubes without any tendency to capsize. Pulling yourself up over the sides while you're wearing full scuba gear won't cause the boat to tip, either.

Inflatable boats are virtually unsinkable because of the multiple and separate buoyancy compartments into which low air-inflation is pumped. They are ideal for divers. The inflatable shown is the 12-foot Avon Redshank in service in a Central American jungle during a marine archaeological research expedition. Such a venture faces incredibly high and continual heat and the dangers of coral reefs.   *Photograph courtesy of Avon Inflatable Boats.*

Good inflatables are virtually unsinkable because they have multiple and separate buoyancy compartments. Their tough but resilient construction makes inflatables less vulnerable to dents and damage than hard boats. And portability is their primary feature, with trailering and mooring no problem at all. They are equally well transported on the back of a mule, a camel, or a human, even on paths around anthills or over fallen jungle tree limbs. Assembled in a few minutes, inflatables can be launched and recovered wherever you can reach the water—from jetty, beach, riverbank, or deck.

Even in bad weather when a rigid dinghy would be of little use, I have found my inflatable boat safe and seaworthy. Though it flooded full at times, it still supported a complement of divers and their gear. The tremendous buoyancy combined with the raised bow and well-tested hull shape allows it to operate in rougher conditions than rigid craft of similar size.

Inflatables suitable for divers are made from eight to eighteen feet in length. They break down to an average forty-pound package, inflate from a hand/foot bellows, and are powered by a 25-to 65-hp. engine. Cost teeters in the vicinity of $800 or better, depending on size and optional features.

The Pontoon Boat
Another small support craft excellent for divers is the *pontoon*

Divers operating from a small Riviera cruiser on an Indiana lake show that the pontoon-type boat is quite adaptable for scuba diving. Divers like the ample deck-space for their equipment and for resting between dives.

Photograph courtesy of Winius-Brandon. Inc. of Indiana for Riviera Cruisers.

boat. It simulates a diving float with big built-in pluses. The pontoon boat is buoyant, shallow-drafted, highly versatile, fast-powered, and tremendously stable, and it can be made as palatial or Spartan as you wish.

A major argument in favor of the motorized pontoon platform is that it can't be surpassed, dollar for dollar, for sheer quantity of square-foot open-area deck space. It costs a fraction of the price of a conventional boat of near-equal utility. The manufacturers' prices of most pontoon boat models—$500 to $15,000—are within the same comparative range of each other, plus or minus a few dollars.

The pontoon boat is an ideal base for a diving operation, since it is easily moored close to the dive site. The motorized platform can immediately be cast off to recover a diver in difficulty, and readily carries a mounted ladder in place at all times. The ladder permits easy entrance into the water and return from submersion without the expenditure of excess energy—a real consideration for all skin divers.

It further fulfills a special need of scuba divers: a line marked at ten-foot intervals, rigged over the side to provide a convenient measure of decompression stops. Finally, a necessity for any dive boat, it gives ample room to dress and store extra equipment, and keeps aquanauts warm and comfortable before and after dives. The luxury appointments that can be added to a pontoon platform enhance every one of a diver's basic requirements magnificently.

The Kayak-Paddleboard

For sheer sport and skin-diving fun, you might try the unique hybrid kayak-paddleboard called the *Royak.* It is a one-person boat that is stable for ocean cruising in rough water, easy to paddle, and no problem to leave and reenter after spearfishing. This kayak is only fourteen feet, seven inches long, with a twenty-three-inch beam; it displaces 425 pounds of water. This craft will hold all your skin-diving gear and picnic trappings in its storage compartment. Its price is in the $400 range.

Skin divers find it simple to climb into and out of this kayak

The kayak-paddleboard called the *Royak* is a fun boat for diving. It is suitable for one person to paddle and ride in and from which to embark on some fancy skin diving. The craft fills all the requirements of a float.

Photograph courtesy of Royak, Inc.

while in the water, far from shore. It's comforting to know that you can self-rescue. The Royak fills all the requirements of a float that you can paddle and ride in. Tipping the craft is tough to do. At boatside, a scuba diver can unhook his weight belt and reach over to drop it into the wet-storage compartment. He hands in his tank, backpack, and harness with one hand while holding the kayak body steady in place with the other. Then with a kick of the flippers the diver can mount his cockpit and slide relatively gracefully into the snug comfort of the enclosed chamber. He takes off his fins, removes his mask and snorkel, reaches back to detach his regulator from the tank valve, secures all gear within the storage space with elastic straps, closes the compartment, picks up the paddle, and dips it into blue water to head for shore.

The Rotork Sea Truck (above) is the perfect dive boat since it is extremely stable and almost totally unsinkable, even with the bow ramp down, which obviously makes it particularly attractive for diving. Equipment can be loaded on where jetties do not exist, and access to the water is made easy by use of the same lowered ramp. The boat operates in very shallow water, and due to its shape there is a huge area of deck space available.

Photograph courtesy of Jim Dailey, Surfside Water Sports, Grand Cayman, B. W. I.

The Remora, shown below, is a new and exciting, diver-oriented pontoon craft intended to vastly improve diver performance, safety, and enjoyment. It is home-built by the experienced and novice alike through use of low cost (approximately $400 to build) materials. Plans for this simple construction can be acquired by payment of $20 to the inventor, Frank Deveney, 240 Quartz Lane, Sun Valley, Nevada 89431. *Photograph courtesy of Frank P. Deveney.*

4

Scuba-Diving Gear

The scuba system comprises three basic pieces of equipment together with their supplementary accessories. The open-circuit system makes use of the compressed-air cylinder or scuba tank, its filler valve, and the demand air-flow regulator. Supplementary gear includes the backpack and harness, exposure suit and accessories, weights and weight belt, diver's knife and other tools, underwater gauges, and the buoyancy compensator described in chapter 3.

The regulator is the heart of the scuba system. The compressed-air tank with its pressure valve lets you swim underwater free as a fish because you are carrying your air supply with you.

Compressed-Air Tanks

Air cylinders, or tanks, or bottles, are made of chromed steel or aluminum. Every five years they must be hydrostatically tested, and each year they should be visually inspected.

What "hydrostatically tested" means is that once in five years an examiner fills your cylinder with water, connects it to a high-pressure pump, seals it in a testing chamber also full of water, and pumps air into the tank to measure its expansion capacity. The amount it expands is measured by a burette water level attached

Scuba compressed air cylinders (also called "bottles" and "tanks") are cold-drawn from high-strength chrome molybdenum steel or aluminum. Each tank is heat treated and tested to D. O. T., *Department of Transportation,* requirements. Hot galvanizing covers the exterior of steel cylinders with a protective coating of zinc. This material has unique self-healing properties that serve to recoat scratched and abraded areas before serious corrosion can occur. In some cylinders, such as the two standing Healthways products shown, hot dipped vinyl coating, applied only after galvanizing, results in a tough, mar-resistant coating ten times thicker than paint. Interiors are sandblasted clean and protected against corrosion with a special moisture-absorbing capsule until valve installation. Positively buoyant when nearly empty, they are rated for 2250 psig service pressure and 2475 psig fill pressure. *Photograph courtesy of Healthways.*

to the testing chamber. The amount of liquid forced out by tank expansion determines the viability of your scuba tank. It has to be able to reach five-thirds of the tank's working pressure. Thus, a tank marked 2250 expanded to five-thirds has a viable 3.750 pounds per square inch (psi). The expansion pressure is held there for thirty seconds and the amount of burette spillage recorded. To pass its hydrostatic test a tank cannot expand more than 10 percent.

Results of the test are stamped on the neck of the tank as numbers and letters. These markings are easy to interpret. "DOT" means "Department of Transportation," the federal agency that sets safety standards for gas cylinders. Also recorded are the type of metal used, the working pressure in pounds per square inch, the tank's serial number, the maker's identifying mark with the government inspector's mark, the date of the first hydro-test before the tank left the factory, the symbol of the tank seller, and the date of the last test with a plus sign. A gas cylinder not marked with an up-to-date hydrostatic test stamp may not be filled by a conscientious air supplier. His refusal is for your safety—a compressed-air cylinder weakened by rust can explode.

Compressed-air tanks come in many sizes: 38 cu. ft., 53 cu. ft., 71 cu. ft., 80 cu. ft., and 100 cu. ft. Here, Captain Don Stewart stands in front of the tank rack inside the Aquaventure dive shop at Bonaire, Netherlands Antilles.

Photograph by Morton Walker.

For visual inspection, the tank is emptied and the tank valve removed, and a light is lowered inside. The examiner looks for rust, which weakens gas cylinder walls. He removes the tank boot and checks for pitting and other weaknesses in the outside metal that might arise from denting or salt corrosion.

Tanks are made in 71-cubic-foot, 38-cubic-foot, 80-cubic-foot, and 53-cubic-foot capacities; U.S. Nemrod makes a 100-cubic-foot steel tank. The numbers indicate how much air a filled tank will supply at atmospheric pressure. Usually, this is also the number of minutes it will last at one atmosphere. Remember, though, that as atmospheric pressure increases, more air molecules are used up with each inhalation. Thus, at 66 feet of depth, three atmospheres of pressure, three times as much air is inhaled into your lungs than on the surface and the tank's cubic-foot capacity is reduced to one-third of its stated capacity.

Filler Valves

Sport divers are supposed to use the nonbacked type of filler valve. This is a tank valve that ruptures if a cylinder is overfilled to 166 percent of capacity. It is called the *burst-disc assembly* and protects divers against overexpansion of interior gas in case the filled tank is left baking in the sun. That way, the metal cylinder won't explode; only the burst-disc assembly ruptures. The tank becomes inoperable, but it won't have turned into a bomb.

Some of the better valves have extra features. One is the *safety hole,* which hisses if you begin unscrewing a valve attached to a half-empty air cylinder. The *valve snorkel* holds contaminating material inside the tank and prevents impurities from ruining your regulator. An underwater pressure gauge can be attached to a valve featuring a *high-pressure air outlet.* You can breathe off a

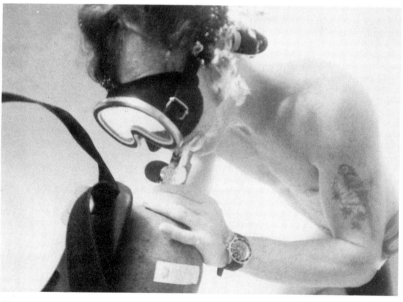

You can breathe off a filler valve the same as you can from a regulator. Shown is a student diver practicing breathing off the air tank valve. This demonstrates that there are safe alternatives if a regulator fails. Also, this practice procedure helps a student learn how to control his glottis.

Photograph courtesy of Ed Brawley's Skin Diving School, Ed Brawley, Inc.

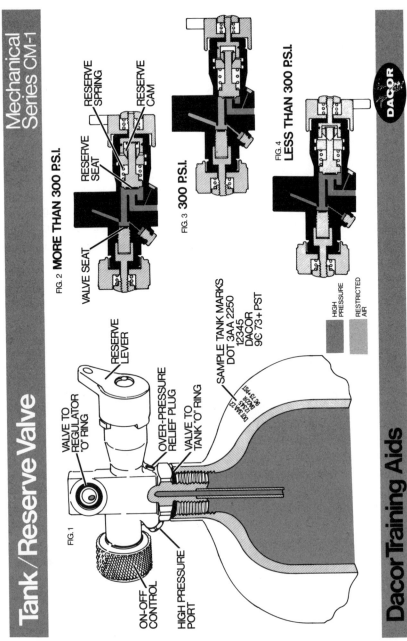

Tank/Reserve Valve

Mechanical Series CM-1

Dacor Training Aids

FIG. 2 **MORE THAN 300 P.S.I.**

RESERVE SPRING

RESERVE CAM

RESERVE SEAT

VALVE SEAT

FIG. 3 **300 P.S.I.**

FIG. 4 **LESS THAN 300 P.S.I.**

RESERVE LEVER

VALVE TO REGULATOR "O" RING

OVER-PRESSURE RELIEF PLUG

VALVE TO TANK "O" RING

SAMPLE TANK MARKS
DOT 3AA 2250
12345
DACOR
9C 73+ PST

ON-OFF CONTROL

HIGH PRESSURE PORT

FIG. 1

HIGH PRESSURE

RESTRICTED AIR

DACOR

Diagram of the Dacor Training aide for the Tank/Reserve Valve.
Mechanical Series CM-1 Training Aide courtesy of Dacor Corporation.

LECTURE OUTLINE FOR TANK/RESERVE VALVE CHART

Fig. 1 - Is a cutaway view of a standard 2250 p.s.i. steel cylinder, plus a partial cutaway of a tank valve, drawn so the instructor can show and explain the "O" ring seal from cylinder to valve, the extension tube used to reduce the possibility of foreign materials entering the valve from the tank, and the preliminary passage of air from cylinder to the final valve port and into a regulator. The basic parts of the valve are labeled for easy identification and explanation to students.

    (A) High pressure port, for installation of underwater gauge or accessory.

    (B) On-off control, should be closed when tank is empty; should be open completely when regulator is being used.

    (C) Val to regulator "O" ring, is the seal between regulator and valve, and should be checked for damage regularly. A spare should be carried by the diver in the event of loss.

    (D) Reserve lever, is in an up position, the normal position when starting a dive.

    (E) Over pressure relief plug, will release if tank pressure reaches 3200 p.s.i., which is the standard disc setting for a 2250 p.s.i. rated cylinder.

    (F) Sample Tank Marks:

        DOT...Department of Transportation (ICC, on older cylinders means Interstate Commerce Commission)

        3AA...Indicates type cylinder, in this case, chrome molybdenum steel.

        2250...Indicates working pressure of cylinder at 70 F.

        12345...Is a sample serial number.

        DACOR...Is the mark registered with the Bureau of Explosives, as the company for which the cylinder was made.

        9℃ 73...Is the hydrostatic test date of the cylinder, in this case, September of 1973. The symbol ℃ indicates Cochrane Laboratories, the testing agent.

        The plus (+) indicates the cylinder can be overfilled 10% of the rated pressure, (if the valve has a frangible disc relief valve.)

        PST...Indicates the manufacturer of the cylinder; in this case, Pressed Steel Tank.

Fig. 2 - Is a cutaway of a typical, spring loaded 300 p.s.i. reserve valve, with the lever in an up position, and air pressure in excess of 300 p.s.i. in the cylinder. The instructor can note the reserve seat being held open by this pressure, and the further flow of air past the open valve seat into the high pressure port, and out the final valve port.

Fig. 3 - Indicates the restriction of air past the reserve seat when the tank pressure reaches 300 p.s.i., and the reserve spring begins to hold the reserve seat down. Further lowering of tank pressure will close this valve completely.

Fig. 4 - Indicates the tank pressure, at less than 300 p.s.i. when the reserve lever has been pulled down, activating the cam, and removing the restriction caused by the spring loaded reserve seat in Figure 2. It can be noted that free air flow is now restored.

filler valve the same as you can from a regulator. This may be valuable information for a time when regulator failure forces you to buddy-breathe from a low air supply while you take time to unhook your regulator and breathe from the cylinder's filler valve.

Scuba tank valves come in two types: J and K. With a submersible pressure gauge in working order attached to your regulator—and you should not dive without one—the K-valve is sufficient. The J-valve warns when your air supply is down to 300 psi. The way you recognize the reduction is that it becomes really hard to pull air from your regulator into your lungs. You will feel as if you are sucking through a bent straw. That's when you'll feel the compulsion to pull the J-valve's reserve lever and give yourself the rest of the tank's air. If you do that, it's time to ascend and not dawdle.

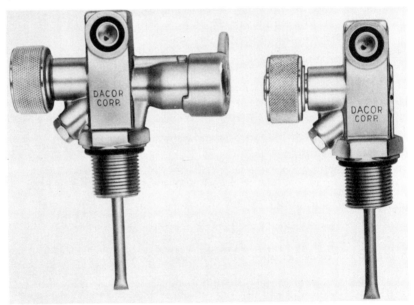

Scuba air-tank valves come in two types: J and K. Shown is the Dacor J-valve (left) with the reserve tilted upward in the activated position. This is a spring-loaded valve in a bright chrome finish, ¾-inch O ring seal, and a knurled on-off knob. It allows 300 psi reserve air supply. The K-valve (right) should be used with a submersible pressure gauge attached to your regulator.

Photograph courtesy of Dacor Corporation.

A word of caution about J-valves: sometimes they slip and release themselves, and so you don't have the reserve you anticipate. Sometimes, too, they stick and won't release when you pull on the wire rod attached. That's when you'll be forced to frantically reach behind your left shoulder and attempt to push down on the reserve lever—or get your buddy to do it. Another problem with J-valves is that sometimes a bump (into a coral ledge, for example) can knock down the lever without your knowing it. The moral of this story is that you should habitually check the J-valve reserve, topside before the dive and periodically underwater, to make sure the valve works and is positioned as you expect. *For J-valve positioning it's up to dive and down to fill.*

Ascending from a New Jersey coast wreck dive, I discovered that my J-valve reserve was down when I thought it was up. I needed air ninety feet down and there was almost none left. I rose the full depth expelling from my lungs, and managed to inhale the little air remaining in the tank. After that incident I gave up using J-valves. I avoid them now, and use K-valves with a submersible pressure gauge attached to my regulator.

The costs of scuba tanks and filler valves vary with the number of extra features you require. For example, a bare galvanized tank, new, is priced at $120. If the tank comes assembled with a K-valve, it will jump in cost to $150. Attach a J-valve instead, and it increases to $170. Coat it with colorful nonchip, nonscuff vinyl, add an unconditional one-owner, lifetime warranty, and the tank cost will rise about $15 more.

Be aware that all prices quoted are subject to a steady upward move annually. The increases have been 10, 15, and 20 percent even with more equipment sold to an ever-expanding diving market. There is no leveling off in sight.

Any time you transport a tank by automobile or boat, tie it securely and lock it or block it to prevent movement. Avoid leaving the cylinder standing or unattended, even in your garage or storage area. Don't carry the cylinder by the tank valve or reserve mechanism. Hold it by the backpack handle. Remove the regulator attached to the cylinder when you finish diving.

If you are not going to use your cylinder for three or four months, bleed the air pressure down to between 100 and 600 pounds (psi). Lay the tank in a horizontal position and rotate it every few months so that no moisture collects on any one part of the interior at the bottom. Otherwise a corrosive action will start inside. Keep the reserve mechanism lever at the up position even if the tank has only a small amount of air pressure left. Take off the bottom tank boot to eliminate sand and water, which can get trapped within seams. At least once each year have your cylinder visually inspected by the personnel of a dive shop.

Scuba Regulators

An air-pressure reduction valve, the scuba regulator attached to the scuba tank valve, allows divers to swim freely without being dependent on air hoses leading to a surface air supply. The scuba regulator was developed in 1943 by Emile Gagnan, a French

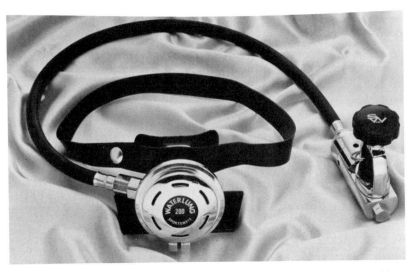

The scuba regulator, invented by Emile Gagnan and Captain Jacques-Yves Cousteau, is an air pressure-reduction valve. The Sportsways model W-200, shown, provides simplicity and efficiency. It features a balanced air flow through a piston of stainless steel, a teflon wiper backing up the O ring to prevent foreign particle entry, and a reversible teflon high-pressure seat. The G. E. Lexan Second Stage and soft, silicone mouthpiece allows for comfort.

Photograph courtesy of Sportsways.

engineer, and Captain Jacques-Yves Cousteau, the now famous underwater naturalist and film maker. It supplies air to the diver "on demand," at a pressure corresponding to the water pressure in which it is used.

The deeper you go, the greater is the ambient pressure and the less the regulator is forced to reduce the high-pressure air in the tank to a safe, breathable pressure. This action takes place automatically with no knobs to adjust and no buttons to push. A regulator of the single- or two-stage type does this under the same principles developed by Gagnan and Cousteau.

Although the early version of the scuba regulator was made as a single stage with two hoses that reduced the air pressure in one step from high to ambient, this is becoming an increasingly unpopular design. No longer are single-stage regulators being manufactured in the United States.

Most sport divers use the newer two-stage, single-hose air-pressure-reduction valve. This is a hookup of two regulators on

Most sport divers currently use the two-stage, single-hose air pressure-reduction valve—two regulators hooked up by means of one sturdy rubber hose such as Poseidon System's Cyklon 300 shown here. The Cyklon 300 has three air outlets, an antifreeze cap that can be filled with an antifreeze solution, and adaptation to 4500 psi. *Photograph courtesy of Poseidon Systems U. S. A.*

one sturdy rubber hose. It reduces the pressure in two stages. The first stage produces an intermediate level of pressure, usually around 100 pounds.   The second stage further reduces this pressure to ambient. Thus, the first stage is fitted into the tank valve and the second stage is located at the mouthpiece.

A two-stage regulator is also available in the two-hose design. The two stages are housed in a large metal container attached to the tank valve, and the mouthpiece holds no pressure-regulating mechanism.

The two-nose regulator conforms to either the single-stage or double-stage version of the scuba reduction valve. Of these two types, the single-stage regulator is no longer being manufactured in the United States. The two-hose, two-stage regulator as represented by this Nemrod Snark III Silver with a multi-port Venturi valve system provides maximum air flow with minimum inhalation effort. It is often preferred by underwater photographers and work-divers because exhaust air is vented behind the head, thus assuring unobstructed vision.

Photograph courtesy of U. S. Nemrod, Inc.

Both kinds of regulators, single- and double-hose, achieve the same easy air delivery underwater. When you want air it comes on demand.   You don't ever rebreathe the same air because exhalation sends air from your lungs into the surrounding environment. This is open-circuit scuba. It mechanically filters the air by means of a small filter screen, and it provides the proper volume at ambient pressure. There is no wastage of air; it delivers a low flow for relaxed diving and a high flow when you do hard underwater work.

Follow these steps for proper use of the scuba regulator:

1. Before attaching the regulator to the tank valve, open the valve a quarter-turn for a moment to rid the air valve of impurities.

2. Close the valve.

3. Check the amount of pressure in the air bottle with a tank-pressure gauge. See that the pressure in the bottle is not higher than the capacity stamped on its neck.

Check the amount of pressure in the air bottle with a tank pressure gauge as illustrated by the Healthways Tank Pressure Gauge and Yoke, as shown here.   *Photograph courtesy of Healthways.*

4. Mount your single-hose regulator to the tank valve so the single hose glides over your right shoulder. This is the only way an American-made regulator can be mounted and still work properly. If you mount it with the single hose sliding over your left shoulder, the regulator will be upside down and you won't be

able to exhaust it of water. Even "experts" sometimes mount a regulator upside down.

5. Finger-tighten the yoke—not too tight or you'll flatten the screw threads. The tank valve O-ring does the sealing.

6. Make sure the reserve valve is turned up, if your regulator features one or if the tank valve is of the J-type.

7. Turn on the tank valve at its handle all the way and then reverse a half-turn.

8. Draw air from the regulator to make sure it works.

For the double-hose regulator, mounting is performed with both hoses pointing upward. The exhaust hose is on your left side and the air intake hose on your right. When you need to clear a double-hose regulator underwater, roll to your left side and gravity will help you exhale the water. Turning on your back exhausts water, too, because air free-flows by rising upward toward the surface where pressure at the level of the tank is less than below you.

Scuba regulators vary widely in price. The costs range from $80

The elaborate and expensive "octopus" scuba system is an emergency back-up or alternative to "buddy breathing." In an editorial printed in the December 1975 *Skin Diver*, publisher Paul Tzimoulis said, "The trend is most definitely toward the octopus regulator concept, and buddy breathing may very well be obsolete in three years. Every major regulator manufacturer in the U.S. now manufactures, advertises, and promotes an octopus model. Practically every resort underwater guide and every instructor conducting open-water training sessions now wear octopus rigs as a regular part of their scuba dress. And octopus usage has become a standard in most all advanced diver training programs." The U.S. Divers octopus model 1099, shown, is a second-stage regulator and hose assembly that allows the diver to convert any regulator with multiple low-pressure ports to an octopus style. It has a 39-inch hose length.

Photograph courtesy of U.S. Divers Co.

for an old-fashioned single-hose two-stage to $210 for the elaborate "octopus" scuba system. What you buy will finally be determined by the options you desire and their extra cost. In general, it's known that the more options attached to a scuba regulator, the less ease of breathability it has.

Attention to your air delivery system is essential. Proper storage is the most important maintenance operation you can carry out between diving seasons or even between individual dives. After diving in salt water, contaminated water, muddy

Diagram of the Dacor Training aide for the First Stage-Piston regulator.

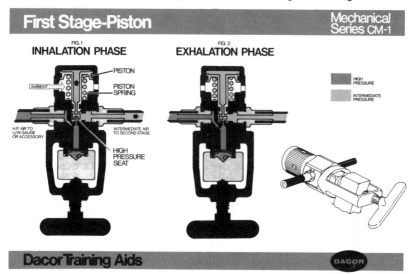

LECTURE OUTLINE FOR FIRST STAGE PISTON CHART

Fig. 1 – Is a cutaway of a typical piston regulator in the inhalation phase. The instructor can note the passage of cylinder pressure through the filter to the accessory port, and past the high pressure seat, where the different shaded area indicates the pressure breakdown from high pressure to intermediate pressure. Further passage of the intermediate air can be followed through the hollow shaft of the piston and into the dome of the unit, a flow which will continue until the intermediate pressure reaches a predetermined figure. This pressure is normally 120 p.s.i. to 140 p.s.i. over ambient depending on cylinder pressure. Further air flow to the second stage should also be noted, and location of "O" rings separating ambient from intermediate pressure can be mentioned.

Fig. 2 – Is a cutaway of a typical piston regulator in the exhalation phase. The instructor can note the high pressure seat is now closed, forced down against the piston spring tension by the predetermined intermediate pressure now in the dome of the unit. It can also be noted that upon inhalation, the intermediate pressure in the dome will drop, the spring will lift the high pressure seat, and air flow from the cylinder will resume for as long as inhalation continues.

Mechanical Series CM-1 Training Aide courtesy of Dacor Corporation.

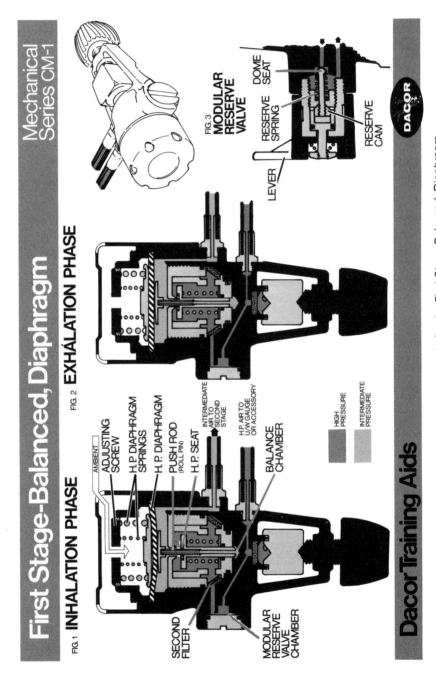

First Stage-Balanced, Diaphragm

Mechanical Series CM-1

FIG. 1 **INHALATION PHASE**

FIG. 2 **EXHALATION PHASE**

FIG. 3 **MODULAR RESERVE VALVE**

RESERVE SPRING

DOME SEAT

RESERVE CAM

LEVER

AMBIENT

ADJUSTING SCREW

H.P. DIAPHRAGM SPRINGS

H.P. DIAPHRAGM

PUSH ROD (ROLL PIN)

H.P. SEAT

INTERMEDIATE AIR TO SECOND STAGE

H.P. AIR TO U/W GAUGE OR ACCESSORY

BALANCE CHAMBER

SECOND FILTER

MODULAR RESERVE VALVE CHAMBER

HIGH PRESSURE

INTERMEDIATE PRESSURE

DACOR

Dacor Training Aids

Diagram of the Dacor Training aide for the First Stage-Balanced, Diaphragm.

LECTURE OUTLINE FOR FIRST STAGE, BALANCED–DIAPHRAGM CHART

Fig. 1 - Is a cutaway of a balanced first stage, adjustable diaphragm unit in the inhalation phase. The instructor should note the passage of cylinder air through the filter, to the accessory port, through, on this unit, the modular reserve chamber, through a second filter, and into what is actually a high pressure module. Location of the three "O" rings separating high pressure air from intermediate pressure air might be mentioned. Further flow of air past the high pressure seat, where reduction to intermediate pressure occurs, then into the area below the high pressure diaphragm and then to the second stage should be described. The mechanical action is as follows. The high pressure seat is being held open by the tension exerted on the push rod through the high pressure diaphragm by the high pressure diaphragm springs. It is important to note that the intermediate air is allowed to flow through the hollow push rod (roll pin) through the hollow shaft of the high pressure seat, and into the balance chamber located below the high pressure module. This means that the high pressure seat will have the same intermediate pressure exerted on both ends, and will be, in fact, balanced between the two. It also means that cylinder pressure should have no effect on the opening or closing of the high pressure seat at any time, so that intermediate air pressure will remain constant no matter what cylinder pressure might be. Intermediate pressure can be increased by turning down the adjusting screw, decreased by turning up.

Fig. 2 - Is a cutaway of a balanced first stage, adjustable, diaphragm unit in the exhalation phase. The instructor can note that the high pressure seat is now closed, and air flow has stopped. This is because the intermediate pressure under the high pressure diaphragm has reached a predetermined figure, usually 120 p.s.i. At this point, the high pressure diaphragm springs are forced up, removing the tension of the push rod and allowing the high pressure seat spring to close the seat. Upon inhalation, the intermediate pressure will drop, the springs will again exert tension on the push rod, the seat will open, and air flow will resume for as long as inhalation continues.

Fig. 3 - Is a cutaway of a modular reserve valve. The instructor may refer to the tank/reserve valve chart for a full description of its operation, with one notable difference. Due to a slight difference in application, a dome seat is used, rather than the flat reserve seat of the reserve valve. This is to allow a smooth flow of air past the seat when the reserve is in the restricting position and therefore prevent turbulence of the air flow to the high pressure seat. *Mechanical Series CM-1 Training Aide courtesy of Dacor Corporation.*

water, or chlorinated water, take the following actions to safeguard and preserve the tank valve and the regulator:

- Rinse the tank valve and reserve mechanism at the top of the cylinder.
- Wash the regulator hose.

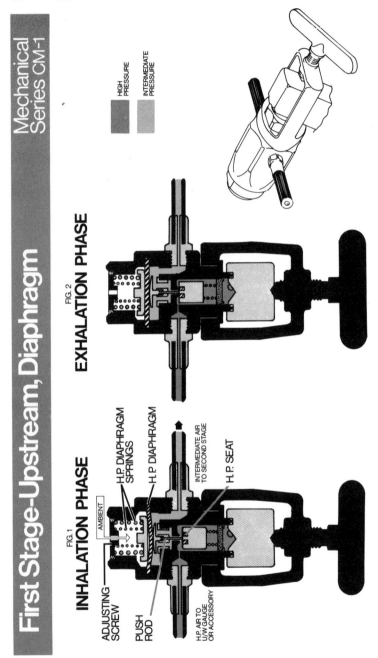

First Stage-Upstream, Diaphragm

Mechanical Series CM-1

HIGH PRESSURE

INTERMEDIATE PRESSURE

INHALATION PHASE
FIG. 1

EXHALATION PHASE
FIG. 2

ADJUSTING SCREW

PUSH ROD

H.P. AIR TO U/W GAUGE OR ACCESSORY

H.P. DIAPHRAGM SPRINGS

H.P. DIAPHRAGM

AMBIENT

INTERMEDIATE AIR TO SECOND STAGE

H.P. SEAT

Dacor Training Aids

Diagram of the Dacor Training aide for the First Stage-Upstream, Diaphragm.

LECTURE OUTLINE FOR FIRST STAGE, UPSTREAM–DIAPHRAGM CHART

Fig. 1 – Is a cutaway view of a typical upstream valve, adjustable, diaphragm unit, in the inhalation phase. The instructor can note the passage of cylinder pressure through the filter, into the high pressure seat chamber, to the accessory port, and past the high pressure seat, which is being held open by the high pressure spring tension being transmitted thru the high pressure diaphragm to the push rod. Intermediate air pressure can be determined by the lighter shades, and normally will range from 110 p.s.i. to 140 p.s.i. over ambient, depending on the unit and cylinder pressure. Tightening the adjustment screw will increase intermediate pressure, reversing will decrease it. The flow of air to the second stage should be noted.

Fig. 2 – Is a cutaway view of a typical upstream valve adjustable, diaphragm unit, in the exhalation phase. The instructor should note the high pressure seat is now closed, caused by the fact that the tension brought to bear on the push rod by the high pressure diaphragm springs was removed when the intermediate air under the high pressure diaphragm reached its pre-determined pressure and forced these springs up. The high pressure seat spring then closed the seat, and the air flow stopped. Upon inhalation, the intermediate pressure will drop, the high pressure springs will take over and open the seat, and air flow will resume for as long as inhalation continues.

Mechanical Series CM-1 Training Aide courtesy of Dacor Corporation.

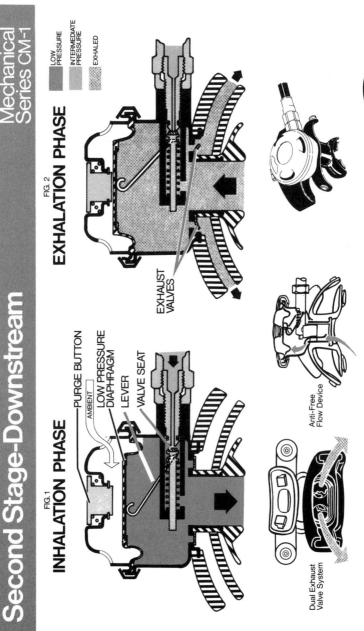

Second Stage-Downstream

Mechanical Series CM-1

LOW PRESSURE

INTERMEDIATE PRESSURE

EXHALED

FIG. 2
EXHALATION PHASE

EXHAUST VALVES

FIG. 1
INHALATION PHASE

PURGE BUTTON

AMBIENT

LOW PRESSURE DIAPHRAGM

LEVER

VALVE SEAT

Anti-Free Flow Device

Dual Exhaust Valve System

Dacor Training Aids

DACOR

Diagram of the Dacor Training aide for the Second Stage-Downstream Valve.

LECTURE OUTLINE FOR SECOND STAGE—DOWNSTREAM CHART

Fig. 1 – Is a cutaway of a typical downstream valve second stage in the inhalation phase. The instructor can note that intermediate air flows to the second stage valve seat where it will be reduced to slightly less than ambient pressure. This is necessary to allow the ambient pressure to push down the low pressure diaphragm, therefore depressing the lever, which in turn will raise the low pressure seat, and allow the air to flow to the diver for as long as inhalation continues. Action of the purge button on the L.P. diaphragm may also be mentioned.

Fig. 2 – Is a cutaway of a typical downstream valve second stage in the exhalation phase. The instructor can note that on exhalation, the exhaled air pressure will push the low pressure diaphragm up, or out, thus allowing the lever to rise, and in turn allowing the valve seat to close, and stop the flow of intermediate pressure air. Further mention should be made of the exhaled air passing through the exhaust valve(s), and then into the surround media, air or water.

NOTE: Also shown on this chart, is a more comprehensive drawing of the flow of exhaled air thru the exhaust valves, and into the media. Also, a diagram of the operation of an anti-free flow device on a high-volume flow unit, which will control the flow of water into the second stage when this part of the regulator is removed from the divers mouth underwater, or when the unit is dropped into the water at the surface.

Mechanical Series CM-1 Training Aide courtesy of Dacor Corporation.

Table 1.-- Comparative features of certain diving regulators

Features	Dacor 400	Scubapro Mark V	Regulators tested U. S. Divers Calypso IV	R. Aquamaster	Poseidon Cyklon 300
Balanced first stage	yes	yes	yes	yes	no
First stage mechanism	diaphragm	piston	piston	diaphragm	diaphragm
Rated pressure input, psi	3000	3000	3000	3000	4500
Octopus port	yes	yes	no[1]	no	yes
Extra tool or utility port	no[1]	no[1]	no[1]	no[1]	yes
Submersible air gauge port	yes	yes	yes	no[1]	yes
Anti-freeze protection available	no	no	no	--[2]	yes
Use on foreign tanks	limited	limited	limited	limited	worldwide
Intermediate pressure setting	adjustable	fixed	adjustable	adjustable	adjustable
Type of exhaust valve	dual disk	single disk	single disk	duckbill valve	circular membrane
No. of exhaust ports	2	1	1	1	13
Weight of 2nd stage, oz.	11.5	11.5	11.0	---	8.5
2nd stage special features	anti-free flow device	adjustable breathing device	special exhaust chamber	---	has flow ejector

1 Can be provided by special adapters.
2 Double hose regulators resistant to freeze-ups.

Table 1. Comparative features of certain diving regulators undertaken by Dr. Richard J. Boyd, Petrie Scubalab, Madison, Wisconsin 53713.

Table 2. -- Initial inhalation resistance of certain diving regulators[1]

Manufacturer	Model	Replicate	Resistance (cm of H_2O)	
			Per unit	Average of 3
Dacor	400	1	3.6	3.3
		2	2.6	
		3	3.6	
Scubapro	Mark V	1	3.3	3.2
		2	2.6	
		3	3.6	
U. S. Divers	Calypso IV	1	3.1	2.9
		2	2.8	
		3	2.8	
	Royal Aquamaster	1	3.8	3.2
		2	2.8	
		3	3.1	
Poseidon	Cyklon 300	1	1.1	1.2
		2	1.1	
		3	1.3	

1 Input pressure was 1200 psi.   *Tables 1 and 2 courtesy of Ron Ribaudo, President, Ribaudo & Schaefer, Inc.*

Table 2. Initial inhalation resistance of certain diving regulators studied by Dr. Richard J. Boyd, Petrie Scubalab, Madison, Wisconsin 53713.

- Make sure that any wash water is sparkling clean, non-soapy, and fresh.
- Make sure the dust cap or waterproof cap is in the high-pressure opening of the regulator so as to keep water or other substances from entering the high-pressure side.
- Putting the dust cap onto the first stage of the regulator, of course, means that you have detached it from the tank valve. Always do this immediately upon ascending from a dive into the boat or onto dry land. Never leave a regulator attached to the tank valve of a potentially rolling cylinder.
- Make sure the hose and mouthpiece are completely drained of wash water.
- Don't ever grease a regulator, even for long-term storage.

Table 3.-- Inhalation resistances of certain diving regulators at a flow rate of 15 cubic feet per minute[1]

Manufacturer	Model	Replicate	Lockup pressure (psi)	Resistance (cm of H_2O) Per unit	Average of 3
Dacor	400	1	140	5.1	4.3
		2	145	3.1	
		3	142	4.6	
Scubapro	Mark V	1	130	3.1	3.3
		2	135	3.6	
		3	135	3.3	
U. S. Divers	Calypso IV	1	130	2.6	2.8
		2	125	4.1	
		3	128	1.5	
	Royal Aquamaster	1	110	10.1	9.0
		2	110	8.6	
		3	115	8.2	
Poseidon	Cyklon 300	1	140	0.5	0.3
		2	145	0.0	
		3	145	0.4	

1 Input pressure was 1200 psi.

Table 3. Inhalation resistances of certain diving regulators at a flow rate of 15 cubic feet per minute studied by Dr. Richard J. Boyd, Petrie Scubalab, Madison, Wisconsin 53713.

Occasionally, remove the hoses of a double-hose regulator and wash them thoroughly with a mild solution of warm fresh water and detergent. Rinse thoroughly and dry completely before reinstalling the hoses.

When you wash out the mouthpiece of a single-hose regulator, do not depress the purge button. Pushing that front button permits the water to go back through the second-stage valve into the hose. Additionally, you won't be able to remove the regulator from the tank valve unless you have turned the tank pressure off. Before trying to remove the regulator from your cylinder valve, make sure all air pressure is vented from the regulator.

Store a single-hose regulator by hanging the first stage from a nail or hook to permit the second stage and hose to hang down.

Table 4.-- Comparative exhalation resistances of certain diving regulators in water

Manufacturer	Model	Orientation of second stage Resistance (cm of H₂O)		No. of exhaust ports	Total functional[1] exhaust area (sq. cm.)
		Swimming position	Upside down		
U. S. Divers	Deepstar I (Comparative control)	6.1	6.1	1	1.7
U. S. Divers	Calypso IV	4.3	5.6	1	3.9
	Royal Aquamaster	5.1	5.2	---	---
Scubapro	Mark V	4.8	4.6	1	3.2
Dacor	400	4.8	4.8	2	3.4
Poseidon	Cyklon 300	3.3	3.4	13	3.9

[1] Exhaust port area minus area blocked by valve support spiders X no. of exhaust ports.

Tables 3 and 4 courtesy of Ron Ribaudo, President, Ribaudo & Schaefer, Inc.

Table 4. Comparative exhalation resistances of certain diving regulators in water studied by Dr. Richard J. Boyd, Petrie Scubalab, Madison, Wisconsin 53713.

Make sure the dust cap is securely in place. To store your two-hose regulator for a long period, lay it flat with the back of the regulator down and the hoses on the same level. Wrap the whole thing in a plastic or cloth bag. Don't let the hoses get twisted, kinked, or bent.

Do not tamper with the interior of a regulator. Have it serviced annually by an expert.

Buying High-pressure Air

The air you breathe as a scuba diver must be free of toxic impurities or it will make you sick. Impure air can be downright hazardous. Contaminants in compressed air are not uncommon, and only the nature of those contaminants and their quantity can be regulated. Compressed air under high pressure may contain carbon monoxide, oil vapor, varying tastes, odors, oxides (like nitrogen dioxide), metal dust, carbon oil, pollen, dirt, and other unhealthy things.

The primary danger of impure air is that a scuba-cylinder air filling station may allow its air compressor to draw in fumes from sewers, chemical storage tanks, internal combustion engine exhausts, or lubricating oil from the compressor itself. In addition, the smog in city air can contain carbon monoxide in excess of the safe maximums listed by individual states. How can you protect yourself against this hazard? Where does your scuba tank air come from? Do you have rights as a compressed-air consumer?

As the purchaser and inhaler of air that has the potential to

The Haskel ScubAmp Air Booster system, a high-pressure air filling station, is shown on the opposite page. On the left, illustrated schematically, is a typical bank of storage cylinders being supplied from a high-pressure air compressor system of some type. The ScubAmp assembly makes it possible for a dive-shop operator to immediately fill 3000 to 5000 psi dive tanks with no change in his existing high-pressure air system other than to connect the ScubAmp assembly directly in series between his storage and his customer's dive tank. The air will pass directly through the free-flow condition of the check valves in the 28720 booster and continue on out the air outlet and into the dive tank until the dive tank pressure is equalized with the storage cylinder pressure.

This drawing courtesy of Haskel Engineering and Supply Company.

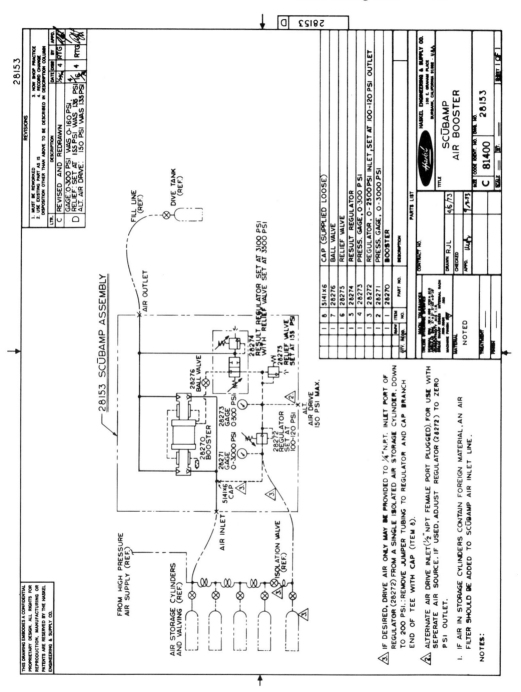

cause harm, you have every reason to question its purity. Consequently, the dive shop manager is under an obligation to open his air filling station for inspection to any diver who will be breathing air from its compressor. *If the filling station site is closed to public inspection, don't buy that air.*

What should you look for during an inspection? Check whether a setup is inside or outside. If it's outside, the air intake pipe should be stainless steel, plastic, or copper. Watch for metal intake pipes that sweat, yielding moisture and corrosion. Beware of galvanized intake pipes because of deposits of zinc oxides. Even worry about birds perching or nesting around an outside installation.

For an inside setup, the air intake line should be away from equipment rooms where temperatures are high, where there is little air circulation, where solvents are stored, or where water heaters, boilers, or other combustion equipment is used. All these are sources for potential contamination. Worry about excessive human habitation and tobacco smoking. Look to see if the air intake is located near the floor—it must not be. It shouldn't be near a garage for fear of carbon monoxide from automobile exhausts.

The average high-pressure compressor is good for a maximum pressure of 3000 psi. It is air-cooled and compresses air in four stages, or it is liquid-cooled and compresses air in three stages. In the first stage the air is compressed in one cylinder to a low pressure, about 80 pounds; in the second cylinder it is compressed to approximately 500 pounds; and in the third stage it is compressed to 3000 psi. Between these stages the air is cooled, because compression creates heat buildup.

A filling bench with a water bath is necessary. It ensures that the air cylinder stays cool during the filling operation. The bottle is filled from a cascade system connected by copper, stainless steel, or flexible hose pipe. But the hose should be breathing air hose of medical grade, not hydraulic hose.

If the air filling station seems not to meet standard qualifications, take your air to a state agency for testing. Find out

(Above) Captain Don Stewart makes an adjustment on the air compressor machinery at Aquaventure dive shop, Bonaire, N. A. *Photograph by Morton Walker.*

(Below) To insure that the air cylinder will stay cool during the filling operation, a filling bench with a water bath is necessary. The bottle is filled from a cascade system connected by piping which is copper, stainless steel, or flexible hose of the "medical grade" type. Here, Daniel Greenblatt, scuba instructor at Aquaventure fills five air cylinders at the same time. The large gauge shows a filling pressure of 2250 psi. *Photograph by Morton Walker.*

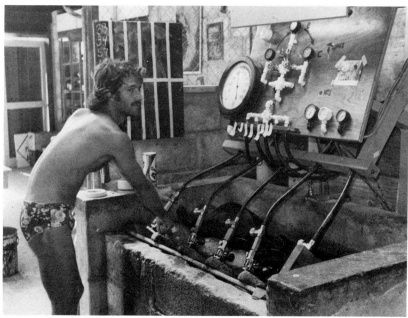

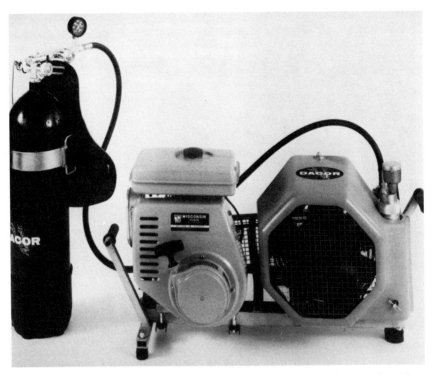

A portable, lightweight compressor that will travel in the car trunk, or boat, is manufactured by a number of companies. This type of compressor is ideal for individual divers or dive clubs or for small dive shops. The Dacor Turbo Compressor model CP-3G, shown, weighs 110 lbs. yet fills tanks to 3,200 psi at 3-cu.-ft-per-minute. It is powered by a 4.6 hp air-cooled engine and features an auto relief valve, deluxe filling attachment, separator, filter, and a rugged steel frame with four rubber-suspension shock-absorbing legs.

Photograph courtesy of Dacor Corporation.

where testing agencies are by inquiring at your local fire station, the city health department, or the state office building. Complain to the authorities if the air you are buying to breathe underwater is contaminated and detrimental to your health.

And follow this final bit of advice: *Never have your tank filled where you have any doubt about the purity of the air.*

Backpack and Harness
For comfort and an even distribution of weight when wearing a

For comfort and an even distribution of weight when wearing a scuba tank attached to your back, the backpack and quick-release harness are necessary.

Photograph by Morton Walker.

scuba tank attached to your back, the backpack and quick-release harness are necessary. Assemblies to hold your air cylinder might be made of plastic, hard rubber, galvanized steel, or aluminum. Harnessing straps are nylon, with stainless-steel buckles for quick releasing. These harness arrangements resist the corrosive and deteriorating effects of salt water.

Of the backpacks, the newer clamp-on type is handiest to use. It lets you change air cylinders in just seconds with easy tank positioning. But a word of caution about clamp-on backpacks: *The clamp can slip, which loosens the band and lets the tank float free.* This happened to me at 65 feet in the waters of Bonaire, Netherlands Antilles. Unknown to me, my tank had come loose; the clamp had let go.

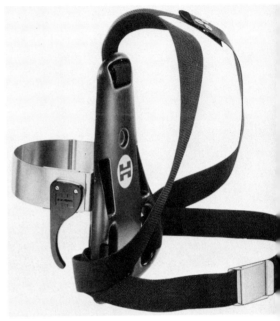

Of the backpacks, the newer clamp-on type similar to the Healthways Quick Cam Scubapak, shown, will let you change air cylinders in just seconds with easy tank positioning.
Photograph ccurtesy of Healthways.

At first I felt a repeated tapping on my hip, as if someone were trying to attract my attention underwater. But no one was near me as I traversed the cliff face of the drop-off at Carl's Hill. Not even my buddy was around. I felt annoyance at myself for losing sight of him. Realizing I had broken a prime rule of diving, I set about looking for my buddy, but circumstances interrupted me. Just a few moments later I felt a tug at my mouthpiece, on which I tightly clamped my teeth; my head was jerked sharply to the right. I looked down and discovered my scuba tank floating down around my ankles, prevented from falling to the bottom only by the stretched regulator hose held by my teeth. This was not a very desirable situation to be in!

I reached down to gather the air cylinder into my arms and sought help from the nearest diver in my group. He and his buddy worked steadily at depth, replacing the cylinder correctly in its backpack, and I continued with the dive. My only feeling of

This photograph, taken in 50 feet of water at Bonaire, N. A., shows a potentially serious accident being prevented. Scuba instructor Ebo is replacing the air cylinder that he caught just as it was slipping out of the lady's backpack. Warning: The clamp can slip in a cam-type band to let the tank float free. Make sure it is tight enough. *Photograph by Morton Walker.*

upset was with my own rule-breaking and with my remiss buddy. The comment he made when I complained of his neglect was a shrug of the shoulders and the words, "You should have clamped your backpack on tighter!" About that, he was correct!

The better backpacks possess a vinyl-coated, all-metal back plate that is contoured to evenly distribute the weight. With use of this plate, you'll find there is less pressure per square inch on your back. Make your personal strap adjustments slip-proof by tightening the wing nuts at the side of the waist. Critical suiting-up time can be reduced to a minimum if you lock your harness to your own adjustment.

Check all quick-release buckles, and have your buddy set your pack in a comfortable position. If your tank is fastened properly,

Make your personal strap adjustments slip-proof by tightening the wing nuts at the side of the waist. Check your straps and quick-release buckles. Shown here, a diver is adjusting his own backpack straps for a proper and comfortable fit.

Photograph courtesy of Ed Brawley's Skin Diving School, Ed Brawley, Inc.

the valve's outlet will be facing you. In that way, being mounted on the valve, your regulator will set smoothly into the high-pressure port. Make sure the tank is positioned within the backpack so the valve won't bump your head and the boot won't bump your butt.

Some backpacks comprise a totally integrated all-in-one diving system, combining all life-support equipment in one fully-equipped unit for diving freedom and mobility. This U. S. Divers UDS-1 System that takes three air cylinders is such a pack. It is capable of holding 105 cu. ft. of air at 3,000 psi, 12 cu. ft. of reserve with a quick-release buckle system and attached regulator and valve mechanism with two low-pressure ports.

Photograph courtesy of U. S. Divers Co.

The most economical combination of backpack and harness, sold new, is priced at about $20. It probably won't have the handy clamp-on release. That fancier backpack and harness costs $40 and more.

Exposure Suits and Accessories

To keep you warm underwater, two types of exposure suits are manufactured—the *dry suit* and the *wet suit*. In the earlier days of diving the dry suit was quite popular. It was patterned after the successful commercial diving suit, made from thin sheet rubber. Within it, the diver wore long underwear and other woolens with which to provide insulation and warmth. It is not the most effective dress for holding back the coldness of water at depth, and was largely abandoned in favor of the wet suit.

There is now, however, a new kind of inflatable dry suit, the sort of diving suit commonly used for descending under ice and

A new kind of inflatable dry suit permits comfortable descent under ice and other cold water diving. It is the inflatable dry suit that the U. S. Navy has tested with refrigerated water in pressure chambers, pointing up the unusually effective insulating qualities of these inflatable exposure suits.

Photograph courtesy of Poseidon Systems U. S. A.

other cold-water diving. The U.S. Navy has, in fact, made pressure-chamber tests with refrigerated water that point up the unusual insulating qualities of the inflatable suits.

Ten different brands of these new diving suits are now manufactured, all capable of being partially inflated to prevent squeeze and to provide insulation against cold. Jack McKenney, former editor of *Skin Diver,* reported on them in the magazine's October 1975 issue. The manufacturers and their products (addresses are listed in Appendix 5) are:

- BayleySuit, Inc.—The Aquastatic
- Harvey's—Viking Variable Volume Suit
- Imperial Manufacturing Company—The Bubble Suit
- O'Neill, Inc.—The Supersuit
- Sea Suits—The Inflatable
- Seatec—Third World Suit
- Sub-Aquatic Systems—Comfort System Suit
- U.S. Divers Company—The Dry Suit
- White Stag Water Sports—Thermal Dry Suit
- Poseidon Systems, U.S.A.—The Unisuit

The best-known inflatable dry suit is the Unisuit, which was imported as a unique product from Sweden in 1966 by Poseidon Systems, U.S.A. Inflatable dry suits are competitively priced in the vicinity of $300.

Diving in temperate climes can be a chilling experience unless you wear a well-designed, perfectly fitting exposure suit. Most of today's insulating suits are wet suits made of unicellular neoprene rubber about 3/16 inch thick. Better wet suits have a backing of stretch nylon or some other synthetic nondeteriorating material to prevent tearing and add strength. A personalized tight fit is critical for this piece of anti-exposure equipment. You should have a custom-designed wet suit made to your exact specifications. Your dive shop dealer can make the arrangements.

A neoprene exposure suit lets the diver get wet, as its name implies. A layer of water is allowed to seep inside the suit upon your entry into the medium. That's the only time a cold-water shock will startle you into acute awareness of where you are. But

Photograph courtesy of U.S. Divers Co.

Photograph courtesy of O'Neill Inc.

Ten different brands of dry, inflatable exposure suits are being manufactured. Among them (above, left) is U.S. Divers' innovative styling with entry through the neck opening and sealed by the neck ring. The suit is easily inflated through the low pressure supply hose which has a quick-disconnect fitting. The dump valve with extra large push button and gas passages allows rapid suit depressurization with precise buoyancy control capability. This is the Aqua-Lung Professional Dry Suit. The O'Neill Supersuit (above, right) approaches the neoprene, inflatable dry suit idea from a flexible free-flow vantage point. It is a protection garment that is easy to wear, allows free unencumbered movement, provides safety for the novice, is durable, and is unbelievably warm. Entry is through an opening across the shoulders.

Most of today's exposure suits are wet suits made of unicellular neoprene rubber about 3/16 inch thick. They have a stretch-nylon backing to prevent tearing and usually should be custom fitted to your personal specifications. The various types shown are manufactured by Parkway Fabricators who contour design suits with arms and legs shaped in a natural swimming position.

Photograph courtesy of Parkway Fabricators.

your body very quickly warms the layer of water under the suit. The skintightness of custom-fitted wet suits prevents the water from circulating and being lost as an insulator. Insulation and protection against cold, then, derive from the neoprene and the layer of water warmed by body heat. Pressure won't build up inside the suit even with submersion to depth because of a free passage of water.

Wet suit thickness needed varies with the temperature of the water you intend to dive in. Suit material is offered from the thickest, 3/8-inch, to the thinnest, 1/8-inch. Although the thicker material offers more insulation, it is very bulky and restricts movement.

The complete custom package for a wet suit—including deluxe Farmer-style suit, cold-water hood, high-top boots, and gloves

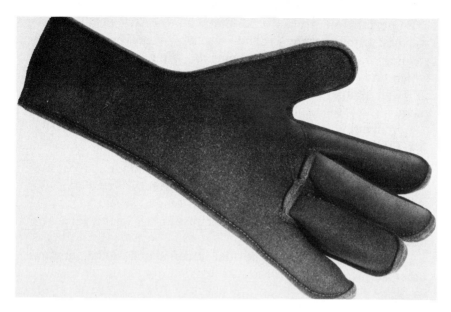

Mittens or gloves of the five-finger type help to prevent frigid hands and retain manual dexterity under water. Shown here is the Scubapro five-finger glove that combines dexterity with durability. It is a pliable ⅛" neoprene for comfort and warmth with nylon lining inside and out for rugged wear.

Photograph courtesy of Scubapro.

(all done in an elegant sharkskin finish), with knife pocket—made to order, can cost you $285, plus. Heavy-duty nylon gloves cost about $15; five-finger gloves are around $17; molded-sole boots are in the $25 range.

Fins invariably fit more comfortably if they are worn over neoprene rubber boots with hard soles, molded soles, or foam soles. Diving boots need to be a lot more than comfortable. They should be warm and durable and provide a secure walking surface that also minimizes slipping when you wear them topside. A foam-neoprene hood will keep your head warm, too.

Unfortunately, unfitted wet suits and accessories make some people look like unreal store-window mannequins. It isn't the diver's shape that's wrong. More likely it's a lack of good fit and construction to the highest standards. It's best to have your wet suit fitted at your area dive shop.

Some form of protective clothing is necessary in all but the warmest tropical waters. The wet suit, by preventing warmth-stealing water exchange, prevents the draining of body heat, which brings on early diver fatigue. As a general rule, skin diving in water temperature below 78°F. demands an insulating garment.

For maintenance and repair of your form-fitting suit-for-the-sea, follow this checklist:

• Repair any rips with a suitable rubber bonding agent such as neoprene cement, probably available from the same dive shop where you purchased your wet suit.

• Avoid storing or drying your subsea suit in the wind or in direct sun.

• Sprinkle nonscented powder or cornstarch on the outer and inner surfaces of the rubber and nylon for longer periods of storage.

• Hang the suit pants and top on wide wooden hangers in a cool place.

Hang the full exposure suit, pants and top, on wide wooden hangers in a cool place. Photograph taken at Aquaventure, Bonaire, N. A. Note the tote boxes for scuba gear stored on shelves above the exposure suits. This is a convenient storage system for diving tourists at warm-water resorts. It permits them to store full diving gear at the dive shop without having to tote equipment back and forth to their guest rooms.   *Photograph by Morton Walker.*

• An alternate method is to store them flat with tissue paper placed between the rubber folds.

For the short term between dives, a standing clothes tree conveniently stores equipment not in use, in the least space practical. Zippers should be of nylon or stainless metal. Pay particular attention to proper maintenance of zippers at the crotch piece and at the chest and arms, especially for putting the wet suit away for a long time. Here's your procedure:

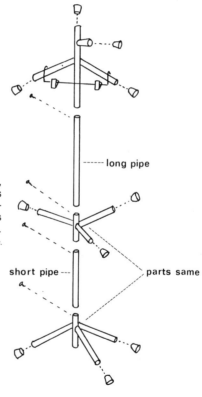

long pipe

short pipe

parts same

For short term storage between dives, a standing clothes tree such as this Duncan's Divers Valet will conveniently hang equipment not in use. It's a space saver.

Diagram courtesy of Duncan Dive Products, Inc.

• Rinse the zippers with fresh water.
• Wipe them dry to make sure the moisture is out from between the zipper teeth.
• Grease them lightly with a silicone or graphite lubricant.
• Don't let the lubricant get on the rubber.

Weights and Weight Belts

Even in salt-water diving, less attention to maintenance is required for lead products and webbed materials. Care of weights and weight belts consists merely of fresh-water rinsing and complete air-drying. Nothing in ordinary diving use can damage lead weights to cause their destruction.

To descend quickly with a minimum of effort against your own buoyancy, particularly when you must remain at about the same depth along the bottom or for a decompression stage, you will need weights on a belt. You should wear a weight belt with a

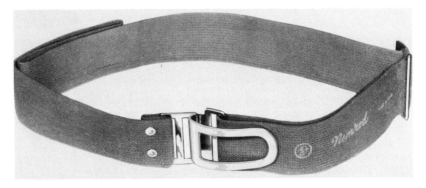

You should wear a weight belt with a safety-release buckle made of noncorrosive metal, to release fast with just a flip of the wrist at the buckle clasp. The Nemrod belt shown is constructed of 2-inch-wide nylon webbing. For ease of fit, it is adjustable.   *Photograph courtesy of U.S. Nemrod, Inc.*

safety-release buckle, usually attached to the various webbed straps holding equipment to your body. The buckle is made of noncorroding metal and releases quickly with just a flip of the wrist at the buckle clasp. A weight belt costs about $7 and lead weights, about $3 per pound.

An absolute safety rule is: *Never attach weights to your body by tying them on with a rope.* An occasion may arise when you must ditch your weight belt fast. Untying the knot in a water-soaked rope can be deadly slow. You may find it necessary to quickly drop your weight belt, a monetary loss though it may be.

Moreover, weights should be interchangeable to adjust buoy-

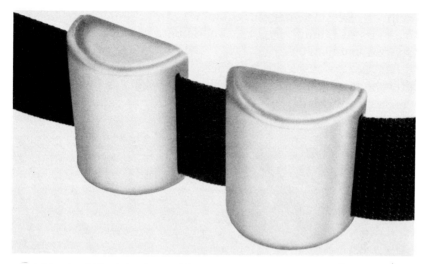

Weights should be interchangeable to adjust buoyancy as you need it. These Scubapro two-and-one-half-lb. weights can slide onto a weight belt with ease. They are slotted, allowing them to be added or removed as required.

Photograph courtesy of Scubapro.

ancy as you need it. For easier sliding along the belt webbing if the slit in a lead weight is too narrow, file or slice slivers of lead out of the weight's slip opening to widen it. Inventor Dana B. Duncan has patented a flexible weight belt filled with lead shot, which lets you eject a small amount of lead to change your buoyancy.

Captain Don Stewart and Bruce "Teacher" Bowker of Aquaventure, Bonaire, Netherlands Antilles, are dead set against overweighting. Captain Don says, "Please don't overweight. Everyone seems to think that you need all that lead to put you down. Not true! Lead smashes up the reef—causes extra exertion—gives you less time on a dive."

The Diver's Knife and Other Tools

A sharp diver's knife can be an indispensable underwater tool. But contrary to movie adventure films or pulp fiction, a diver's knife is not useful for fighting off sharks or cutting away octopus arms. Rather, its use comes from cutting oneself out of tangling kelp or releasing snagged equipment from antler coral, or for purposes of bottom digging. The knife and sheath will run you approximately $20.

The underwater knife is predisposed to rust. Your best bet to prevent this common problem is to buy only a high-tempered chrome-steel blade. The blade should be attached into a

Diving equipment manufacturers make knives in many shapes and sizes, but overall the diver's knife primarily is a digging or prodding tool underwater. Many knives have measurement markings for determining the size of objects. Some of these markings can be seen on the U. S. Divers knives shown here.

Photograph courtesy of U. S. Divers Co.

nonfloatable, easy-to-grip handle. A floatable knife is an inconvenience because if you fumble with it, and it gets lost from your grip, the knife will float up to the surface. You may, for some reason, take the easy way out and buy a cheaper diver's knife without a rustproof blade. In that case, after each exposure to water, fresh or salt, oil it well. Otherwise, you will doubtless discover that it has lost its edge and is rusting into powder.

Storage of the underwater knife for a long period of time demands that you coat the blade with petroleum jelly. Always pack your knife away in its sheath.

Captain Don Stewart suggests using an underwater hand pick or geologist's hammer rather than a knife. He finds it more useful for digging, holding yourself on the bottom, hauling yourself along against bottom currents, breaking open a sea urchin to feed the fish, and holding the pick head in your hand to push yourself off from underwater obstacles with the handle.

Underwater archaeologist Aaron Furman prefers a mountain climber's ice ax. "The ice ax," he says, "is an implement useful as

Underwater archaeologist Aaron Furman prefers a mountain climber's ice axe as an underwater implement in place of a diver's knife. The ice axe is useful for ramming, as a wedge, or as a lever, and it has a needle point for killing a dangerous animal if necessary.

Photograph by Jo Furman.

a battering ram, for holding as a wedge, or as a lever. It has a needle point useful for anything that an ice pick would be good for, but it has enough weight in the head to let you get a fairly good swing. The other end is flat. It is a fine implement for a wreck diver working on an archaeological project in strong current. It will act as a lever to move beams. A holster on your hip is the best way to carry the ice ax underwater."

Scuba Gauges

The various scuba gauges should, wherever possible, possess large numerals and be color-coded for instant underwater reading. Gauges give you vital information, and the mere accessibility of scuba gauge readouts offers a feeling of security underwater.

This is the Aquastar Navigator Panel. This divers' instrument panel is delivered with compass module, oil-filled depth gauge module, and also has a seat for a diving watch. All Aquadive watches will fit in watch seat (except Combination Time/depth). The advantage of this modular concept is that the instruments can be exchanged if necessary.   *Photograph courtesy of Aquadive.*

These are the gauges you may want close at hand: the depth gauge, a scuba diver's watertight wristwatch, a submersible regulator gauge, the nitrogen decompression meter, and a liquid-filled underwater compass.

The diver's watch is represented here by four models from Favre-Leura of Geneve.
Photograph courtesy of Favre-Leura.

Scuba gauges need meticulous care after diving, but even more so after exploring in salt water or contaminated water. The depth gauge requires perhaps the most attention. This is the maintenance program to follow after each sport dive wearing the depth gauge:

• Shake the gauge well to make sure all the water has left the bourdon tube or the diaphragm area.

• Soak it in fresh water.

• Don't just rinse it; rather, wash thoroughly around the diaphragm opening or bourdon tube opening to exert a pressure.

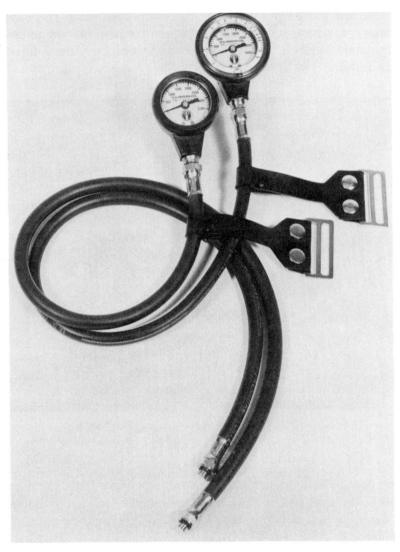

The U. S. Divers products shown are a right angle 3,500 psi pressure gauge (on the left) to measure cylinder pressure. It has a 360° swivel, replaceable O-ring seal and lens, a rubber cover and blow-out plug. The gauge on the right is a combination pressure and capillary depth gauge.   *Photograph courtesy of U. S. Divers Co.*

For proper cleaning after using gauges in muddy or polluted water, submerge them in fresh water for a minimum of thirty minutes. Wash off any clinging debris from a compass, nitrogen meter, underwater watch, submersible pressure gauge, or depth gauge. Again, salt water is the most destructive element that can come into contact with the sensitive mechanisms of one of these gauges. Don't allow corrosive salt to remain in contact with any of the delicate parts.

The prices of gauges run all over the map. For instance, watches can cost anywhere from $25 to $225; depth gauges are $8 to $50; an automatic decompression meter is about $85; a submersible pressure gauge can run about $45; the new combination pounds per square inch diving timer costs as much as $100; compasses range from $5 to $75. Remember that prices are increasing each year for every piece of diving gear. Be prepared to spend more than the prices quoted here.

The Scubapro Contoured Capillary Depth Gauge has a large dial for quick reading at a glance—without turning the wrist. *Photograph courtesy of Scubapro.*

5

Preparing to Use Scuba

The compressed-air open-circuit self-contained underwater breathing apparatus (scuba) has liberated innerspace travelers, novice and advanced sport divers, who explore the wonders of the subsea world, submerged for long periods without attachment to the surface. The basis of scuba, the demand regulator, is used in combination with a compressed-air cylinder and a high-pressure cylinder valve. This is the aggregate gear popularly known today as scuba.

Demand-type or open-circuit scuba is the only form of underwater breathing apparatus recommended for a sport diver's use, and the only one described in this book. The other type, closed-circuit scuba, consists of a breathing bag from which the diver inhales and a purifying canister through which he exhales. This closed-circuit scuba is considered too dangerous for recreational purposes. Very little of the gas supplied to the system is exhausted from the system; it is recirculated. For that reason the closed-circuit system is recommended only for the U.S. Navy or professional underwater workers.

With compressed-air open-circuit scuba, there is little risk of oxygen poisoning. A novice needs only a relatively short time to

Demand-type or open-circuit scuba is the only form of underwater breathing apparatus recommended for a sport diver's use and the only one described in this book.   *Photograph by Morton Walker.*

become familiar with compressed-air breathing. In addition, a diver finds it comforting to see expelled air bubbling upward, a sign that all is well with one's breathing device.

One precaution deserves mentioning: *Don't use pure oxygen in open-circuit scuba.* An explosion can occur if a residue of oil vapor comes into contact with an oxygen charge. Also, breathing pure oxygen lets you dive only in shallow waters because of its partial pressure danger.

The oxygen partial pressure (the percentage of O_2 in the breathing mix multiplied by the ambient pressure) determines oxygen toxicity. If you dive to just 33 feet, you double the ambient pressure and double the O_2 pressure. This increased pressure drives more O_2 into the body, with resultant oxygen toxicity. Symptoms include convulsions, transient constriction of retinal blood vessels, and other minor symptoms, such as nausea, muscle twitching (especially at the lips), vertigo, visual abnormalities (particularly reduction of peripheral vision), irritability, and numbness. Susceptibility to oxygen poisoning varies, but the danger arising from the use of pure oxygen in open-circuit scuba at depth is certain, so be wary of using it. You could forget the precautions necessary with oxygen inhalation when using open-circuit scuba.

How to Mount the Regulator on the Tank

When mounting the regulator on an air tank you will immediately come into contact with the regulator yoke and the protective cap. These items are located at the high-pressure stage. Before turning the thumbscrew to loosen the yoke and remove the cap, first check your regulator for leaks. *Never dive with a leaking regulator.*

Check for Leaks

Take the mouthpiece of your breathing regulator in hand while the protective cap is still sealed in place. Attempt to inhale from the mouthpiece. You should come up completely short of air. If you pull in air, check the hose for breaks or cuts, especially where connectors hold rubber hose to metal parts.

Next, use your tank-pressure gauge to determine how much air is compressed into the cylinder. *Always check cylinder air pressure before diving.* Do this even if you have just finished filling the cylinder. Avoid using any tank that's filled to less than 70 percent of capacity.

With all equipment checked and functioning well, turn the thumbscrew to unscrew the regulator yoke. Remove the protective cap from the regulator's high-pressure orifice. Seat this high-pressure output valve in place at the top of the cylinder. Make sure you fit them together exactly so that no leaks occur. To check the air flow, turn the knob of the tank valve to let air into the high-pressure port of the regulator. Improper placement or a worn O-ring may allow leakage.

An O-ring lost from the tank valve is a common and frustrating problem. This is generally a result of abuse of your equipment—excessive jostling, or the insertion of an O-ring of the wrong size, one that's outworn, or one that is not securely seated in the valve. For this reason, most diving stores and dive resorts put a piece of masking tape on the filler valve to hold in the O-ring and keep the high-pressure port sealed against dirt. You will discover that the most common problem is a badly seated regulator. When this happens, air under increased pressure when you turn on the valve will take the course of least resistance. The valve's O-ring may be forced out of the valve and be lost or damaged or rendered otherwise useless.

Always carry a spare O-ring. Often, the regulator's protective cap contains a channel that readily holds a spare O-ring. There are several other places where spare O-rings can be stored on a diver's equipment:

• At the mask—on the strap, on the snorkel holder, between the purge valve and cap.

• At the regulator—between the yoke and the yoke screw.

• At the personal flotation device—on the oral inflator, on the CO_2 inflator line, between the knob and inflator, on the straps.

• At the wet suit—attached to the zipper tab.

• At the compass, depth gauge, diving watch—attached to the strap, used in place of a strap loop.

After the regulator is well coupled to the air cylinder, open the tank valve and listen for leakage. Another way to check for air leakage is to submerge the top of the cylinder in water with the regulator attached; you'll be able to spot any escaping air bubbles. Mount a single-hose regulator so that the hose passes over your right shoulder when you don the tank.

Summary procedure for tank attachment of your regulator:
    1. Turn the thumbscrew to open the regulator yoke.
    2. Slip the yoke over the tank valve.
    3. Line up the input orifice on the regulator with the O-ring on the tank.
    4. Seat the orifices exactly into each other.
    5. Turn the yoke thumbscrew finger tight to secure regulator and valve together.
    6. Let air enter the regulator by turning the valve handle.
    7. Check your regulator's monitor pressure gauge for a reading similar to the tank gauge reading from before.

A few regulator rules are vital. Be cognizant of your regulator as a delicate instrument on which your life depends. Therefore, don't stow a tank with the regulator attached. Keep dirt, salt, barnacles, corrosion, sand, water, and other impurities out of the high-pressure inlet to the first stage. Thoroughly dry the dust cap and place it over the high-pressure orifice as soon as you are finished diving. Make sure you wash your regulator with its dust cap in place in warm water. Let it soak for a few minutes while you run water through the second stage and out the exhaust ports. Do not depress the purge button or you'll be pushing impurities up into the interstate hose. If by accident the purge is pushed, replace the regulator on the tank and again blast air through it.

How to Don Your Tank

The easiest way to put on the aqualung apparatus is to have your diving companion hold the rig while you slip your arms into the harness. As you put your hands behind you to support the cylinder, your buddy can adjust the straps to fit your body. Make sure your chest strap is not overly tight.

For donning the tank yourself, the following technique is best. Sit in front of the tank, slip your arms through the straps, and check them for proper size. Adjust the straps to conform to the needs of your shoulders. Fasten the shoulder straps; leave the waist strap unfastened. Place the tank standing upright on its tank boot so that the straps and backpack are facing away from you. Slip your hands inside the straps and grasp the backpack at its handles, if any. The straps will be lying over the backs of your hands or wrists. Lift the tank up and over your head and flip it

To don the tank by yourself or with some assistance, lift the tank up and over your head and flip it gently so that the backpack touches against your back and the straps have slid down your arms to your shoulders. Putting a tank on over-the-head is a matter of coordination more than muscle.
Photograph courtesy of Ed Brawley's Skin Diving School, Ed Brawley, Inc.

gently so that the backpack touches against your back and the straps slide down your arms to your shoulders. Make sure the shoulder straps lie flat and untwisted. Fasten the waist strap until it is comfortable.

A double-hose regulator will flop over your head into position if you simply duck forward quickly. You'll find the single-hose regulator dangling at your right side. Grasp the regulator by its neck strap and bring the mouthpiece to your mouth.

Do not fasten the regulator neck strap around your neck. The steel snaps on a neck strap tend to corrode after a few dives and are almost impossible to remove in an emergency, especially if you're wearing gloves underwater or if hands are numb from cold. Buddy breathing is hindered by an attached neck strap, too. You might be fiddling with the fasteners on a neck strap while your buddy is bursting for a breath—and he might decide to help you cut the neck strap with his diving knife.

Pre- and Postdive Tips for an Equipment Check

Before donning your tank and entering the water, a predive checkup of *all* your equipment *every* time you dive is advisable. The first item to look over should probably be your personal flotation device.

A predive life vest inspection consists of removing the CO_2 cartridge and ensuring that its threads are still lubricated with silicone. Operate the detonator pin a few times to make sure it will puncture a cartridge that's in place. Inflate the vest orally and watch for leaks. Deflate the vest to flatten it and replace the CO_2 cartridge.

Before slipping into your wet suit, look it over for weak spots or tears. Rubber cement or liquid latex strategically applied to areas that need treatment will help prolong the life of this garment.

Make sure your weight belt will hold you in neutral buoyancy. Take into account that your wet suit fills with air and adds to your body's natural buoyancy. Add or subtract weight so that you gently sink after exhaling and gently float after inhaling. To overcome the problem of weights that slide on the belt, put a machine screw through the web belt into the lead weight. The screw can be removed for weight adjustment.

Keep diving boots and gloves handy for use in cold-water diving. The neoprene of these accessories can be repaired in the same way as a wet suit can. For foot blisters on tender toes from fins that have rubbed, Band-aids or moleskin applied before diving will give preventive protection while you're in the water.

Make sure fins are in best shape. A few simple adjustments may be required. Drainage holes may be blocked; cut the extra rubber from those holes. A few taps with a hammer to spread and secure the end of the buckle pin will prevent a buckle from coming loose. Tape a piece of old wet suit on the inside of each fin strap to insure comfort at the Achilles tendons. This simple procedure involves cutting the wet suit material in the shape of the fin strap and applying liberal amounts of electrical or water-hose repair tape to keep it in place.

Make sure your fins are in good shape when you perform your predive checkup. To insure comfort, tape a piece of wet suit material on the inside of the fin strap. A small piece of nylon line attached to the heel strap will let you more easily slip on the fin heel straps.

Photograph courtesy of Ed Brawley's Skin Diving School, Ed Brawley, Inc.

To more easily slip on fin heel straps, attach a small three- or four-inch piece of nylon line to the heel strap. To put on the fins, you need only slip your foot firmly into the pocket, reach down, grasp the nylon line, and pull.

For easy identification underwater when you're swimming away from your group, paint a distinctive design on the bottom of your fins. The marks can also be used to indicate which are left and right in the case of custom-made fins.

To make more drain holes in either the top or the sole of the foot pockets to allow less slip-on resistance, heat a sixpenny nail over a charcoal brazier, grasp it with a pair of pliers, and make a few well-placed thrusts to produce small holes. Small holes are better than large because they let water run out without too much sand seeping in.

To prevent rubber and plastic deterioration—cracking and hardening from salt, ozone, and ultraviolet radiation—after diving equipment has been used in salt or chlorinated fresh water, two maintenance methods are worthwhile. Fill a tub, sink, or clean trash can with warm water. To this add one teaspoon of Shaklee Basic-H,® a concentrated organic cleaner from Shaklee Distributors that is not a soap or detergent but a softening agent to make water wetter. This allows deeper penetration into the rubber pores, especially of wet suits, where salt or chlorine deposits build up. Put all the rubber items into the solution and let them soak for about twenty minutes. Then rinse with fresh water and allow to dry away from direct sunlight.

For the straps of mask and fins, apply ArmorAll GT-10®, which is available at most hardware and automotive supply stores. This is a polymeric formulation of deterioration inhibitors, excellent for protection and preservation of natural and synthetic polymer materials in an adverse environment. It is a safe, nontoxic water solution that is waterproof. ArmorAll GT-10 absorbs the agents that cause cracking, weakening, hardening, and decay. It can improve equipment appearance while stretching and giving with the material.

For instrument protection, use your wet suit, gloves, boots, and hood to pad your gauges before you place them into your dive bag. This will prevent them from being jarred, and saves room in your dive bag for other items.

An excellent equipment checkout idea suggested by the NAUI Diving Association is to count the number of items of equipment you are using and to remember the number. Then, when you are packing your equipment for a dive trip and just before you go into the water, take a quick recount. You might have thirteen items—hood, gloves, buoyancy compensator or life vest, weight belt with weights, knife, boots, fins, mask, snorkel, compass, depth gauge, wet suit, and diver's watch. The last number you counted is the important one to remember. Most divers keep track by the sequence in which they put on their equipment.

Equipment-Donning Sequence

The sequence you don your equipment in before the dive will likely always be the same. Consequently, it's best to formulate good habits from the novice stage onward. After you've assured yourself that your gear is in the best of diving condition, put it on in a precise sequence. Put on the various gauges. Slip on your exposure suit; first if it is the type without a nylon lining, sprinkle it liberally with talcum powder. The powder will prevent its binding and catching at your skin as you pull on the pants or jacket. However, an exposure suit with nylon on the inside will slide on smoothly without powdering.

Slip the flotation vest or buoyancy compensator over your head

Shown here is Captain Don Stewart of Aquaventure, Bonaire, N. A., who wears his safety vest against his body, under his wet suit. Note that he has made a hole through the wet suit jacket through which he has passed the inflator valve of the life vest. The air is distributed evenly all around his body that way. You see him under water ditching and shifting air cylinders in this picture.

Photograph courtesy of Bonaire Tourist Information Office.

and fasten its strap loosely around your waist. Captain Don Stewart wears his safety vest against his body under his wet suit. He has made a hole through the jacket through which he passes the inflator valve. That way, the air is distributed evenly all around his body. No straps fastened on land should be secured snugly; they will constrict your movements or retard your breathing under water. To prevent recurrence of any prior chafing around the neck from straps or from a wet suit, use a piece of kitchen plastic wrap. Cross it once like a scarf where the irritation occurs at your neck and tuck the ends into the wet-suit jacket. This will eliminate friction rub.

Don the tank and regulator assembly as described, where you can sit down near your fins, mask, snorkel, gloves, boots, and so

Put on the tank and regulator assembly where you can sit down near your fins, mask, snorkel, gloves, boots, etc. While sitting, don the equipment in this order: boots, weights, fins, gloves, and mask attached with snorkel. In the picture, the diver in the foreground is putting on gloves after slipping the mask on his face. These divers are preparing for a back roll, tank first water entry over the gunwhale of a small boat.

Photograph by Morton Walker.

on. The filled cylinder will make you feel top-heavy and clumsy. While sitting down, don these items in order: boots, weights, fins, gloves, and mask with attached snorkel.

How to Enter and Exit the Water

A frequent result of getting fully suited up for diving is that you will feel overheated, awkward, and weighted down. You'll sense yourself using up valuable energy before diving, which must finally result in fatigue even before you enter the water. You can avoid this predive fatigue by suiting up correctly and by getting into the water right away.

Entering and exiting the water are often the hardest work connected with the whole scuba experience. The one entry that I do not recommend is the "Mike Nelson" headfirst entry. *Do not dive in headfirst while wearing scuba gear.* The faceplate of the diving mask could crack or the mask be ripped over your nose and mouth. The air tank could smash the back of your head or the regulator mouthpiece loosen some teeth. A headfirst entry will leave you momentarily disoriented when you hit the water, and this has been known to panic some new divers.

In 1972 underwater archaeologist Fred Dickson died of a severed artery in the head, resulting from a skull fracture incurred while jumping from his dive boat into the water. In a freak accident, the impact of the water against his face mask fractured his skull. He had been searching for Columbus's flagship *Santa Maria.*

The three most popular ways to enter the water wearing scuba equipment are the "front step, feetfirst" approach, the "back step, feetfirst" entry, and the "back roll, tank first" method. The technique used is determined by the site you are embarking from.

The *front step, feetfirst approach:* stand on the edge of the pier

The front step, feetfirst water entry calls for you to make sure your front step is a long one so that your tank clears the edge of the pier or large boat gun-whale. Note that the diver is outfitted with the octopus rig as a regulator to preclude the need for sharing air with a diver in trouble by means of buddy breathing. More and more, octopus rigs are being used by sport divers. *Photograph by Morton Walker.*

or a large boat gunwale and step out into space. Your front step should be a long one to ensure that your tank clears the edge. Hold yourself standing upright to prevent yourself from bellyflopping forward or from being carried backward by the weight of the air cylinder.

A *back step, feetfirst entry* is used only when the distance between the land base and the water's surface is less than six feet. There is no particular advantage in this entry over the front approach; the back step requires more attention to where and how you're landing. You will hit the water on your seat and on the tank.

This diver is about to make a back step, feetfirst water entry wearing scuba. The back step requires your attention to where and how you are going to land in the water so that you hit on your seat and on the tank.   *Photograph by Morton Walker.*

The *back roll, tank first method* causes less wear and tear on the diver; this is a water entry that's used when the boat is small and the gunwales low and narrow. Sit on the boat rail, hold your mask against your face, and roll backward. You will flop over the side and be able to orient yourself in the water rather quickly.

A variation on this method is the *side roll technique.* To retain balance on a tossing boat in rough water, this entry is best. Instead of sitting on the gunwale, crawl up to it on all fours and fall sideways over the rail.

For any water entry while wearing snorkel or scuba gear, *always hold your mask close against your face* with one hand. Your fingers can be placed with palm on the faceplate and fingers braced against the top of your head or with fingers on the faceplate and thumb under your chin. The point is that just holding on to your mask won't keep it in place—when you hit the water your arm jars and moves the mask unless your hand is braced. Hold your free hand to your waist or use it to support the bottom of your tank to keep it from bobbing in its harness. If there is no one to hand a camera down to you in the water, your free hand could also hold camera equipment close against your body to prevent it from being jarred as it hits the water.

Climbing a ladder up or down for exit or entrance is another practical way to get in the swim. The problem with this method is that the weight of the tank and associated gear saps your strength when you are out of the water.

In general, a few guidelines should be followed for safe and effective water entry.

• Don't jump up and out from a boat or dock with heavy gear on; gravity will pull you down to hit the water's surface harder.

• Don't carry a spear gun or camera or other loose piece of equipment; you might lose it when you hit the water. Carrying something sharp is dangerous. Enter the water first and have a boatman or dockside person hand you the gear after you are in.

• Wear the snorkel in your mouth rather than the regulator.

• Secure your mask to your face by holding it on with one braced hand. The faceplate will be protected against jarring that way.

• Make sure your air cylinder is snugged into its backpack so it won't smack your head when you hit the water.

To exit the water into a boat, it is best to remove your weight

To exit from the water into a boat, it is best to first remove your weight belt and used air tank before attempting to climb a Jacob's ladder or boarding ladder. Hand up your fins, too, so you can fit your booted or bare feet into the ladder rungs.

Photograph by Morton Walker.

belt and used air tank before attempting to climb a Jacob's ladder or boarding ladder. Hand up your fins so you can fit your booted or bare feet into the ladder rungs. If the boat is small, exit the water over the transom. If the motor is in the way so that you must pull yourself in over one side, ask your boat tender to counterbalance your weight by sitting on the other side.

6

How To Operate Underwater

Preparing to Submerge

Having entered the water at your dive site, make these surface observations: the visibility distance, the strength of currents and their direction, and the water temperature. Look at cloud formations, water ripples, wind velocity, and the weather you are temporarily leaving. Remember these conditions—any changes in their pattern will be a sign that you should be alert to possible hazards. Satisfy yourself that the situation is right for a dive.

Set the mouthpiece comfortably, and with your regulator delivering compressed air for breathing at regular intervals, signal your buddy that you are prepared to submerge. Premeasured lead weights should make you slightly positive on the surface and neutrally buoyant ten feet under the surface. In order to submerge you will have to expend some effort with a surface dive. If you are lucky enough to be outfitted with a buoyancy compensator, you'll be able to lower yourself as if you were on an elevator.

When diving from a boat, you can steadily submerge by pushing yourself down the anchor line. As a more advanced diver, you will feel confident enough to face head downward and kick steadily in descent. In either case, equalize pressure in your ears with ambient pressure—otherwise you could feel pain.

(Above) Having entered the water at your dive site, make surface observations relating to visibility, current strength and direction, water temperature, cloud formation overhead, water ripples, wind velocity, and the kind of weather you are temporarily leaving. Remember these conditions because any changes in their pattern will be a sign that you should be alert to possible hazards. Satisfy yourself that the situation is right for a dive.

Photograph courtesy of Ed Brawley's Skin Diving School, Ed Brawley, Inc.

If you are outfitted with a buoyancy compensator (BC), you will be able to lower yourself as if you are on an elevator. Merely dump the air in your vest for a descent by raising the valving mechanism on the BC and compressing the mouthpiece. *Photograph courtesy of Ed Brawley's Skin Diving School, Ed Brawley, Inc.*

When diving from a boat,
you can steadily submerge
by pushing yourself down
the anchor line.

Photograph by Morton Walker.

Descending

Clearing Your Ears

To clear your ears while descending it is important to start the process even before you enter the water. Yawn to open the eustachian tube valves inside your head. After you enter the water, provide air to the middle ear from your scuba by breathing steadily. This will provide air at different pressures to the middle ears at two feet, four feet, six feet, and so on. As you go deeper, keep pace with the ambient pressure at your new depth. Don't get behind or you will have to stop and do the *Valsalva Maneuver,* an emergency trick of holding your nose and blowing. If you make a faster descent, inhale faster with smaller breaths.

Eardrums push in or out when there is a difference between the water pressure outside your eardrum (ambient pressure) and the air pressure inside the middle ear. But two throat valves at the

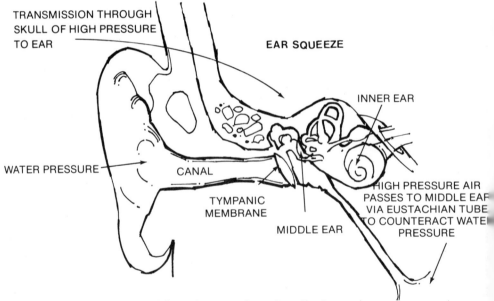

Pressure is exerted from the water inward on the tympanic membrane, and within the middle-ear space, from the surrounding tissues. High-pressure air entering the mouth and nose passes directly through the eustachian tube, raising the pressure to that of the water. Blockage of the eustachian tube eliminates this route of equalization and a pressure gradient develops with capillary dilation and possible rupture, and flexion inward of the tympanic membrane and possible tearing of it.

lower end of your eustachian tubes, away from the ears, open when you swallow, yawn, or breathe. Divers new to the sport seem not to take advantage of their physiology. They feel pain upon descending because by the time they begin to equalize, the valves are already closed against pressure. From all sides the surrounding water squeezes the internal valves shut, and a diver in pain must stop and face the risk of eardrum rupture by holding his nose and blowing. This nose-blowing technique forces air through the eustachian tube to the middle ear and relieves the problem, but it's at the expense of the flexing eardrum. This bit of anatomy, possibly out of flexing practice from your sitting behind a desk all season, will protest after a time with pain or "ear block."

Besides breathing steadily, holding your nose, and blowing, you can relieve ear pressure by snorting into your mask, swallowing, and wiggling your jaws. Do this continuously throughout your descent. Never wear earplugs while scuba diving or skin diving. Water pressure can drive earplugs into the outer ear canal and even into your eardrums.

In addition, a hood or a bathing cap covering the ears can cause external ear squeeze. Do not punch holes in your wet suit hood to make it easier to clear your ears. Once you've done that, the holes do nothing but allow cold water to circulate for the entire duration of the dive. Instead, just lift the hood away from the ears a couple of times to equalize during the descent.

Clearing Your Mask

As you submerge, regardless of how snug a fit your mask appears to make on your face, water is likely at some time to leak inside and obscure the faceplate. You'll experience discomfort and distorted vision from this, but the problem is easily rectified.

To clear your flooded or leaking mask underwater, consider the physical law involved. The lighter-weight air, blown into your mask through your nose, will go to the top of the mask and force the water out through the bottom. To accomplish this, merely look up at the surface, push the top of the mask against your face,

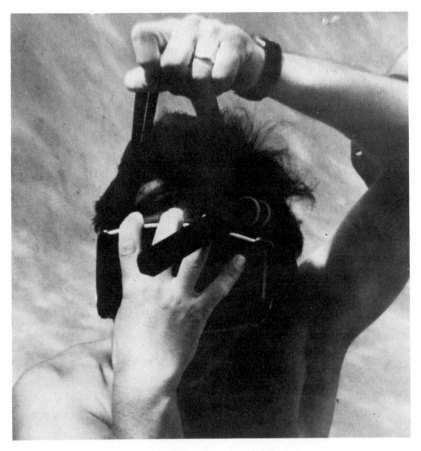

To clear your flooded or leaking mask under water consider the physical law involved—lighter weight air, blown into your mask through your nose, will go to the top of the mask and force the water out through the bottom. To accomplish this, merely push the top of the mask against your face and exhale.

Photograph courtesy of Ed Brawley's Skin Diving School, Ed Brawley, Inc.

and exhale through your nose. Another way to perform this mask-clearing technique is to roll to your side and push your mask against your face at the higher side while exhaling through your nose. The water will be forced out through the tiny opening on the bottom of the mask because of the air pressure you are exhaling.

The purge device built into the faceplate of some masks acts as a one-way exhaust valve for this purpose, too. You don't have to roll onto your back or lift your face to the surface to push water out of your mask. Simply exhale air through your nose to force water out through the purge.

Clearing Your Mouthpiece

It isn't unusual for a diver to remove his regulator mouthpiece to slip a camera strap around his neck. Because of this possibility, it is mandatory to be able to clear your water-filled mouthpiece so you can inhale from it again.

Underwater, it is not unusual for a diver to remove his regulator mouthpiece for the purpose of slipping a camera strap around his neck—or for some other reason—as illustrated here by Aaron Furman, Jr. at a depth of 65 feet.

Photograph by Jo Furman.

While scuba diving among strangers off Baja California, using a two-hose regulator rented from one of the local dive shops, an accident occurred to me that pointed up the importance of being able to clear water from a regulator. I was diving over a drop-off at a depth of 120 feet. During inhalation as usual the presence of water in my air system became apparent. Combined with some air, it gushed into my mouth. At first I thought the leak came from the mouthpiece. I began my ascent expelling air in a hum. At 60 feet I felt compelled to inhale again. This time I received no air but a lot of salt water. I realized then that I was in serious trouble. I wanted air and had none to breathe.

I kicked steadily upward, all the while holding myself in check against panic. During the few seconds I rose, I ran my hand along my right intake hose and came to a portion where the rubber attaches to the metal air-delivery part of the regulator. I felt the hose where it had come away from the metal of the regulator. Ordinarily it should have been attached by a clamp. The clamp had come undone and disappeared.

Grasping the hose end, I guided it onto the air-delivery output and held it in place, my right thumb and index finger squeezing tight and acting as the clamp. Those next split seconds forty or fifty feet underwater called for sureness in the next few actions. I didn't know if the hose would deliver air. As I finned steadily upward, I removed the mouthpiece and raised it higher than the regulator—and air flowed freely. The escaping air forced water out of the intake hose. My hand clamping was working.

All this time I was slowly rising and expelling my breath; I now had nothing left. I faced the surface, still holding the mouthpiece high, and turned the mouthpiece opening downward. Then I stretched my neck, reached up with my face, and replaced the bubbling mouthpiece between my lips. Using any vestigial remains of lung air, I exhaled sharply and chanced an inhalation. Whether I lived or choked at that moment depended upon my old-fashioned, nonreturn valve, two-hose regulator functioning again—and it did! I pulled in air mixed with some water spray.

I rolled to the left to drain the remaining water into the exhaust hose. Then I exhaled with short, forceful breaths to clear the exhaust hose altogether.

Buddy Breathing

No diver should ever dive alone. This means that the buddy system is used in diving. If possible, you should be accompanied by a partner whose skills and behavioral psychology are well known to you. The buddy system is employed alike by novice divers, advanced divers, and most professionals.

Inherent with this system is the buddy rule: *Always stay within close support range of your buddy.* An excellent arrangement to follow, especially if your buddy is a stranger (which occasionally happens during diving vacations), is to agree in advance to surface at once when you lose contact with your partner. It is proper for buddies to check each other's equipment operation underwater and to watch out for odd behavior from nitrogen narcosis. Master diving instructor Ed Brawley offers this advice: "If your buddy is fifty feet away at the bottom of a 100-foot ascent, you would be foolish to try swimming to him with the need to buddy-breathe. Not understanding, he may turn and swim away from you. Do a proper free ascent instead. If at all possible, buddies should remain within half-a-dozen feet of each other below."

Buddy breathing is assisting your partner with air from your own tank, or being assisted by him, in the event that one of your

Buddy breathing involves assisting your partner with air from your own tank in the event that his system malfunctions.

Photograph courtesy of Ed Brawley's Skin Diving School, Ed Brawley, Inc.

systems malfunctions. The four-cycle breathing technique —exhale, inhale, exhale, inhale and hold it—will let you share a single air supply with a buddy. Follow these steps if your breathing apparatus fails and you suddenly feel a block in your ability to inhale:

1. Attract your buddy's attention and tell him your air supply is cut off: use the "cut-throat" gesture; swipe your turned-down palm across your throat.

2. Show your need to buddy-breathe by pointing to his mouthpiece and then to your mouth. Remove your failed regulator mouthpiece to emphasize your meaning.

3. Approach your buddy to half an arm's length. Put your left hand on his right shoulder and his left hand on your right shoulder. Hold each other's shoulder harness strap so as not to drift apart.

4. Do *not* grab for your buddy's mouthpiece; let him decide to hand it to you. Take it and exhale, inhale, exhale, inhale; hand back the mouthpiece so that he can also go through the four-cycle breathing technique. As he inhales and holds his second breath, he will pass the mouthpiece back to you.

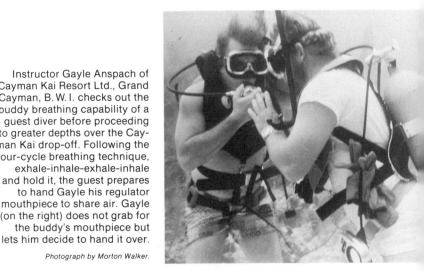

Instructor Gayle Anspach of Cayman Kai Resort Ltd., Grand Cayman, B. W. I. checks out the buddy breathing capability of a guest diver before proceeding to greater depths over the Cayman Kai drop-off. Following the four-cycle breathing technique, exhale-inhale-exhale-inhale and hold it, the guest prepares to hand Gayle his regulator mouthpiece to share air. Gayle (on the right) does not grab for the buddy's mouthpiece but lets him decide to hand it over.

Photograph by Morton Walker.

The sharing buddy's hand is on his own mouthpiece with the borrower's hand (Gayle Anspach, right) lying over his only to guide its direction into the mouth.
Photograph by Morton Walker.

5.   Your buddy's hand should be on the mouthpiece with your hand lying over his only to guide its direction into or out of your mouth. As both of you steadily ascend, do not hold your breath—exhale during the ascent. Making a moderate humming sound is a good way to exhale while ascending.

As both air-sharing buddies ascend steadily, neither one holds his breath. They exhale during the ascent, making a moderate humming sound.

Photograph courtesy of Poseidon Systems, U. S. A.

6. Try to relax and use as little air as you can as you make your way to the surface.

7. If for some reason of panic you refuse to allow the return of your buddy's regulator, he will be perfectly justified in placing one hand on your faceplate and pulling the regulator out of your mouth with the other.

How to Ditch and Don Scuba

To develop skill and confidence in your ability to handle yourself underwater, the drill exercise of scuba ditch and don is sometimes carried out. Many scuba instructors use this as a final swimming-pool test before taking you for your open-water dive. Ditch and don may serve the purpose of preparing you to perform this feat in the open water, too, in cases where you need to change tanks during the long wait of a decompression stop. I should point out, however, that this ditch and don exercise has lately been criticized as serving no real purpose unless you become entangled in kelp or other obstacle and must remove your scuba to unsnarl yourself.

At the deep end of the pool while you are wearing the full scuba pack, remove your equipment underwater. Stay in a kneeling position; this allows you to depart from the equipment once you've ditched it. Follow this procedure exactly:

An instructor teaches his diving class how to ditch a tank underwater. After removing and laying fins together on the pool bottom, he assumes a kneeling position, removes weight belt, lays it over legs to hold them down, unbuckles the scuba harness at the waist and begins to pull it over his head.

Photograph courtesy of Ed Brawley's Skin Diving School, Ed Brawley, Inc.

Remove your fins and lay them side by side on the pool bottom. Assuming a kneeling position, remove your weight belt and lay it over your legs to hold you down. Unbuckle the scuba harness by pulling the quick-release mechanism at the waist and one shoulder. Slip out of the harness and rebuckle the open shoulder

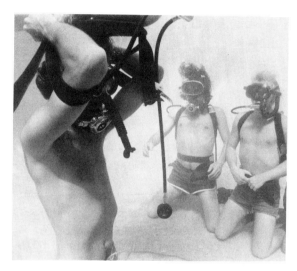

The diving instructor has taken hold of the backpack handgrips to steady the tank as it slides over his head while he's on the bottom of the pool. His students are preparing to follow his example.

Photograph courtesy of Ed Brawley's Skin Diving School, Ed Brawley, Inc.

The tank moves forward to float downward in front of the diving instructor. He has demonstrated the correct method of ditching a tank underwater.

Photograph courtesy of Ed Brawley's Skin Diving School, Ed Brawley, Inc.

strap—not the waist strap. Place your weight belt over the scuba pack to anchor it on the pool floor. Inhale a breath and hold it while you shut the valve to cut off the tank air supply. Tuck the mouthpiece under the regulator if it's a two-hose model and on top of the first stage if it's the one-hose type. Remove your mask, leave it lying on your backpack, which is facing upward, and while exhaling make a free ascent from the bottom. As you ascend, make a 360-degree turn as if looking for obstacles. Remember to constantly exhale, and do not surface faster than sixty feet per minute.

In open water, students practice donning scuba tanks over their heads the way they were taught to perform in a swimming pool.
Photograph courtesy of Ed Brawley's Skin Diving School, Ed Brawley, Inc.

The procedure to don scuba equipment is a reversal of what you've just done. Dive to the equipment. Find the tank valve and turn it on. Put the mouthpiece in your mouth and breathe from the regulator. Slip your mask onto your face and clear it of water. Being able to breathe and see will allow you to take your time with donning your equipment. Place the weight belt across your legs as you kneel. Slip your hands inside the harness straps and pull the tank over your head, the way you learned to don the tank yourself. Make sure all unit straps are secure. Replace the weight belt around your waist, slip on your fins, and ascend as usual, making a 360-degree turn.

Making a Free Ascent

In most underwater emergencies there is no reason to ditch your breathing apparatus to make a free ascent without it. If you must ditch, though, here is how to do it:

Draw your buddy's attention to what you must do. Pull the quick-release belt mechanisms that hold your tank harness to your body. As the tank floats upward behind you, reach back and pull it over your head. Take a last inhalation, lay the tank on the floor, and cover it with your weight belt to prevent it from drifting away. You may be able to go back to fetch it later.

Begin your ascent without kicking faster than one foot per second. *Don't ascend faster than your smallest air bubbles.* Exhale the compressed air from your lungs as you rise. A good practice is to tilt your head toward the surface in order to open your air passages. Remember—it is the last fifteen feet of ascent that are dangerous. Where you might start fast from the bottom on a free ascent, slow down about twenty feet from the surface.

Guiding a group at 50 feet, a dive tour leader was confronted by a diver stricken by panic when his breathing apparatus failed. No octopus rig was being used, and the tour guide went through the usual four-cycle breathing routine preparing to buddy-breathe. His second inhalation came just in time as the panicked diver grabbed for the guide's mouthpiece.

Jamming the regulator bit into his own mouth, the stricken fellow swam for the surface, dragging the diving guide behind him. Being experienced, the guide tried turning the diver in order to buddy-breathe, but panic seemed to prevent any responsive action. The stricken diver just kicked and clawed upward while the tour leader could only hum in exhalation and follow.

Uncomfortable with the situation and knowing that he would ascend faster alone, the guide decided to make for the surface. He dropped his weight belt, pulled the quick-release buckles holding the harness onto his back, and let the tank drop away as the panic-stricken diver held it clamped by the mouthpiece between his teeth. Air volume in the guide's lungs increased as he made a free ascent. Boyle's Law came to his aid, although a slight pressure pain hit his chest, either from rising too fast or from exhaling inadequately. He slowed his ascent near the last fifteen feet, using the force of his will as he expelled any remnants of air from his lungs. He made the surface none the worse for wear.

Underwater Orientation

The magnetic wrist compass for underwater direction is invaluable for orienting where you are and where you wish to go. There are certain inherent inaccuracies, but overall, the compass will lead you if you use it right.

Poor visibility or far distances to travel underwater are two reasons for relying on compass readings. These readings can prevent your getting lost underwater. Follow three rules to easily manage underwater compass readings.

The magnetic wrist-compass such as this U. S. Nemrod lubber-line-type model with markings on the face and gun-sight-type sight will lead you where you want to go under water. Follow the easy rules for underwater compass readings: have the lubber line lying in the direction in which you wish to travel, sight over the compass and not down at it, and wear the compass on a wrist with no other ferrous metal objects present. *Photograph courtesy of U.S. Nemrod, Inc.*

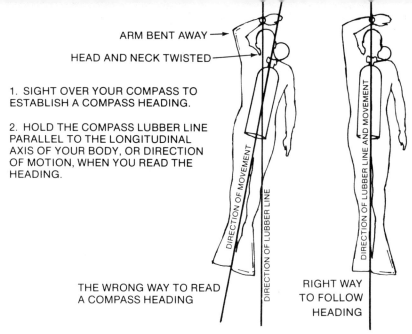

ARM BENT AWAY →

HEAD AND NECK TWISTED →

1. SIGHT OVER YOUR COMPASS TO ESTABLISH A COMPASS HEADING.

2. HOLD THE COMPASS LUBBER LINE PARALLEL TO THE LONGITUDINAL AXIS OF YOUR BODY, OR DIRECTION OF MOTION, WHEN YOU READ THE HEADING.

DIRECTION OF MOVEMENT

DIRECTION OF LUBBER LINE

DIRECTION OF LUBBER LINE AND MOVEMENT

THE WRONG WAY TO READ A COMPASS HEADING

RIGHT WAY TO FOLLOW HEADING

1. Make sure the compass's lubber line is lying in the same direction as your body is traveling through the water. If it is not, you will be following a heading that's right but a direction that's wrong. This will put you far away from your intended object.

2. When sighting, don't look down at the compass; rather, sight over it. Hold the compass up in front of your eyes when you take a bearing on an object.

3. Wear the compass on your wrist with no other ferrous-metal objects on the same wrist. Other iron gadgets will throw off a correct reading by causing a magnetic variation.

Using the formula **speed × time = distance,** a scuba diver's watch can also be used for orientation. First determine your underwater swimming speed. Lay out a 100-foot-long or longer course. Swim the course at your usual cruising speed and time yourself as you do it. Divide the distance by the number of seconds it takes to cover it to learn your feet-per-second velocity.

If 200 feet (back and forth your 100-foot course) takes you fifty seconds, you swim underwater at the rate of four feet per second. If a distant object takes you five and a half minutes of underwater swimming to reach, it can be judged to be a quarter of a mile distant.

Using your diver's watch and compass, you'll have the ability to navigate and orient yourself in different directions underwater.

7

Underwater Physiology

To dive safely it's important to follow nature's laws. Violating them won't just bring you some minor slap on the wrist from a sitting judge; punishment can be permanent in the form of bodily changes. Skin-diving physiology demands constant care. Diving is great fun, filled with exciting experiences, but divers must follow certain established rules.

Working and playing underwater puts physiological stress on the whole human system. This is permissible within limits; the body can take stress of relatively short duration and allowable circumscribed physiology. It has great adaptive powers, and will refunction as usual when it finally returns to the conditions under which you normally live. Only when stress is severe or overly long does diving present a physiological problem.

Chief among various stresses are the forces of pressure from two sources, air and water. This chapter covers the human physiology associated with these sources of underwater stress. This is not a medical text, however, and its information assumes that you have at least some scientific knowledge of how your body works. The anatomical or physiological information presented here is cursory. I may, for instance, refer to the circulatory system and show how

Working and playing underwater puts physiological stress on the whole human system. But the body has great adaptative powers and will refunction as usual when it finally returns to conditions under which you normally live. Only when stress is severe or of overly long duration is there a problem in diving.

Photograph by Morton Walker.

an air embolism can travel through the arterial system because of improper breathing during ascent. Or I may describe how blackout can occur from insufficient oxygen circulated to the brain. What follows is an explanation of the physiological functionings and requirements underwater.

The Circulatory System

A friend of mine who dives professionally for a large Florida boatyard averages six hours a day underwater. He attributes his virility to the quantity of oxygen he takes in from breathing compressed air. Hemoglobin, a substance held by the red blood corpuscles, forms a loose chemical combination with oxygen. The higher the partial pressure of oxygen in the air inhaled, the more oxygen is soaked up by hemoglobin. As the red blood cells travel through my friend's circulatory system, they come into contact with a much lower partial pressure in the tissues and give up their oxygen. This, declares my friend, gives him more energy and vitality than other men, and women are attracted to his better performance. Surprisingly, he may be correct!

One of the medical theories connected with diving is that hyperbaric intake of air furnishes more oxygen for use by the body tissues. Under ordinary breathing conditions, hemoglobin takes up about 98 percent of the total amount of oxygen it is possible to carry. But breathing compressed air multiplies the partial pressure of all its gases, so the deeper a diver descends the more oxygen is absorbed into his hemoglobin. Consequently, the 500 million red blood cells present in just one cubic centimeter (cc.) of blood fluid, if increased in their oxygen-carrying efficiency by just 1 percent, will give the diver the equivalent of five million more red blood cells per cc.—and there are 6,000 cc. of blood in the average male's body. It would seem that scuba diving offers the body cells a tremendous quantity of extra oxygen.

In addition, hemoglobin carries carbon dioxide waste away from the tissues. The gas is dispelled from the blood into the air sacs of the lungs and exhaled out of the body. Buffering agents in the blood prevent overacidity.

The simple act of inhalation from scuba underwater sets up an amazingly complex interchange within the tissues. The body cells give up their wastes and take in new nutrients. The fluid portion of the blood, the plasma, contains a material dissolved in it that is vital to life. It is circulated by means of the heart pump and streams under pressure throughout the vast circulatory tree. If some obstacle blocks the passage through a branch of this arterial tree, the portion of the body that would ordinarily be nutrified with oxygen and dissolved substances would die.

Thus, the examples cited previously, air embolism as the obstacle and anoxia as the cause of tissue death, are important hazards to avoid in scuba diving. These processes and precautions are discussed in detail later.

The Respiratory System

The crux of physiological life for man is the alveolar air spaces of his lungs. Air breathed is a mixture of gases that exerts a total sea-level pressure of 760 millimeters of mercury. Before the metric system was popularly used this was given as 14.7 pounds per square inch (psi). In this book the two measurements, mm and psi, are used interchangeably or jointly.

The ultrathin membrane of the alveolae exposes blood to the air mixture—recorded in millimeters of mercury, oxygen 100 mm, nitrogen 570 mm, water vapor 47 mm, and carbon dioxide 40 mm. It becomes arterial blood on its way out to the tissues, carrying life-giving nutrients for the cells. A gas exchange takes place between the tissues and the plasma. It then turns into venous blood, with oxygen pressure dropping to 40 mm and carbon dioxide pressure increasing to 46 mm. The venous blood travels back to the pulmonary capillaries to again become exposed to the alveolar air. On its way it gives up waste products to the kidneys and takes on hormonal chemicals to deliver from the endocrine glands.

At the lung membrane lining the air sacs, blood is held on one side and air on the other. An exchange of gases takes place between them. Venous blood, through gas diffusion, again becomes arterial blood. Nitrogen and water vapors remain at an unchanged proportion, since they are inert. But oxygen and carbon dioxide continue to alter their millimeter pressure, because they are life-sustaining gases.

A person at rest goes through between ten and twenty respiratory cycles a minute. Each cycle expels only about one-half of one liter of gas, whereas the total lung capacity of an individual is between five and six liters. A hyperventilating skin diver, on the other hand, can expel between four and five liters of air from his lungs after a full inspiration. The residual volume, the amount of air that remains in the lungs even after the most forceful expiration, is between one and one and a half liters. As a result, when you're spearfishing and holding inspired air on the bottom, as you head for the surface feeling as though you are going to implode for want of breathing, you'll find more in your lungs as the pressure reduces with your ascent. The residual air will expand.

Yet even though this is an advantage for surface-bound skin divers, it can be a source of danger to compressed-air-breathing divers. Holding the breath while rising can pressure a lung. Overinflation of the lungs can also cause mediastinal emphysema, the forcing of air into the tissue spaces in the middle of the chest; subcutaneous emphysema, air settling under the skin; or pneumothorax, air lodging in the space between the lungs and the lining of the chest wall on either side. Again, all of these problems are described for symptoms and treatment later.

The Sinus Cavities

The bones of the face and head contain cavities called *sinuses.* There are four paired sinuses: the *ethmoid,* between the eyes, the *sphenoid,* back under the brain, the *frontals,* in the forehead above the bridge of the nose, and the *maxillaries,* in the cheekbones. They are lined with a mucous membrane that is continuous with the nasal cavity membrane.

Any pressure applied to these hollow air pouches when their passages are obstructed by mucus from an upper-respiratory-tract infection causes pain at the obstruction site. Sinusitis can develop from subjecting swollen sinus membranes to the pressure of diving.

An obstructed sinus suffers from squeeze between normal atmospheric pressure within the cavity and ambient pressure outside in the water. The lower pressure inside the sinus equalizes itself with the greater pressure outside the cavity; this increased pressure is likely to be accomplished by an infusion of blood into the chamber. If this happens at depth, as the diver ascends he will experience frightful pain, because as blood tries to exit from a sinus, overabundant pressure develops. With the sinus passage blocked, the blood can't escape. Thus, a diver's ascent must be very slow to avoid the excruciating pain and the possible nose-bleeds that go with a blocked passage. The moral: *Never dive when you have a cold or other upper-respiratory infection that could block your sinus passages.*

Ear Squeeze

The source of at least 50 percent of all medical complaints in diving is the middle ear. It sometimes becomes subjected to a problem divers commonly call "the squeeze."

Middle-ear squeeze occurs on descent when the air inside the middle ear contracts. This contraction on body-space walls causes ear enclosure rupture, for two reasons: vacuum suction from within and ambient pressure from without. You don't have to descend very far to suffer the painful feeling of squeeze. You can develop ear pain at about ten feet from the surface, and can even experience dizziness and some hearing loss afterward.

You can prevent middle-ear squeeze from happening by remembering that the greatest pressure changes take place within a few feet of the surface. Don't ignore sudden ear or sinus pain; don't keep right on descending to make eardrum rupture inevitable.

Realize instead that when your ear vent is blocked by an acute cold or chronic sinusitis, you're asking for trouble. Blockage creates a negative pressure within the closed cavity as you descend. Air constricts inside the cavity and attempts to occupy less space. Conversely, upon ascent, the blocked cavity creates a positive pressure and the air within tries to expand and blow out the membranes. Thus, bleeding from a rupture or mechanical damage can result.

The body spaces, such as the middle ear, equalize pressure through vents to the outside. The eustachian tube is the vent for the middle ear. Only if both your eustachian tubes remain unblocked can you dive free and easy. One solution may be to suck in through your nose within the vacuum of the mask to put negative pressure on the eustachian tube and cause reversal of the blockage.

How Diving Affects the Eyes

Underwater fishermen often tell taller tales than land-based fishermen, and the reason is not that lies come more naturally to them. They just visualize fish as looking bigger—a three-foot-long barracuda actually seems four feet long underwater.

Underwater eye effects on a person wearing a diving mask cause a one-third enlargement of objects and appears to bring them one-fourth closer than they actually are. The top of objects will look higher and the bottom will seem lower since light rays bend when traveling from air to the denser water. Refraction of light brings slightly false impressions as you swim underwater, and your usual field of vision shrinks.   *Photograph courtesy of Parkway Fabricators.*

Underwater, without benefit of a face mask, vision is magnified. Human eyes are built physiologically to function in air; opening the eyes directly in water causes a distortion of images because of an inability to compensate for the light refraction.

A diving mask has a faceplate that lets you see the tiny details of a lake, river, or sea bottom by keeping out the water and enlarging objects by one-third. It tends also to bring them 25 percent closer than they actually are. The tops of objects look higher and the bottoms seem lower in water, because light rays bend as they travel from the air to the denser water. Refraction of light brings slightly false impressions as you swim under water, and your usual field of vision shrinks. But the skin diver, from experience, quickly adjusts to the changed sizes and distances, and makes automatic reflexive allowances for them when judging underwater.

A diver's eyes see odd color changes, too. Underwater the color spectrum quickly loses red; it begins to dull at 15 feet and vanishes altogether at 30 feet. Orange is lost at 35 feet and green at 80 feet. Only blue-green is sensed by the diver's eyes at 90 feet, and that is lost deeper than 100 feet. The balance of color deep underwater remains gray-blue. Beyond a depth of 200 feet, all objects organic or inorganic take on varying shades of black and white. Only the shining of artificial light on objects or animals at depth restores their actual color.

Hearing at Depth

Cousteau has called it the "silent world," but sound travels well under water, and you do hear it. The main thing that keeps you from conversing with your diving companion is the regulator mouthpiece and the inrush of water that greets any attempt to open your mouth to speak. Much speech is dissipated under water, but if you put your head to your buddy's or touch faceplates, you can bridge the underwater sound barrier. Sound penetrates water at a usual rate of 4,800 feet per second, as compared to its speed through air, 1,090 feet per second.

Divers can signal each other by making metallic sounds.

Rapping your metal air cylinder with the metal blade of a diving knife is quite an effective way to call out.   A handy signaling device one dive tour leader uses to call together a group of divers underwater is to bang a small aluminum frying pan, which he lets dangle from his weight belt.   It makes a good scraping or digging tool, too.

The newest in underwater verbal communication among divers and between divers and the surface is the Hellephone, designed by underwater electronics manufacturer and oceanographer Jim

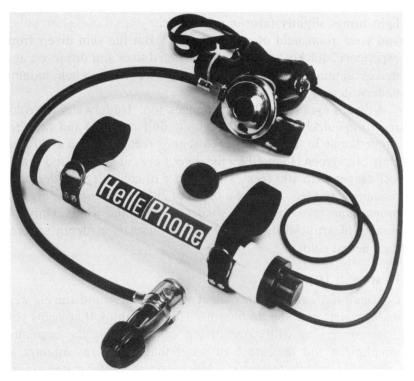

Hellephone is a wireless underwater communications system for sport diving and commercial diving. Using a simple "push to talk" switch, divers can talk clearly to each other or to the surface over distances of up to ½ mile and to depths of 200 feet. Shown is the diver unit #3110 worn attached to the regulator. The electronics cylinder straps to the tank, the earphone slips under a mask strap or hood, and the microphone attaches to the voice cavity.

Photograph courtesy of Helle Engineering Inc.

Helle, of San Diego, California. Rugged yet lightweight, the Hellephone promises to give a new dimension to safety, training, and time-saving in sport diving. It has been checked out in research diving under the Arctic ice, placing instruments in the swift-flowing Columbia River, exploration of an underground lake in Missouri, investigating the physiology of an off-Florida reef, and to depths of 200 feet and at distances of a quarter-mile and greater.

The Hellephone is a complete communications system, but it can be purchased in units and expanded as needed. It is wireless like a two-way radio, but it uses sound waves rather than radio waves for transmission. It provides clear voice communication underwater, for divers to talk to other divers and to their surface vessel.

Underwater Heat Loss

Body energy is used up as divers lose heat underwater. A diver burns calories to help maintain an equilibrium of temperature over the surface of his body. Prolonged immersion in cold water dissipates too much heat energy and lets exhaustion set in. This is serious; if rest and reduction of overexposure do not follow quickly, unconsciousness hits. Sometimes death is the result.

Most of the time the water you'll be diving in will be between 60° F. and 85° F. in temperature. The ocean does not get any warmer than 85° F. The most comfortable skin temperature for a person is 93° F., and if your skin temperature falls below 88° F., discomfort starts. This occurs when the water temperature drops to between 70° and 75° F. You should not dive bare-skinned in water this cool. Wear outerwear in the form of ski pajamas or woolen underwear to reduce the amount of bare skin surface coming in direct contact with the water. This will reduce the transfer of heat from the body surface to the surrounding water so that you can dive longer without exhaustion.

The United States Naval Institute illustrates the effects of underwater heat loss in various degrees of water temperature in Table I.

TABLE I

Water temperature in degrees F.	Approximate time in hours to exhaustion or unconsciousness	Death in hours
32	¼	¼-1½
50	¼-1	1-2
60	2-4	6-8
70	3-7	unknown
80	12	relatively safe

An obese person can remain in cold water longer than a lean one simply because his greater volume of flesh offers more insulation against heat loss. The human body stores heat and doesn't lose it all at once. The duration of exposure determines the deleterious effects of energy loss from calorie burning. The body shunts blood away from nonvital parts to keep its life-sustaining organs functioning, and this includes upkeep of temperature too.

At a skin-surface temperature of 86° F., a person develops goose bumps and starts shivering. This is an involuntary protective mechanism: shivering involves muscle action that increases calorie consumption and keeps up heat production. Wearing at least a wet suit top or "shortie" wet suit of the type worn by water-skiers will ensure that you are not diving and shivering simultaneously. A good rule to follow is to *always dive wearing at least a shirt.* Not only will the garment reduce heat loss by preventing the skin surface from being directly exposed to cool water, it will also protect your shoulders against scuba strap friction and ward off too much sun.

Gastrointestinal Functioning

Diving does not demand more strength and agility than other sports. Yet the unnatural environment a diver puts himself into calls for good health and a certain amount of fitness. Paul Tzimoulis, publisher of *Skin Diver,* has written editorials about divers who have gotten into trouble underwater simply because they engaged in diving in less than the best physical shape.

For example, a person subject to high blood pressure, tuberculosis or emphysema, asthma, heart disease, poor circulation, or another formidable illness should not try deep diving. Becoming ill or breaking down under water takes on consequences of great magnitude from the associated multiple traumas the body is being subjected to within innerspace. It's certainly riskier to get sick 100 feet underwater than having it happen while engaged in camping, bowling, golfing, or some other sport or hobby that's land-based.

Even healthy divers had better watch themselves before going out for a day underwater. Precautions should include not eating gas-forming foods or drinking carbonated beverages and liquor or beer. If you eat cabbage or imbibe beer, the gas given off by these foods while you are under pressure will remain static inside your stomach. As you rise from deep ambient pressure, expanded gas can cause distension of the bowel or discomfort from an inability to expel flatulence fast enough. You can feel mighty uncomfortable coming up at four atmospheres with a belly full of gas, and gas pockets can form outside the lining of the lungs if the gas is unable to escape through natural passageways because of environmental pressure.

Thus, a rule to take seriously is: *Eat or drink only lightly and of non-gas-forming products before a dive.* A diver in good health who takes the rules of diving seriously could even pursue the sport to an age of four score and ten.

Aspirin and upset-stomach medicines containing aspirin, like Alka-Seltzer®, should not be taken before diving. They cause an antipyretic effect that reduces body temperature to cause heat loss. The skin blood vessels dilate from their direct action on the heat-regulating center of the brain, and with an increased blood flow, heat loss takes place.

All underwater swimmers and scuba divers should satisfactorily pass a routine diver's medical examination of the type recommended by the Council for National Cooperation in Aquatics in its 1974 edition of *The New Science of Skin and Scuba Diving*. In addition, the examining physician is correct in carrying out chest

X-rays, an electrocardiogram, a complete blood count, urinalysis, fasting blood glucose with two-hour postprandial sugar determination, fasting cholesterol and triglyceride tests, VDRL, uric acid, and selected individual tests. These will help establish the guidelines for future evaluations, which should be performed annually.

The medical requirements of diving are predicated essentially upon the demands of physical laws on the diver. These medical requirements must be strict enough to protect the health and safety of an underwater participant, but not of the stringent nature common to military and commercial diving. Simply stated, one's bodily functions must respond to various foreign conditions underwater dictated by the properties and behavior of the environment. The very minimum a diver can do to preserve his life is to learn the essentials of what is known in physics as they affect his physiology before, during, and after diving.

8

Physical Law Demands Underwater

How Safe Is Scuba Diving?

Open-circuit-compressed-air-breathing divers must follow certain physical laws—if you don't, you can kill yourself. The characteristics of solids, liquids, gases, pressure, and buoyancy must be known and taken into account in every underwater action. If you ignore the physical laws when you dive you will pay the consequences.

Having offered the above warning, let me add that skin and scuba diving are relatively safe sports. There are very few fatalities, primarily because of the precautions divers take and because their understanding of the physical principles of diving is adequate. For example, reporting in *Skin Diver* for the National Scuba Advisory Committee, Ralph Shamlian says: "A comparison of the statistics on certification and scuba fatalities indicates that not only is diving a safe sport, but it is getting safer each year." Table II is presented to prove that statement.

TABLE II

Year	Total divers certified by national agencies	Percentage increase over 1970	Total scuba fatalities nationally	Percentage increase over 1970
1970	116,125		112	
1971	152,639	30%	114	2%
1972	186,313	60%	118	5%
1973	230,851	99%	118	5%
1974	235,600	103%	132*	18%

* Through October 2, 1974

Out of each 100,000 scuba divers, the National Scuba Advisory Committee figures that there are just 11.9 fatalities. That compares with the National Safety Council's Accident Facts, which indicate 56 deaths per 100,000 for the national average in the United States. That makes diving five times safer than any ordinary activity. These figures are averaged over the past five years. And the certified diver population is increasing five times faster than any scuba fatalities.

Shamlian points out that "the United States Underwater Fatality Statistics compiled by the University of Rhode Island, under federal grant, indicate that 62 percent of the diving fatalities for a three-year period were divers who were classified as having *some experience* to *very experienced,* which indicated at least one to two years experience. The 'early open water' (less than five or six dives) classification represents 27 percent of the fatalities."

How did these experienced divers die? In most cases it was not from poorly-made equipment. The University of Rhode Island report of 1972 states, "The 1972 year was the third year with no verified case of regulator failure. Furthermore, in about one thousand fatal scuba cases during 1946-1972, every case of regulator failure has been due to improper disassembly or clogging by weeds or bottom material."

If equipment did not fail, what could have caused scuba diving fatalities? Two possibilities remain, and both lie with the dead diver. Either he forgot one of the physical laws under which he was diving or he never learned it. Both are connected with improper or incomplete training, for which these divers have paid the ultimate price.

Physical Laws You Need to Know

The laws of underwater physics are named after their discoverers: Boyle, Charles or Gay-Lussac, Dalton, and Henry. They deal with the properties of matter and the way matter behaves under different conditions. The first thing to know is the composition of air and the way it acts under pressure.

Compressed air used in the self-contained underwater breathing apparatus is a simple mixture of 78 percent nitrogen, almost 21 percent oxygen, almost 1 percent argon, less than ½ percent carbon dioxide, and traces of neon, radon, hydrogen, helium, and other rare gases. Under certain conditions almost any of these gases can be dangerous to the diver. For example, nitrogen inhaled at a depth beyond 100 feet can cause a euphoric effect, nitrogen narcosis, sometimes described as rapture of the deep. Carbon dioxide that accumulates disproportionately in the breathing mixture can be toxic. As with all matter, these breathing gases have weight and take up space. It is pressure on this gaseous matter that is the source of danger to a diver.

Types of Pressure

In diving, pressure is a force that is measured in pounds per square inch (psi). Since much diving is performed in the sea and below sea level, another way to express pressure is in feet of seawater and in atmospheres (atm). Thus, we measure atmospheric pressure.

Inside and outside our bodies, we exist under pressure. That's because the weight of the Earth's atmosphere produces a force in all directions on its surface. It consists of 14.7 psi. This is 1 atm and is called *atmospheric pressure*. Since we are born into and spend our lives at this atmospheric pressure, we aren't aware of it.

But that awareness changes as soon as we go under water. That's because water weighs so much more than air. It exerts extra pressure of almost one-half-pound per square inch for every foot of depth—.445 psi, to be exact.

If you descend thirty-three feet underwater, you subject yourself to a combined pressure of air and water amounting to 2 atm or 29.4 psi. That's twice 14.7, the air pressure at sea level. Every thirty-three feet farther you descend in seawater, you subject yourself to another 14.7 psi, an added atmosphere. At 297 feet you are at 10 atm or 147.0 psi. That is your *absolute pressure.*

The only thing a snorkel diver has to consider when he dives underwater to 33 feet is whether his sinus passages and his eustachian tubes are open. If they are blocked, air will not circulate comfortably within his body to all of his air spaces. He will feel head pain. With all air passages working well, body air will stay in equilibrium with the pressure of the surrounding water. Surrounding water pressure at whatever depth the diver descends to is called *ambient pressure.*

Air within the lungs of the snorkel diver compresses from ambient pressure on his chest cavity. The deeper he descends the more lung air compresses. Coming back up, the ambient pressure diminishes and the lung air expands again.

It's not so uncomplicated for the scuba diver. The physical effect pressure has on the compressed air he is breathing makes the discovery of Robert Boyle, a seventeenth-century English physicist, rather important.

Boyle's Law

Boyle discovered that *if the temperature of a gas is kept constant, the volume varies inversely with the absolute pressure while the density varies directly in proportion to the absolute pressure.* In other words, when you double the pressure on a gas its density doubles too. The gas gets thicker because it is being confined to a smaller space. It shrinks, in fact, to one-half its original volume.

Remember Boyle's Law, for it can prevent you from bursting your lungs or from throwing an air embolism. The mate to

Boyle's Law is a physiological rule that every diver follows: *Never hold your breath while using scuba—breathe regularly.*

The two go together this way: if you hold your breath as you ascend from four atmospheres, 99 feet, your lung air will have expanded four times by the time you reach the surface. The air you inhaled at 99 feet will expand by half at 66 feet, double at 33 feet, and double again at the surface. Ruptured lungs or air embolism will likely be the result of this foolishness, because air in the delicate air sacs of the lungs can cause membrane rupture and capillary explosion as it expands. Air enters the bloodstream as bubbles and can cause blockage of major arteries, ending in death or paralysis.

Yet my example of danger from breath-holding at 99 feet should not give you the false impression that depth is the danger. Actually, the nearer you are to the surface the more wary you should be of holding an inhalation. Note that the rise from 99 feet to 66 feet increases the air volume by one-half but the ascent from 33 feet to the surface doubles it. Air embolism from breath-holding can happen as the result of depth changes of only four feet; it is an especial danger while scuba diving in depths of 15 feet or less.

The nearer you are to the surface while scuba diving the more wary you should be of holding an inhalation. Air embolism from breath-holding can happen from depth changes of only four feet and is especially dangerous while scuba diving in depths of 15 feet or less.   *Photograph by Bruce "Teacher" Bowker.*

Using Boyle's Law you can determine how much bottom time a tankful of air will allow you. If you are carrying the standard 71.2-cubic-foot cylinder and breathe at the inordinately heavy rate of one cubic foot per minute (cfm), your tank would last 71.2 minutes at the surface. But if you doubled the absolute pressure to 2 atm (at 33 feet), you would halve your bottom time. At 66 feet you would be diving at 3 atm, with diving time one-third as long. At 99 feet it's 4 atm and only one-fourth as long. Thus, theoretical bottom times with heavy breathing are:

33 feet = 35½ minutes
66 feet = 23½ minutes
99 feet = 17½ minutes

Remember that the force of the currents and the storminess of the sea vary, as do the nervousness and the exhaustion of the diver. These factors make a person breathe faster or slower. The time in which he uses up a tank of air is different for each diver. An average breather consumes air at the rate of 0.6 cfm.

Two theoretical mathematical formulas, used together, can furnish the hypothetical bottom time for any depth you intend to dive.

$$\frac{A_1C_1}{A_2} = C_2 \ and \ \frac{C_2}{A_1} \times T_1 = T_2$$

where:

A_1	=	1 atm of pressure at the surface
C_1	=	the cu. ft. volume of compressed air in your tank at the surface
T_1	=	the number of minutes this cu. ft. volume of compressed air lasts you at the surface
A_2	=	the number of atm of pressure at the depth you intend to dive
C_2	=	the cu. ft. volume of compressed air you need at the depth you intend to dive
T_2	=	the number of minutes this cu. ft. volume of compressed air will last at the depth you intend to dive

Problem: How long can you stay at 132 feet while breathing from a full 71.2-cubic-foot cylinder? Since you know yourself to be an efficient breather getting the maximum from each breath, it has been your experience that your surface tank will usually last for 90 minutes.

Solution: 132 feet is 5 atmospheres of pressure.

$$\frac{A_1 C_1}{A_2} = C_2$$

$$\frac{1 \text{ atm} \times 71.2 \text{ cu. ft.}}{5 \text{ atm @ 132 ft. depth}} = C_2 = 14.25 \text{ cu. ft. needed}$$
$$@ \text{ 132 ft. depth}$$

Then: $$\frac{C_2}{A_1} \times T_1 = T_2$$

$$\frac{14.25 \text{ cu. ft. @ 132 ft. depth}}{71.2 \text{ cu. ft. @ surface}} \times 90 \text{ minutes (surface time for 71.2 cu. ft. of compressed air)}$$

$$= 9.8 \text{ minutes bottom time.}$$

Try to ascend slowly, never faster than one foot per second. Two good rules to hold to are *exhale as you ascend* and *don't come up faster than your air bubbles.*

Charles's Law or Gay-Lussac's Law

The mixed gases of compressed air are affected by Charles's Law, also known as *Gay-Lussac's Law.*   This law states that *at a constant pressure the volume of a gas increases when the temperature increases.* Thus, if you let your air cylinder sit in the hot sun, for each Fahrenheit degree rise in temperature, pressure will increase 5 psi within the tank.   Take a pressure gauge reading topside and compare it with another reading after you've been under cool water for a few minutes, and you will likely be surprised at the dramatic drop in tank pressure from cooling under water.

Charles's Law is one of the reasons cylinders are filled as they stand in a barrel of cool water. The air heats up as it's compressed into the cylinder. An uncooled cylinder would build up pressure as it heated from the filling, and leave the diver with only a partially filled tank when he cooled it underwater.

A personal rule for complying with Charles's Law should be: *Fill tanks while they are submersed in cool water; keep them out of direct sunlight.*

Dalton's Law

The English chemist John Dalton noted that when a mixture of gases is brought into contact with a liquid, each gas dissolves separately into the liquid, as if it were by itself and not part of the gas mixture. *Dalton's Law* states that *the total pressure exerted by a mixture of gases is the sum of the pressures that would be exerted by each of the gases if it alone were present and occupied the total volume.* Briefly, his law means that when you breathe air, oxygen, nitrogen, and the other gases in the mixture are dissolved into your bloodstream and distributed by the blood throughout the body.

The *partial pressure* of a gas is proportional to the number of molecules of the gas present in the cylinder at the time you breathe it in. Since we know that nitrogen in air takes up 78 percent of its volume, we can figure out how much nitrogen will enter the bloodstream at a depth of 99 feet. To learn the partial pressure of any gas, multiply the percentage of that one component gas by 14.7 psi (1 atm).

At the surface, the partial pressure of nitrogen is 14.7 x 78% = 11.45 psi. At 33 feet, multiply the surface psi by 2 atm—22.90 psi. At 66 feet, multiply by 3 atm—34.35 psi. Thus, at 99 feet the amount of nitrogen being inhaled into your bloodstream with each breath is under a pressure of 45.80 psi.

This information is important when you apply it to carbon dioxide. With CO_2 taking one-half percent of the total number of molecules in compressed air, its partial pressure at 99 feet, inhaled at 4 atm of pressure, is 2 psi. Any increased concentration of this gas, introduced as an impurity or otherwise, could cause carbon dioxide poisoning.

You have only yourself to blame in most cases of CO_2 poisoning. Its rare occurrence with scuba comes about when a diver breath-holds for ten or twenty seconds as a means of preserving his air supply. This is a false economy; the higher the concentration of CO_2 allowed to accumulate in the lungs, the higher the rate of breathing climbs. And should the level of carbon dioxide reach as high as 10 percent, you are likely to lapse into unconsciousness.

Surface air breathing is the most effective way to reduce the level of carbon dioxide in the lungs. On reaching the surface after scuba diving, it's good practice to immediately switch air intake from the regulator mouthpiece to the snorkel.

Henry's Law

The American physicist Joseph Henry discovered that the gases contained in air are absorbed into the bloodstream only in accordance with ambient pressure. So *Henry's Law* is: *With temperature constant, the quantity of a gas that goes into solution of any given liquid is in direct proportion to the partial pressure of the gas.*

A narcotic effect takes hold of the diver's central nervous system when the increased partial pressure of nitrogen becomes more than he can handle. This can take place anywhere beyond a depth of 100 feet. It's known as nitrogen narcosis, sometimes called the rapture of the deep, and it causes intoxication akin to overimbibing alcohol. In fact, people who can't hold their liquor and have a low tolerance for alcohol may be more prone to early nitrogen narcosis. Thin divers also seem to have more problems with nitrogen narcosis than corpulent divers, because fatty tissues absorb about five times more nitrogen than water. Fat acts like a sponge, keeping the partial pressure of nitrogen low for a longer period of time. Some divers, however, have been known to be stricken at the relatively shallow depth of 75 feet.

Like narcosis, decompression sickness—also known as "the

bends" or caisson disease—comes from a buildup of blood nitrogen. A Frenchman named Paul Bart observed hard-hat divers in pain after some deep dives and discovered that their subsequent deaths came from the presence of gaseous nitrogen in the bloodstream and tissues.

For nitrogen narcosis and decompression sickness, Dalton's Law and Henry's Law simultaneously come into play. Putting together the two laws at a constant temperature, the volume of nitrogen varies inversely as the absolute pressure, and its density varies directly as the ambient pressure. A volume of nitrogen goes into blood solution in direct proportion to its partial pressure. Thus, a greater depth produces greater pressure and diffuses more nitrogen into the blood. The human respiratory function is adapted to taking only a certain saturation of this gas.

Tissue saturation with nitrogen can only be counteracted underwater by stage decompression. That's because a quantity of nitrogen is taken up by the body during every dive. The amount absorbed depends upon the depth of the dive and the exposure (bottom) time. If the quantity of nitrogen dissolved in body tissues exceeds a certain critical amount, the ascent must be delayed to allow the body to remove the excess nitrogen. Decompression sickness results from failure to delay the ascent and to allow this process of gradual desaturation. A specified time at a specific depth for purposes of desaturation is called a decompression stop.

Decompression stop information is given in the U. S. Navy Standard Air Decompression Tables, included in Chapter 11 of this book. It is absolutely mandatory before you go diving that you familiarize yourself with these tables. However, it is recommended that you *avoid ever diving so deep or for so long that you will have to resort to using the air decompression tables.* No-decompression dives are the only type generally recommended for sport divers.

Dives that are not long or deep enough to require decompression stops are no-decompression dives. Dives to 33 feet or less do not require decompression stops. As the depth increases, the

This diver is waiting at a stage-decompression stop. Tissue saturation with nitrogen can only be counteracted by holding at a specific depth for a specified time for purposes of desaturation. Decompression-stop information is given in the U.S. Navy Standard Air Decompression Table included in Chapter 11. Familiarization with its use is absolutely essential before you go diving.

Photograph by Bruce "Teacher" Bowker.

allowable bottom time for no-decompression dives decreases. Five minutes at 190 feet is the deepest no-decompression dive time.

The inference of "bottom time" should be corrected. It really is not the time you actually spend on the sea bottom. Rather, *bottom time is the number of minutes that elapse from the moment you leave the water's surface to the moment you begin your ascent.*

Archimedes' Principle

The laws of buoyancy are expressed by *Archimedes' Principle,* which states that *any object wholly or partially immersed in a liquid is buoyed up by a force equal to the weight of the liquid displaced.* Thus, if you weigh 192 pounds wearing all your scuba equipment, theoretically you will displace about 3.25 cubic feet of water and be buoyed up by a force equal to the weight of that same volume of water. Because seawater weighs 64 pounds per cubic foot, the buoyant force acting on you is 3.25 x 64, or 208 pounds. But this is only a theoretical concept—no fixed rule exists, because bone density, fatty tissue, muscle, and so on are all different factors in different people. The theory is used in this example to illustrate the workings of Archimedes' Principle.

According to the example, the force of buoyancy is sixteen pounds more than your total weight, and extra poundage is positive buoyancy. It would cause you to be lifted and float with one-quarter cubic foot of your volume out of the water. The volume of water you then would displace would be three cubic feet. The weight of three cubic feet, 3 x 64, is 192 pounds, which just equals your total body weight wearing scuba dress. To give yourself negative buoyancy beginning at about ten feet under the surface and sufficient to submerge without fighting to stay down, you would have to don a weight belt bearing sixteen extra pounds of lead, more or less. Obese individuals may have to wear even more extra weight, because fat molecules are farther apart and hold more air to give greater buoyancy than do muscle and bone molecules.

Diving in fresh water requires less weight to produce negative buoyancy. That's because fresh water weighs 62.4 pounds per cubic foot and its displaced volume weighs less. A skin diver is buoyed up better in salt water than in fresh water. He will, however, become less buoyant the deeper he descends on a lungful of air.

Archimedes' Principle encompasses other laws of flotation:

1. *A body sinks in a fluid if the weight of fluid it displaces is less than the weight of the body.* Some people find they don't need

extra lead to achieve negative buoyancy because their average body density is greater than that of the water, and their bodies thus weigh more than the water they displace.

2. *A submerged body remains in equilibrium, neither rising nor sinking, if the weight of the fluid it displaces is exactly equal to its own weight.*

3. *A floating body displaces its own weight of a liquid.* If a submerged body weighs less than the volume of liquid it displaces, it will rise and float with part of its volume above the surface. This is illustrated in the 192-pound example given.

Gauge Pressure Compared to Absolute Pressure

The really important pressure in diving is ambient pressure within the surrounding water medium, plus 14.7 psi at the surface. This combination is *absolute pressure,* measured as pounds per square inch absolute (psia). A depth gauge measures absolute pressure as you descend, but as you rise in the air (increase altitude) the measurements grow smaller.

For example, suppose you dive in Lake Tahoe, on the boundary between California and Nevada, which lies at the base of the Sierra Nevada at an altitude of 6,225 feet. Atmospheric pressure at this altitude is lower than that at sea level, so pressure on the various instruments that make up your diving gear is also lower. The depth gauge is calibrated at a depth of water starting at zero (0) at sea level, and pressures are expressed as so many atmospheres or pounds per square inch *gauge* (psig). Thus, the depth gauge records a built-in error—a backing off—predicated on the lower air pressure. As you dive into the 1,650-foot waters of Lake Tahoe, your gauge will indicate less depth than you have actually attained.

A diver maneuvering at a depth of 99 feet is under a pressure of 3 atmospheres gauge (44.1 psig) or under a pressure of 4 atmospheres *absolute* (44.1 psig plus 14.7 psi = 56.8 psia). You should distinguish between the two atmospheric pressure readings when you quote them.

Your depth gauge works in this way. Since every foot of depth in water exerts .445 psi, you can determine the ambient pressure by multiplying the feet in depth by .445. For example, a diver swimming at a depth of 99 feet is surrounded by an ambient pressure of 44.1 psi. To learn the absolute water pressure at this same depth, merely add onto this ambient figure the pressure of the atmospheric air at sea level (14.7 psi). Thus, the diver is subjected to 56.8 psia.

Conversely, you can learn the depth in feet by dividing the psi gauge water pressure by .445 psi. The depth gauge does this automatically and gives you the reading on its dial in calibrations marked as feet of depth.

9

Diving Know-how

My diving buddy from Florence resented my suggestion that he should wear a buoyancy compensator or life vest. He considered advice to dive with a personal inflation device almost an affront to his manhood. Although he is brave, tough, and physically fit, I think my buddy is a little foolish too. Wearing a buoyancy compensator, even more than other items of diving gear, makes diving pleasant, easy, and less fatiguing. It could even be a lifesaver. In short, my buddy's attitude indicates that he is not thinking like a good diver.

Yet the tough scuba divers of Israel who dive in the Red Sea near Eilat don't wear life vests or buoyancy compensators. Their diving know-how just does not include employment of a personal flotation device. Underwater technology and procedure differ quite a bit for divers around the world.

Red Sea diving technique, for example, varies in certain ways from our methods in United States waters. Divers swim from the beach to the reef's edge, where they drop to depths of 100 feet. They descend as a group and follow a Dive Leader. That procedure is similar to our American method of shore-based diving. But their technique is different when they enter the water

Large and small inflatable boats may be used as diving platforms as is the practice among Israeli divers in the Red Sea near Eilat. Note that these divers are not wearing life vests or buoyancy compensators, making this an unacceptable technique for diving in the United States. Because diving technique varies in accordance with the area you are in and with the people you accompany, some basic systems and rules should become common practice for all.

Photograph courtesy of Studio 41.

from a boat. Israeli divers gather in a group in the water, and the boat's captain takes away the means of safe surface transport to wait upwind. He leaves behind a large inflatable boat (sometimes it is a huge inflatable raft) anchored in place as a safety platform.

After a no-decompression dive the divers follow prearranged instructions to rise from the bottom at an ascending speed of slightly less than sixty feet per minute and take a mandatory three-minute decompression stop at ten feet. Upon surfacing and while still in the water, they doff their compressed-air tanks over the head, roll into the inflatable, and lift the tanks in after themselves. The boat merely drifts downwind toward them upon spotting a signal. As the Israelis climb the boat's ladder, they follow the Red Sea diver's habit of continuing to wear masks and snorkels as a safety measure in case a misstep should dump one of them back into the sea.

Because diving technique varies in accordance with the area you are in and with the people you accompany, some basic systems and rules should become common practice for all. That way, a lack of communication won't be the cause of avoidable accidents. This chapter concentrates on suggestions to make diving easier and safer.

The Buddy System

Most accidents or fatalities that occur in diving can be directly attributed to at least one diving companion disregarding his responsibility to his buddy. *Correct diving procedure presently includes following the buddy system.* That means that you should *never dive alone.* Under any circumstances, a diver is responsible for the safety of his buddy. Having a buddy is no substitute for expert training and complete diver competency; if you are an unsafe diver a buddy won't change your tactics. The real purpose of being a diving buddy is to help the other person out of entanglements and to share your air in the case of equipment failure.

The buddy system calls for close, continuous visual contact with your companion. Where diving conditions such as strong current or poor visibility demand it, use a short rope line, hand-held, to stay linked together. A line seven to ten feet long is best. Under even the best conditions, never stray more than ten feet from each other. If your buddy is in distress, never leave him, and always work to help him. Only severe, unmanageable entanglement in kelp or some other underwater hazard might be an excuse to temporarily leave your buddy in order to fetch other divers to his aid.

Sometimes conditions demand that you and your buddy tie yourselves together, as for ice diving, descending into murky water, or entering total darkness without a light.   But be cautious—a tied line can get tangled around rocks, submerged trees, wreckage, or other obstacles. To prevent such entanglement make up a rope attached to a quick-release belt at both ends. Attach the belt after your weight belt goes on.   If your line gets tangled, all you need do is pull the release mechanism and you will be loose.   Then you can safely follow the rope to where it is caught or to your buddy.

Sometimes a buddy system includes tripling up.   This is sometimes the case on a large dive boat where the divers entering the water are superabundant.   The dive master and the equipment tender might wish to cut down on the number of individual groups earmarked for descent.   As a single individual joining two others

Avoid tripling up in a buddy system where your two buddies are brothers or parent and child or husband and wife, etc. You will be the intruder if trouble develops with simultaneous emergency action required for you and one of the related duo. You are likely to be left to provide for yourself.

Photograph by Morton Walker.

in such a tri-buddy system, here is a hint that you may never hear elsewhere. Never team up as a stranger entering a three-member group whose other two buddies are sweethearts, siblings, parent and child, husband and wife, or any similar combination. This may seem odd, but consider: if trouble developed simultaneously with you and with one of the other members—if, for instance, you both ran out of air—who would the third diver be likely to help first?

I was diving recently at John Pennekamp Coral Reef State Park, Florida, as the third member of a team. I had never before met my buddies, a man and woman who made it obvious that they were lovers. They were ardent underwater photographers as well, and I snapped pictures along with them—for this book, in fact. After we had been submerged for forty minutes at a depth of 35 feet, the male member of the duo rose to the surface—to change film, I later found out. His companion, her eyes ever on him, left me with my macroscopic photographic manipulations. No one gave me a signal or a sign that he or she was ascending or leaving the water; they just left me there.

Discovery came when I flashed my strobe for a photographic close-up of a spider crab. I turned to share the scene with my buddies, and they were nowhere to be found. I rose to the surface alone to signal the dive boat.

The Remiss Buddy and Panic

In my diving travels I have seen some reprehensible actions among diving companions. People who have falsely claimed a knowledge of underwater physiology and technique have been certified to victimize unsuspecting diving buddies. These divers deserve to be censured, expelled from the diving fraternity, and even prosecuted for criminal actions. One such person, whom I label the Remiss Buddy, actually caused the death of his wife, his sidekick of 32 years.

The son-in-law of the Remiss Buddy told me the whole story, and later the killer confirmed it by revealing his ignorance of diving procedure. A few days later, I investigated the accident scene. The unfortunate couple had been diving on the south shore of Grand Cayman, B.W.I., in a group of thirteen, with one instructor diver and two diving guides. Their daughter and son-in-law were included in the party. The ocean surface was choppy and a current ran along the bottom. Entry was made from shore, a short walk through surf on a sloping beach that leveled off at a depth of 30 feet.

It was the habit of this Remiss Buddy to leave his wife, with whom he always buddied, and explore underwater on his own wherever curiosity led him. He had told me previously of his preoccupation with underwater sights, and of how he depended on his wife to stay with him or seek him out if he should stray. "She always has to come looking for me—ha, ha—'cause I get so infatuated with watching the little swimming things," he explained. I had cautioned him then against this dangerous practice.

During that dive, this remiss man had disregarded the buddy system once too often. Just before they embarked, he admitted afterward, his wife had complained of stomach cramps. But he had cajoled her into entering the water anyway, calling her a sissy. On the bottom the current had forced them to hold on to rocks and coral so as not to be pushed out to sea. These alarming conditions, however, did not deter the remiss diver from going his own way as usual and paying no mind to his buddy.

She might have looked for her husband once again, as many times before, but this time it was because she needed his help to save her life. She never found him. Some kind of medical accident struck her under water, and she died alone at 30 feet depth, her regulator working properly, the weight belt still buckled around her waist, an elaborate buoyancy compensator left uninflated, and 600 psi of compressed air remaining in her tank. Panic showed in her dead, open-staring eyes.

Afterwards, the Remiss Buddy sat in the Grand Cayman police station. He hid his face in his hands and cried, "I killed her! I killed my wife!" And he was absolutely correct!

Problems with equipment or trouble with your physiology can and sometimes do develop under the surface. A regulator could block and leave you sucking at a vacuum; abdominal cramps could hit, doubling you over. These emergency situations would alarm anyone, of course. But accidents of near drowning don't actually take place at the bottom, because the diver is usually able to make his way to the surface. It is at the surface that panic strikes and that drowning occurs.

Panic kills, by producing mental confusion and the total disregard for diving rules once learned. Common sense gets thrown to the four winds by panic, with only the instinct for survival taking command. An alarmed diver will struggle to the surface (probably too fast), dog-paddle by reflexive instinct to keep his head out of the water, and be finished off by succumbing to total fatigue. Then he sinks!

What is the physiological process that builds up to this panic? Alarm leads to excitement and overexertion, which cause carbon dioxide buildup in the tissues. Too much carbon dioxide leads to hyperventilation, with the nervous response of the diver feeling difficulty in breathing. More forced breathing causes greater hyperventilation, which finally strikes as panic. The critical time span between the first added resistance of overexertion and panic depends only on the diver's physical fitness. An alert buddy near him is the main safeguard to stave off panic. His buddy could help save the diver's life.

The In-Water Signal System

Before embarking on a dive, you and your companions should agree on stipulated signals. Their purpose is to accomplish underwater and topside communication when speech is impaired.

For example, at least once during a shallow-water dive of 50 feet or less you and your buddy should rise to the surface and give the OK sign, each raising your hands over your heads and then bringing them together. This is a confirmation sign given to the boat tender to show that you and your buddy are together and in good shape. Then the boat tender will indicate that you may again submerge.

Additionally, on the surface at a distance from the boat, you should be able to signal the tender to come and get you because you are in trouble. With buoyancy compensator inflated, raise one arm high over your head to alert the boat person that you are in need but not in immediate danger and that he should come and fetch you as soon as he is able. If you rotate that single upraised arm, you will be indicating acute alarm, that your request is urgent, and that he must get to you fast.

Losing visual contact with your buddy underwater is sufficient reason to ascend to the surface and hold up one arm. Your alert buddy, presumably, will also have noticed that he is missing a diving companion. He too should follow the system and ascend with outstretched arm. Your boat tender can then point out where each buddy is in order to bring the two of you together.

Underwater communication by voice contact is not possible without special equipment, although highpitched shrieks or grouperlike grunts might be heard. The only noise that is really attention-getting is the striking of your air cylinder with a metallic object such as your diver's knife. Such a sound won't tell your buddy your direction, since sound is scattered by the higher speed that it travels under water. So your communication system might include the following:

2 metal taps: low on air, return to the surface.

3 metal taps: danger, leave the water.

4 metal taps: are you all right?

5 metal taps: lost object, help me look for it.

It might be more practical to take down a plastic writing board and a crayon if you want to give instructions or record readings and measurements.

The simplest and fastest in-water system of communication, where visibility permits, is hand signals. The following signals should be universally understood:

"COME HERE"
PALM TOWARD SELF, MOVES BACK AND FORTH FROM WRIST

"STAY BACK"
"GET AWAY"
ARMS MOVE BACK AND FORTH

"STAY THERE"
"HOLD STILL"
"WAIT"
FLAT PALM EXTENDED TOWARD PARTNER

Divers should be able to use these Handtalk Signals in order to communicate underwater.

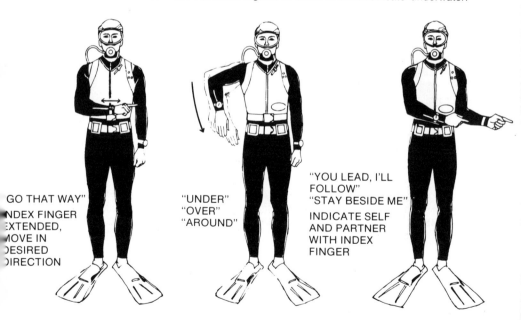

GO THAT WAY"
NDEX FINGER EXTENDED, MOVE IN DESIRED DIRECTION

"UNDER"
"OVER"
"AROUND"

"YOU LEAD, I'LL FOLLOW"
"STAY BESIDE ME"
INDICATE SELF AND PARTNER WITH INDEX FINGER

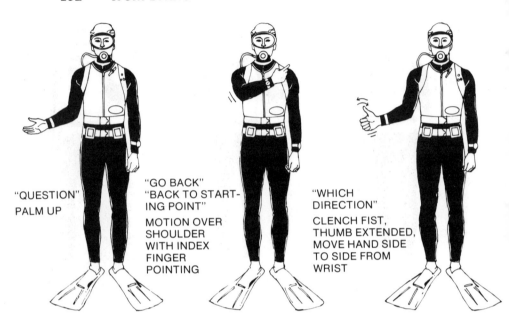

"QUESTION"
PALM UP

"GO BACK"
"BACK TO START-
ING POINT"

MOTION OVER
SHOULDER
WITH INDEX
FINGER
POINTING

"WHICH
DIRECTION"

CLENCH FIST,
THUMB EXTENDED,
MOVE HAND SIDE
TO SIDE FROM
WRIST

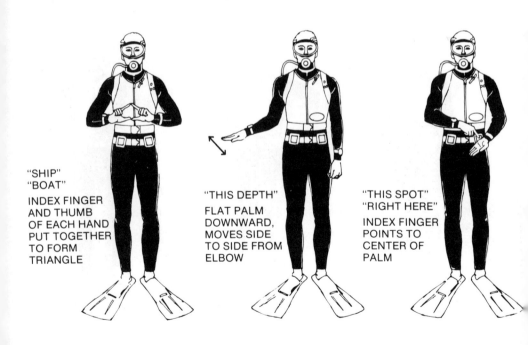

"SHIP"
"BOAT"

INDEX FINGER
AND THUMB
OF EACH HAND
PUT TOGETHER
TO FORM
TRIANGLE

"THIS DEPTH"
FLAT PALM
DOWNWARD,
MOVES SIDE
TO SIDE FROM
ELBOW

"THIS SPOT"
"RIGHT HERE"

INDEX FINGER
POINTS TO
CENTER OF
PALM

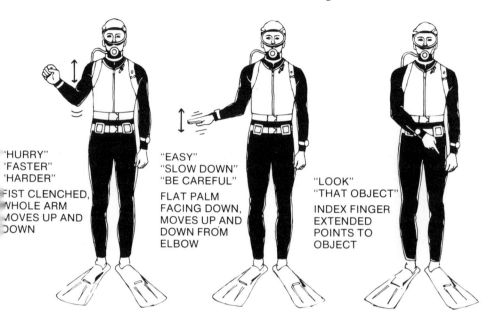

"HURRY"
"FASTER"
"HARDER"

FIST CLENCHED,
WHOLE ARM
MOVES UP AND
DOWN

"EASY"
"SLOW DOWN"
"BE CAREFUL"

FLAT PALM
FACING DOWN,
MOVES UP AND
DOWN FROM
ELBOW

"LOOK"
"THAT OBJECT"

INDEX FINGER
EXTENDED
POINTS TO
OBJECT

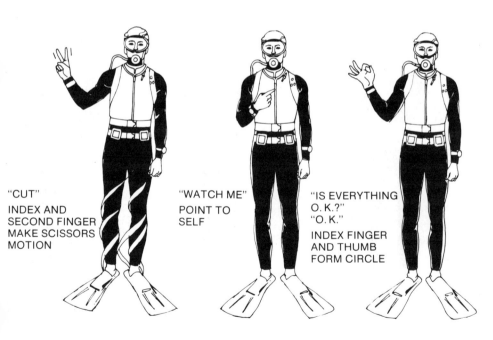

"CUT"

INDEX AND
SECOND FINGER
MAKE SCISSORS
MOTION

"WATCH ME"
POINT TO
SELF

"IS EVERYTHING
O.K.?"
"O.K."

INDEX FINGER
AND THUMB
FORM CIRCLE

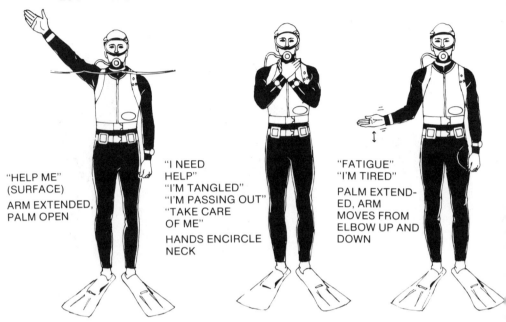

"HELP ME"
(SURFACE)
ARM EXTENDED,
PALM OPEN

"I NEED
HELP"
"I'M TANGLED"
"I'M PASSING OUT"
"TAKE CARE
OF ME"

HANDS ENCIRCLE
NECK

"FATIGUE"
"I'M TIRED"
PALM EXTEND-
ED, ARM
MOVES FROM
ELBOW UP AND
DOWN

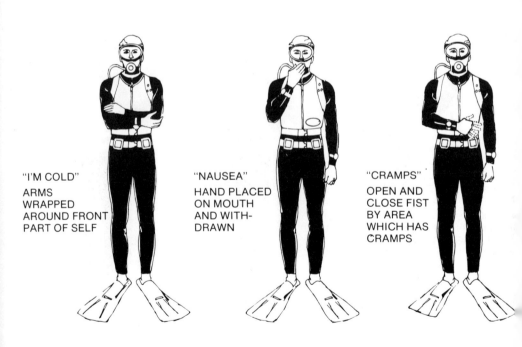

"I'M COLD"
ARMS
WRAPPED
AROUND FRONT
PART OF SELF

"NAUSEA"
HAND PLACED
ON MOUTH
AND WITH-
DRAWN

"CRAMPS"
OPEN AND
CLOSE FIST
BY AREA
WHICH HAS
CRAMPS

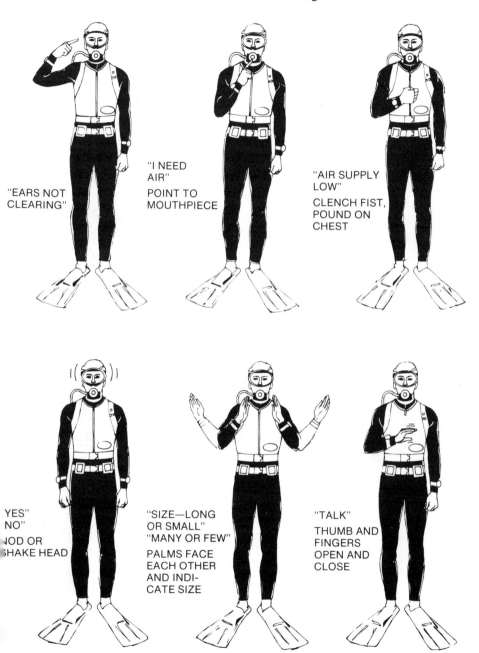

"EARS NOT CLEARING"

"I NEED AIR"
POINT TO MOUTHPIECE

"AIR SUPPLY LOW"
CLENCH FIST, POUND ON CHEST

"YES" "NO"
NOD OR SHAKE HEAD

"SIZE—LONG OR SMALL" "MANY OR FEW"
PALMS FACE EACH OTHER AND INDICATE SIZE

"TALK"
THUMB AND FINGERS OPEN AND CLOSE

"ALERT TO DANGER"
"DANGEROUS"
"SHARK"

ARM MAKES
CIRCULAR
MOTION—UP
TOWARD SELF
AND PUSH
AWAY

"TELL HIM"
"TELL THEM"

USE 'TALK'
MOTION THEN
INDICATE
TO WHOM WITH
INDEX FINGER

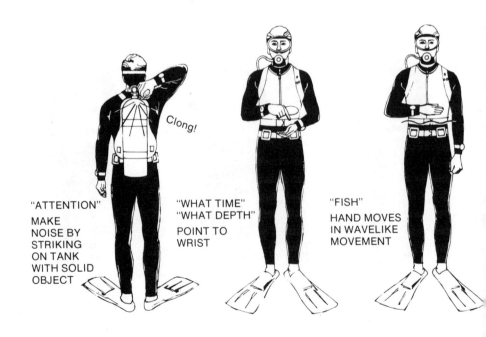

Clong!

"ATTENTION"
MAKE
NOISE BY
STRIKING
ON TANK
WITH SOLID
OBJECT

"WHAT TIME"
"WHAT DEPTH"

POINT TO
WRIST

"FISH"
HAND MOVES
IN WAVELIKE
MOVEMENT

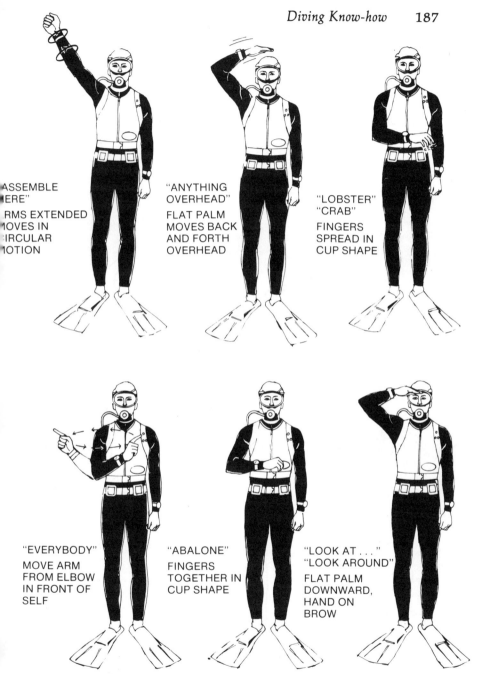

"ASSEMBLE
HERE"

ARMS EXTENDED
MOVES IN
CIRCULAR
MOTION

"ANYTHING
OVERHEAD"

FLAT PALM
MOVES BACK
AND FORTH
OVERHEAD

"LOBSTER"
"CRAB"

FINGERS
SPREAD IN
CUP SHAPE

"EVERYBODY"

MOVE ARM
FROM ELBOW
IN FRONT OF
SELF

"ABALONE"

FINGERS
TOGETHER IN
CUP SHAPE

"LOOK AT . . ."
"LOOK AROUND"

FLAT PALM
DOWNWARD,
HAND ON
BROW

Illustrations for signals courtesy of Professional Diving Instructor College.

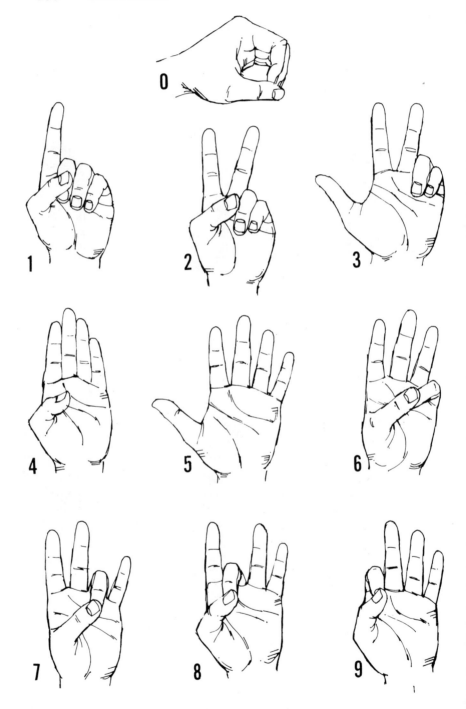

Diver's Down Flag Modified

The four-unit-high by four-unit-long diver's down flag has an orange-red field with a white stripe, which is one unit wide that runs diagonally from the upper left to the lower right corner. It waves from a staff not less than three feet in height and clearly demarcates the area of diving operations. The laws of many states ask surface craft when approaching this displayed flag within 100 feet to proceed at five knots or less and to watch out for divers. The flag protects the diver and the boat operator from coming together in a serious accident. Divers often use scuba *under* their flying flag, but even then they should ascend to the surface with caution.

The diver's flag should be flown from the mast of a dive boat or mounted on an automobile tire inner tube and towed by the diver.

Basic scuba courses sometimes include this sort of instruction in the program and state that the diver's down flag is an important piece of equipment. But common sense and a little experience with towing a fully inflated float might be instrumental in changing that instruction, because dragging a float can be detrimental.

The battle to navigate even moderate surf precludes a diver's adding to his problems. For instance, when a wave breaks on a diver or his float at the surf line, 64 pounds per cubic foot of saltwater weight is striking him at the moment. Since a diver's body surface area is at least two cubic feet, he's dragged down by an extra 128 pounds as he attempts to make his way into or out of the surf. The towed tire inner tube just drags him down.

It's been suggested that a flag float serves well as a resting platform, but the buoyancy compensator vest accomplishes this task better. Floats have been designated as a means of rescue in case your buddy is in trouble; but here, too, one buoyancy compensator with its large air volume is capable of supporting two fully equipped divers. Stuffing yourselves through an inner tube while wearing scuba tanks won't be necessary. Floating flags are, indeed, important, but the best type are manufactured as part of Styrofoam or air-bag models. The only current use for an unattached float is as a holder of your goodie bag for carrying speared fish or shellfish.

You can modify an inner tube float, if you've invested in one, and utilize it more effectively. Streamline the float by attaching a piece of Velcro one inch wide and long enough to wrap around it. Cinch the strap so that the float squashes into a smaller surface volume. If it's a surf mat you're using, probably three strips of Velcro will be necessary to pull it past the surf line. In open water release the Velcro to let the float expand to its normal inflatable size.

To deflate the float with ease, attach an oral inflator. You can get discarded inflator tubes from a dive shop that repairs them. After cutting a small hole in the float, attach the end of the tube opposite the mouthpiece to the cut-out site. Bind it in place permanently with inner-tube cement or surf mat cement. Cover the binding with an extra overlay of attached surf mat material.

If you must tow a float behind you through a surf line, lengthen the towline. This will prevent your being bowled over by a breaking wave that hits a straggling float six or eight feet behind you. Avoid becoming entangled with a long towline as you swim on the surface toward your dive site.

Improved Underwater Optics

The first underwater goggles were tortoise-shell discs scraped very thin and polished. Divers who wore them did not see very well. Some divers still don't see well underwater, simply because they have not incorporated the newest technology to improve their optics.

As I grew older in diving I discovered, year by year, that it was getting increasingly more difficult to read my underwater gauges. By late 1973 it had become almost impossible for me to dive, simply because I couldn't tell how deep my depth gauge was recording, how much time had elapsed while I was underwater, how much air remained in my tank, whether I had entered the danger zone on my decompression meter, or even in which direction I was heading according to my underwater compass. In short, my inability to read my diving gauges endangered my life. This is not an unusual state for divers near age forty-five. Vision in water is restricted by both rapid scattering and absorption of light. If you must view such small details as camera settings at close range, the task becomes almost impossible without spectacle correction.

How can a diver who can't see clearly wear his eyeglasses or contact lenses underwater? New diving technology makes it possible. Some divers may be able to wear their contacts, but they risk the danger of losing them. The process of mask clearing might slide them out of position. Salt water can be irritating to a contact lens wearer, too. The only change in spectacle correction for underwater use is a change in the vertex power due to the lens being farther from the eye than the usual spectacle position.

Underwater technology offers five methods for visual deficiency correction. In one method the correction is ground into the faceplate of the mask. This is useful if you are nearsighted with the same power in each eye, with no astigmatism. The requirement is that the measurement from the center of the pupil of one eye to the center of the pupil of the other eye (interpupillary distance) be close to 64 millimeters. Any substantial variation in your pupillary distance can cause eye muscle strain, especially if the power of the lens is strong.

Your optometrist can take your pupillary measurement, or you can mark your own measurements. To do this simply stand before a mirror while wearing your glasses. Using a grease pencil or lipstick, mark a spot on each eyeglass lens that lines up with your own eye and its mirror image. Measure the distance between the marks as accurately as possible. This is your interpupillary distance. If you are farsighted or have astigmatism, however, this faceplate correction is not useful since the glass can't be tempered.

In another method, you can incorporate unused eyeglasses into your face mask and attach the plastic frames to the faceplate with epoxy cement. You also can buy a plastic insert with a spring hinge, into the frame of which you can place corrective lenses. But this homemade device is practically worthless, for two reasons: the

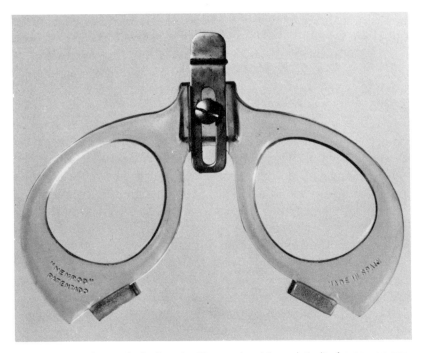

You can acquire a plastic insert with a spring hinge. Into its frame you can place corrective lenses. U. S. Nemrod manufactures an adjustable eyeglass holder with a metal slide which fastens the holder to any face mask (shown).

Photograph courtesy of U. S. Nemrod, Inc.

plastic frames seldom remain in proper position, and there are three glass surfaces instead of one that you have to keep clean and free of fogging.

Corrective lenses can be substituted for the plain glass inserts that come with some masks. Mechanical problems in securing a tight seal do occur, nevertheless, when the lenses are quite strong or when significant astigmatism must be corrected.

The next two methods are the ones I have found most effective. The first of these techniques consists of bonding the lenses you need to the inside of the faceplate. The principal advantage here is that the same vision is achieved underwater as topside, wearing spectacles. No power is too complicated to be accommodated by this means. Bonding material of a flexible type must be used,

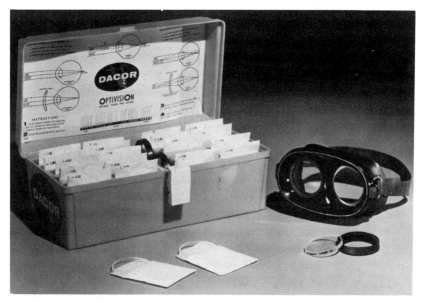

To accompany the DM19K Vedo mask, Dacor supplies a full diopter range of prescription lenses available through the Dacor dealer dive shop.

Photograph courtesy of Dacor Corporation.

since ordinary optical cement will eventually separate because of the different rates of expansion between the plate and the lens.

Four laboratories in the United States specialize in the bonding of lenses to diving mask faceplates:

Aqua Optics, A. S. Newton, O.D., Director, 575 Sixth Street, San Pedro, CA 90731

Leonard Maggiore, Optician for Divers, 1702 Gates Avenue, Brooklyn, NY 11227

Underwater Optics, P.O. Box 933, Temple City, CA 91780

Underwater Vision, Inc., Venice Medical Center-612, 950 Cooper Street, Venice, FL 33595

The price for their bonded faceplates is in the $38 range.

The last and most novel of the five methods for fuller vision underwater is a method of incorporating the normal prescription into the diver's face mask while maintaining the efficiency of the

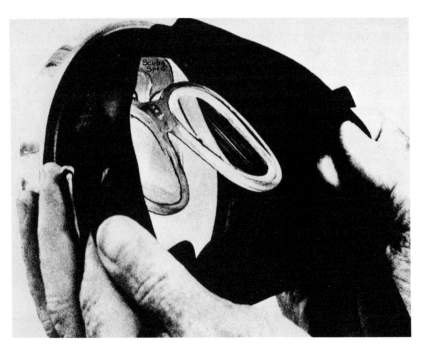

The Scuba Spec Underwater Spectacle™ is a newly patented concept in under-water vision. It does not use bonding of lenses to the mask faceplate or grind-ing of the faceplate. It duplicates the position and function of your habitually worn spectacles in regards to power, distance, and pantoscopicity (tilt of frame and lenses before the eyes), when positioned properly in the face mask. Scuba Spec may be used with single vision and/or bifocal lenses in a unique, corro-sion free nylon frame. Its "locking" arrangement of the frame to the anchor bar allows for easy insertion and removal of your frame and prescription lenses. Masks may be alternated simply by having an additional anchor bar cemented into each mask.   *Photograph courtesy of Scuba Spec, Inc.*

eyeglasses he wears in air. *The Scuba Spec Underwater Spectacle®* duplicates usual optical action and effectiveness of dioptric power, vertex distance, and pantoscopicity (an eyeglass wearer's requirements). It is a unique, new nylon frame into which a diver's most recent visual prescription is edged and inserted. Any type and power of lens, single-vision or bifocal, can be incorporated. It can be removed from the face mask at will and transferred to another mask by use of an anchor bar of rubber silicon cemented onto the faceplate. It is priced at $41 and can be purchased from the Scuba-Spec Company, Inc., S. Shedrow, O.D., President, P.O. Box 3356, Station A, Savannah, GA 31403.

Emergency Actions Underwater

When struck suddenly by a personal underwater emergency, such as vertigo, what is the first instinctive action you feel compelled to take? Without question, it's to get to the surface out of the unnatural water environment, even if that instinctive action might be a wrong one. Emergency actions underwater follow a definite pattern of priorities, just like those of emergency first aid.

Getting rid of the weights that hold you down comes up as the first order of self-help. To gain buoyancy control, drop your weight belt even if the dollar loss will be painful to your wallet. Better that than painful to your ears, lungs, and joints.

Learn to regard the weight belt as your primary emergency flotation device. In case of trouble, get rid of it before it's too late to do anything else. When you don your diving gear, make sure that the weight belt has a "clear drop." It should be able to fall away without getting hung up on crotch straps or your diving knife. A weight belt hanging loose around your fin weighs you down just as effectively as if it were attached around your waist. The belt buckle must be of the quick-release type, able to be opened by a simple pull with one hand.

Topside, you can tighten loose quick-release buckles that don't hold snugly. Strike them with a hammer in the center back. After this, check the flip pivot for excess play. Correct the pivot by tapping its edge again with the hammer.

Any problem with the old-fashioned lead weights that slide onto your weight belt can easily be fixed. Slide the weights to where you want them on the belt, drill a hole through the belt into the lead, and secure the weight in place with a stainless steel screw.

After your weight belt has fallen away, you need not inflate the life vest or buoyancy compensator; you will already be on your way up. Consider the BC as a tool to be worked with, however, and during each dive try to make use of it several times for the sake of practice, if for nothing else. Between dives, of course, maintain your BC with care, as described in chapter 3. Follow the manufacturer's instructions, for the effectiveness it will retain and the amount of safety it will provide is dependent almost entirely on how well you take care of it topside.

Use of the Octopus Regulator

For safety's sake, the newest underwater breathing insurance for settling down the air-starved, near-panic diver is the octopus regulator. Most instructors and dive tour guides use them out of choice. They can't know in advance whether a student's or tourist's own regulator will fail or how that diver will react under

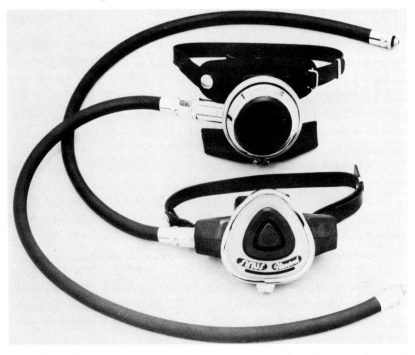

Easy-breathing, downstream regulator second stages are being manufactured for octopus hook-ups such as these Nemrod models Delta II with a 32-inch hose (above) and the Sirius Second Stage (below). These new octopus hook-ups thread into the low-pressure port of your present regulator as a safety backup for all divers.   *Photograph courtesy of U. S. Nemrod, Inc.*

any kind of emergency situation. It's getting to be common practice, as well, for the advanced amateur diver, on investing in a new regulator, to acquire an "octopus" for himself.

Essentially this is a single-hose regulator with an extra one or two low-pressure ports to which additional second stages have been fitted. Only a few types of two-hose regulators can be converted to the octopus outfit. Most divers have found that it is better to abandon the old-style double hoses rather than make the expenditure for the more modern conversion.

Be careful about the tilt valve in the second-stage octopus rig. Sometimes trouble with inhalation develops if the tilt valve does not have an over-pressure valve. Letting your octopus regulator and tank-pressure gauge hang down together during a dive could also be risky; they could get trapped in rocks, coral, parts of a shipwreck, or some other underwater hazard. A trapped hose could hold you to the bottom. A cut hose can lead to myriad problems that are too frightening to contemplate. But some simple solutions to prevent these troubles are at hand.

First, take a look at how cave divers, who specialize in safety and life-support systems, secure their octopus regulators. They use two or three large rubber bands to fasten the hose and second stage to the sides of the scuba tanks. Rubber bands are economical and simple and easily slide up and down on the tank. You can also break them or cut them when you have to.

Another simple solution is to make a rubber belt with a piece of two-inch-wide rubber from an unused automobile tire inner tube. Sew one piece of three-inch-long, two-inch-wide Velcro to the rubber after you have measured the tank at the proper location for fastening it to the tank's sides. Sew another piece of Velcro of the same size to the hose of the second stage of the spare regulator and tank-pressure gauge. The Velcro around the regulator and tank-pressure-gauge hoses can be held against the Velcro attached to the rubber belt around the tank. The Velcro is easily sewn with a large needle and sail thread.

A sure sign of diving know-how is different-colored rings of reflecting tape spiraled around your octopus regulator and submersible pressure gauge hoses. This allows your hoses positive identification and distinguishes the low-pressure inflator hose and second-stage hose, too.

Some divers attach the extra second stage of an octopus rig to their tank harness with smooth alligator clips. There is a problem with this method, though. Even if it keeps the extra regulator from dangling, when diving takes place in strong current or in surf line entry, the regulator can pull away from the clips. Something better, besides using the rubber bands and belts mentioned, is to add a pocket to your wet suit to hold the second stage. Place the pocket in your wet suit jacket at the level of your stomach under your left shoulder. If the pocket is in your wet suit pants, the hose for the octopus will have to be extra long. Material to make the pocket should be colored neoprene so that it will stand out against the rest of your suit. It should be obvious to any diver in need where he has to go for the extra regulator.

Remember though, that some panicky person won't be looking for fancy colors on your wet suit. When the need for air hits he's going to reach for your mouthpiece. All he knows or cares is that you have a regulator in your mouth that is supplying you with what he wants. Upon receiving his windpipe cutoff signal of "I need air," your best action is to immediately give him your main regulator with your right hand. Be generous and let him hold on to it, while you reach into your colored pocket with your left hand to fetch the accessory air supply. Now both of you can safely ascend to the surface without panic while holding on close and breathing from the same tank.

An alternative to purchasing and breathing with an octopus rig for emergency purposes is the use of a pony bottle. Attach a separate regulator to a small-volume pony bottle, which can be mounted in a holder on your twin- or single-tank rigs. Mount a slab of PVC plastic as a holder with a partially open bottom to let the water pass through. The pony bottle can be held in place by a fastened-down regulator neck strap, to be easily unsnapped or released with a pull.

Being able to pass the bottle and regulator to a distressed diver leaves you free to help him to the surface. The concept of an extra source of air is reassuring, since breathing jointly through an octopus rig means that you are both inhaling from the same air source. If inhalation by both of you is done at the same time, it is possible, although improbable, that you can overbreathe the first stage; the result would be that each of the two divers would have to receive less air. A situation like this could start a chain reaction of hysteria leading to deadly panic.

Emergency Swimming Ascent

At a quarry in Ohio, a friend of mine had descended to 80 feet. He was just completing an exhalation when suddenly his mouthpiece was violently torn from his mouth. He reached behind him, frantically searching for his hose and mouthpiece, only to discover that they were gone, along with his air cylinder. His backpack held nothing.

My friend's air tank had slipped through the backpack retaining band. The band had been covered with a rubberized padding material to prevent it from scratching his tank. Topside, the band had been secured just snugly enough to hold the tank in place. Underwater, when exposed to the increase in pressure at 80 feet, the rubberized material compressed sufficiently to let the tank slide completely free.

If the tank had been wrapped with a couple of turns of electrical tape immediately above the backpack band it would have been prevented from slipping. This procedure also marks the height adjustment for the pack to be attached to the refilled tank.

But that was not the case for my diving friend's tank that day. He was left with nothing to breathe, and nearly empty lungs at that. What did he do to save his life? He made an emergency swimming ascent.

The emergency ascent procedure varies, depending on the circumstances under which it must be made. Let's look at my friend's predicament first. Popular sloganing in scuba diving is "blow and go." That means you should blow out all the air it's possible to muster from your lungs, and then ascend to the surface as fast as you can. For my friend, that circumstance was already an accomplishment. At 80 feet, with no air to inhale and gasping for his next breath, he had nowhere to go except up.

His particular emergency ascent consisted of a quick flip of his weight-belt buckle, a pull at the carbon-dioxide-cartridge cord dangling from his life vest, and swimming motions to the surface. His actions took only fractions of seconds, and they saved his life. The pressure of the surrounding water at first prevented the CO_2 from inflating the vest at full capacity, but as he ascended above the 40-foot mark the vest began to fill. He also found new capacity to exhale as he rose, for remaining residual air in his lungs expanded from the 33-foot level to the surface.

Ditching the weight belt gave him positive buoyancy in overabundance and inflating his life vest made him rise in an uncontrolled ascent, too. He went to the surface with more speed than was desirable and only his constant exhalation efforts prevented lung damage or worse. But the diver had followed the rule of *blow and go,* and had added emergency swimming motions to his procedure. He had tilted back his head to keep a clear airway to his lungs, extended an arm to ward off obstacles, and swam to the surface, exhaling all the way.

My friend's judgment in that moment of emergency dictated that he do everything he could in those split seconds to get him to the surface. Actions to be taken in an emergency are always dictated by the particular situation. Suffice it to say, you should get to the surface taking the fewest actions possible. Do not remove your weight belt, do not inflate your life vest underwater, if your speed of ascent is fast enough within the confines of your residual air.

Ed Brawley has told me that over the many years he has watched people act in emergencies he has seen them do always one of two things. Either they think and then fall back on training or they let unthinking survival instincts take over. Training keeps them from panicking and heading for the surface. It is best to practice one form of emergency ascent and act in that way all the

time. Brawley suggests dropping the weight belt so you don't
expend energy and require air in swimming up against it.

Almost the first action you should take, if you discover that your
air is insufficient, should be to tell your buddy you need to buddy-
breathe. Except for the weight belt, *do not ditch your equipment if
you can hold on to it.* As you reach 33 feet, it's likely that the tank
will provide expanded residual air enough to let you inhale
another breath from it.

Log Your Dives

The habit of logging your dives can pay off with increased
enjoyment. For years afterwards, reviewing the records you've
kept for each dive will let you relive the experience. You will
recapture the old thrills and excitement of swimming free in
aquaspace. Again you'll see the wonderments and glory in what
you witnessed then, and the words you read in your log will
become a catalyst to reactivate your interest in the sport.

Knowing that you intend to note down what you see on each
dive will make you more aware of your watery surroundings. No
routine journal entry will satisfy you; you will put out effort to find
something different in each dive. All kinds of phenomena will
come to your attention. Keeping records about the subsurface
world does that.

Your diving log also becomes a measure of your diving know-
how. The idea is to take the logbook with you on each dive and
write in it before you leave the dive site. At first the act of writing
will feel forced. But it gets to be a happy habit after a while as
you find it fun to record your underwater experiences. Your
buddy signing your log becomes a record for him too, and it draws
him into the fun. Don't procrastinate and say that you will write
up the dive experience at home later. This seldom works.

The logbook should record information that is useful for the
future. This might include date, day, time, location, accom-
panying buddies, the purpose of the dive (photographs, game,
discovery, depth, etc.), water conditions (surf, temperature, visibility, tides, etc.), weather conditions (rain, wind, cloudy, sunny,

etc.), and a narrative report of the dive telling about the equipment you used, the problems you met, the sights you saw, and the plan you wanted to follow and did or did not, and why. What you write in your log should please you, so write what you please. But include information that seems useful; you'll appreciate it when you read the logbook over in about five years.

The formerly enacted but since cancelled scuba diving ordinance number 11025 of Los Angeles County required, in Section 404, subsection (d), that "the diver shall produce a diving log documenting a minimum of twelve dives during the preceding twelve months with a witnessing signature for each recorded dive." Since legislation enacted in one part of the country often serves as a model for another, it would be advantageous for you to make logging your dives your habit.

10

Averting the Hazards
of Scuba Diving

One day you may be forced to assume the role of
"aquadoc"—an emergency medical technician for another diver
or for yourself. The National Safety Council reports that 8,700
people drowned in 1973. Of these victims, 2,900, or one-third,
were experienced swimmers. The council stated that "in about
half the cases the water was calm, water temperature was at least
65°, and the weather was clear."

As a scuba diving enthusiast, you are a part of the high-risk
population for whom skill in cardiopulmonary resuscitation is
essential. You may, by chance, be called upon to assist an
unconscious person up from the bottom. This is one of the
realities of following a sport that takes you around bodies of
water. Accidents happen! Coming upon a medical emergency
topside, with a diver or someone else incapacitated just after
leaving the water, is, unfortunately, not as rare as it once was. It is
likely also that you will be needed to patch skin tears, cuts, rips,
slices, and puncture wounds. Rocks, corals, and shells can be
sharp.

You should be able to decipher the signs and symptoms of
medical problems connected with the diving environment. More

than a million enthusiastic people don scuba gear each year, and some sort of emergency care is essential. The aim of this chapter is to help you be prepared to meet some of those more common emergencies.

The Diver's Emergency First-Aid Kit

Chief among the requirements of emergency medicine is having the implements at hand to give you an assist. Since most store-bought emergency medical first-aid kits are inadequate to treat the problems involved with scuba and skin diving, my recommendation is that you assemble your own. The items listed here are dedicated to the ideal fulfillment of first-aid requirements. You will probably be able to find them in a pharmacy, a tackle shop, a dive shop, or a hardware store. As you'll see, some of them are not strictly medical items.

A plastic or metal tacklebox makes a good medical first-aid supply container. Get one that is lightweight and noncorrosive: it should have three trays and be about twenty inches long by ten inches wide by eight inches deep. Mark it plainly with red crosses painted on the top and sides.

Surgical tools for your first-aid kit should be simple and utilitarian to meet the variety of diving or boating emergencies you might be forced to handle. Include scissors of good quality, up to six inches long, and make sure they are keen-edged and sharp-tipped—rounded ends are no good. Pack single-edge razor blades to act as scalpels and 1½ to two-inch-long sewing needles to close wounds or pick out splinters. Keep their tips sharp by inserting them in a cork. Stock 000-size nylon surgical thread to go with the needles.

Enclose fine-tipped tweezers (eyebrow tweezers do fine), but be sure that the tips come to a point. They should not be flattened, and they must meet exactly. Get a small, soft bristle brush to scrub your hands before touching any injury.

For a multipurpose instrument, get a combination fisherman's wire cutter and pliers tool in one. Most tackle shops sell them for handling wire line. You'll discover that this small tool works well for many uses, including minor maintenance on diving equipment.

A plastic airway of the kind sold by Johnson & Johnson is mandatory. Hopefully, you will never have to use one, but it can save lives and is sometimes all you need to start someone breathing again. Before you pack it into your kit, read the instructions and learn how to use it.

Other items needed for emergency health care are cotton-tipped applicators and tongue depressors, which you can buy in a box or get from your doctor in a handful. Tongue depressors make fine finger splints, and they double as spoons for custard and ice cream. Often a five-ounce disposable cup made of paper or plastic will be needed. Assorted safety pins are useful, too, for holding bandages or for making slings.

To hold medications, the best method is to acquire a number of small plastic pill bottles from your pharmacist. This will preclude your having to carry hundreds of pills packed in bigger containers. Label each small pill bottle and pour in a small supply of each medication.

Common Medications for First-Aid Use

Some common, over-the-counter drugs to take along are Allerest, an antihistamine for internal use against jellyfish stings, coral burns, hives, and other allergic reactions; aspirin or Tylenol, a nonaspirin pain killer; and salt tablets for fluid retention. To prevent seasickness or relieve nausea on a dive boat trip, bring along Dramamine. Nupercainal Cream is good for the pain of minor burns from sun, flame, wind, electricity, and rope. Include Visine eye drops for relief of eyes exposed to sun and wind too long.

Minor cuts and wounds require their own special forms of medication. The usual antiseptics are all right to stock, but even better is an antibiotic ointment, preferably with only one medication contained in the tube, such as Bacitracin Ointment. Do not use an antibiotic contained as a spray; this is difficult to use in the wind and rarely goes exactly where you want it. Hydrogen peroxide 3 percent is ideal for wound cleaning. It will stay active and foaming if you keep it in a brown bottle, tightly stoppered.

For abrasions and minor skin breaks, get Betadine Solution, an iodinelike liquid that does not burn. Avoid pouring Betadine directly onto the wound, but use it instead like a soap. A regular bar of antiseptic soap is useful for the first-aider's washing. Anyone will eventually want suntan lotions, such as red petrolatum. The ultraviolet-light-absorbing type, such as Uval, is excellent.

Other Emergency First-Aid Supplies

Important first-aid supplies include Band-Aids or similar adhesive bandages in assorted sizes. Duke Laboratories makes elastic-backed bandage shapes for patching odd places like elbows, chins, and knees. Certainly you'll want individually-wrapped sterile gauze pads in two-by-two, three-by-three, and four-by-four-inch sizes. If you run short of the smaller ones you can cut up the four-by-four size into little squares while they're still in their envelopes. Don't handle the portion that will touch the wound; try to keep them clean for future use. Loosely woven two-inch roller bandage that sticks to itself will hold sterile dressings in place. Elastic roller bandages (Ace bandages) in the two- and four-inch widths are important to stock. Two-inch-wide adhesive tape can be split into any width and cut to any desired length. For cotton, you can get away with the nonsterile kind—once you open the pack, you have contaminated it anyway.

A few final tips for the diver's first-aid kit—keep certain medications on tap all the time for treatment of special diving-related problems. Make it a habit to replace items as you use them and to check the kit from time to time. Find out how long items keep and whether they need to be refrigerated.

One special medication you'll need for particular problems is 100 percent oxygen administered by bag and mask equipment. Afrin by Schering Corporation and Sudafed from Burroughs Wellcome Company are good decongestants to have, and sodium bicarbonate is a good antidote for food poisoning from eating bad fish.

Treating Skin Breaks

Because fresh and salt waters are becoming more and more polluted, germs are everywhere and infection can be the result of any puncture wounds, rips, tears, and slices of the skin. In fact, any break in the skin, even if it's made in the ocean (theoretically nonpolluted), requires some degree of medical attention. Fortunately, most wounds connected with diving can be handled completely with supplies from your self-assembled first-aid kit.

The immediate danger from big wounds is loss of blood. But stopping the bleeding can almost always be accomplished if you don't panic. All that's needed is firm pressure with four-by-four gauze pads applied directly on top of the opening. Press hard and keep pressing for ten minutes or more. This stops skin bleeding 99 percent of the time. Forget about the old-style tourniquets—they're sometimes dangerous. The only time a tourniquet should be used is when bleeding is otherwise uncontrollable and likely to prove fatal. Check a medical textbook or the *Boy Scout Handbook* before you use one.

Make sure the victim lies down, and elevate the wound above the level of the heart, if possible. Keep the pressure applied as long as bleeding continues. If it won't stop, get the victim to medical help fast. Blood colored purplish-red means that a vein is injured, while bright red spurting comes from a cut artery. Both are dangerous, but the artery may be more so.

Some skin breaks, such as puncture wounds, don't bleed. Hemorrhaging is inside from the skin so the wound tends to seal itself off. Don't force it to bleed; this will only damage the tissues further. Allowing a wound to seep blood does not clean it. Occasionally a deep wound will not bleed at all, probably because the blood vessels have gone into spasm from the trauma. Watch out for bleeding when the spasm releases; that's the time blood might gush forth in earnest. Be prepared by piling on dressings in advance.

All the first-aid measures in this chapter should be used in conjunction with one other important measure: *get the victim to professional medical help as soon as possible.* For wounds, however, you can determine if you are able to handle the problem on the spot with physician treatment delivered later. Troubles that surely require medical help fall under the following categories:

- Uncontrolled bleeding.
- Gaping wound edges. Your needle and thread may hold the flesh together until a surgeon is found to sew the wound under anesthesia.
- Wounds with cut tendons or yellow fat or dark red muscle sticking out of them.
- Complicated dirty, or swollen wounds. These may occur with burns, mashed-in dirt, slivers of glass, jagged or crushed edges, or fish bites and stings. Take precautions with any wounds associated with lots of pain.
- Injured areas that entail cosmetic appearance. A physician can usually reduce the amount of scarring that might result from gaping edges.

Emergency medical problems that might come into your area of first aid and allow on-the-spot treatment demand some positive actions. Here's where you will have to dip into your first-aid kit.

Scrub superficial wounds with soap and water to clean them and reduce the risk of infection; when plenty of water is available, ten minutes of vigorous scrubbing are in order. If the wound is deep or if water is in short supply, pour hydrogen peroxide over it or apply peroxide to a couple of gauze pads and soak the wound with them. Do this for five minutes, wipe away dirt, press to stop bleeding, and then repeat for another five minutes with fresh hydrogen-peroxide-saturated gauze. After that, reach for the Betadine, soak another gauze square, and wipe the area thoroughly. Any rehemorrhaging should be pressed again.

Next apply Bacitracin Ointment on a suitable dressing. Hold the antibiotic in place with gauze pads wrapped around by roller bandage and fastened in place with tape strips. Make sure the wound stays dry and change any wet or soiled dressing. Each time you change the gauze covering, reapply Bacitracin. Get a tetanus injection for deep gashes or wounds that result in serious pain or show swelling, redness, or discharge. Do this within two days of the injury.

Deep wounds or puncture wounds are likely to have dirt driven into them. Keep in mind that fish bites, fishhooks in the hand, and nails in the foot are all puncture wounds, and infection can easily develop. Your first-aid treatment should consist of hot soaks in plain or salt water started within a few hours of the injury. Soak the injury for thirty minutes at least four times a day for a few days. Here, too, visit a doctor; there is a risk of tetanus.

Wounds from the water environment carry a slightly higher risk of tetanus because of the changing ecology. Consequently, you have to be on the lookout for redness, swelling, pain, and a feeling of warmth to the touch in any wound contracted in diving. These are the beginning signs of tetanus or local infection. Don't wait for pus to start leaking from the site or for red streaks to form radiating outward from it.

Treating Near-Drownings

The "syndrome of acute asphyxia with varying degrees of arterial hypoxemia, acidemia, and hypercarbia that produces an anaerobic metabolism" is, of course, doctor's talk for *near-drowning*. When progression has gone to cardiac arrest and death, that is drowning, and there's no use treating it.

After accidents involving breaks in the skin, near-drowning is next in frequency among diving medical problems. Drowning is the third leading cause of accidental death in the United States. It happens to swimmers who faint in the water and drown or who overextend themselves and become exhausted far from a boat or land.

A diver suffering near-drowning is undergoing hypoxia, a deficiency of oxygen in inspired air, so your first emergency care should be to clear his airway and begin mouth-to-mouth resuscitation. If there's no heartbeat, combine ventilation with closed-chest cardiac massage. Your job as the emergency first-aider on the scene is to overcome any cardiovascular collapse due to hypoxia. You must ventilate the victim's lungs to improve oxygen supply to the heart. Thus, cardiac output will increase.

Give this resuscitation in preference to wasting time trying to drain water from the lungs. A victim of near-drowning in fresh water will give up a very poor yield of lung water, because within minutes most of the water is absorbed into his circulation. Seawater, on the other hand, is hypertonic, and therefore draws plasma into the lungs. In seawater cases, therefore, you might clear the airway by draining. Use the *Trendelenburg position,* with

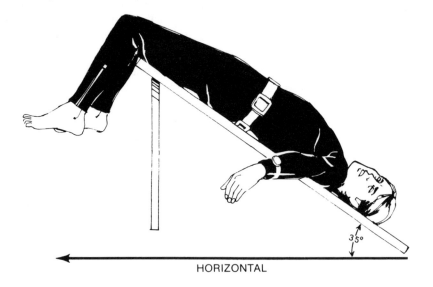

HORIZONTAL

In near-drowning occurring in seawater, you might clear the victim's airway by draining the lungs through the use of the Trendelenburg position. Tilt the entire body on a board elevated to about 35° from the horizontal with the head turned to one side to allow passive drainage during your resuscitation effort.

the victim's head turned to one side. It allows passive drainage during your resuscitation effort.

Keep in mind that with water flowing out of his lungs and air going into them, a near-drowned diver could regain consciousness and maintain fairly normal breathing; but he is not out of danger. He needs oxygen. Here is where the oxygen mask and gas bag mentioned above come into play. Give a high concentration of oxygen and continue this while you travel with the victim to the hospital.

All near-drowning patients should be hospitalized and evaluated. Their blood-gas tension and pH levels should be checked to ascertain whether they have persistent hypoxia and acidosis (blood bicarbonate level lowered from retention of CO_2). Metabolic acidosis occurs in 70 to 75 percent of all near-drowning cases. Thus, although near-drowning is the diagnosis, it is not the only problem faced by the patient. Near-drowning can be precipitated by some of the other mishaps that happen in water.

Shallow-Water Blackout and Hyperventilation

Among near-drowning precipitating mishaps, the commonest is *shallow-water blackout* or fainting under water. Shallow-water blackout primarily affects skin divers and other individuals who attempt prolonged underwater activities while holding their breath. The condition is connected with the carbon dioxide level (CO_2) and the partial pressure of oxygen level (PO_2) within the lungs. It does occasionally affect scuba divers.

Individuals breathing under normal conditions use the partial pressure of oxygen in the lungs. Carbon dioxide, on the other hand, serves as a stimulus to breathing by informing the brain that a person's body requires another breath of air. This process occurs in any prolonged holding of breath, including underwater swimming. The levels of CO_2 and PO_2 are manipulated in one of two ways.

Hyperventilation is one of the manipulative ways, the repeated inhalation of fast, full breaths of air and rapid exhalation in order to lower the beginning CO_2 level. With a lower CO_2 level, the brain does not receive a stimulus to cause quick breathing. This is a tampering with the normal physiological warning system. The individual is thus able to hold his breath longer. But W. D. Snively, M.D., Professor of Life Sciences, at the University of Evansville in Indiana, tells me that hyperventilation can result in unconsciousness, especially in shallow pools.

Professor Snively has studied several drownings that occurred without apparent cause and several near-drownings in which the victims hyperventilated before diving underwater. All the victims were excellent swimmers, but in each case the swimmer blacked out under water. The professor suggested that hyperventilation was likely the deadly danger.

Hyperventilation washes CO_2 out of the lungs, resulting in an extremely low CO_2 level. The diver uses up the oxygen in his blood. Since the normal breathing stimulus, carbon dioxide, is lost, breathing stops; a lack of oxygen to the brain (called hypoxia) causes the diver to lose consciousness. And underwater fainting can result in drowning.

Dr. Snively points out that the danger of hypoxia has not been sufficiently stressed. Some underwater swimmers are extremely sensitive to even a mild degree of hypoxia and could easily get into trouble. He recommends that you should be informed of the hazards of hyperventilation before diving. You should know the basic physiological concepts involved and should be aware that in many cases the victim drowns before potential rescuers even realize he has lost consciousness.

The second manipulation of breath happens when a diver prolongs the time it takes to breathe by descending to such a depth that the PO_2 is raised because of the increased water pressure. His problem here begins when he has used most of his oxygen. As he begins to ascend, the O_2 level begins to drop as water pressure decreases; because of the great lack of oxygen the diver can lapse into unconsciousness before he reaches the surface. Dives to great depths by spearfishermen are the common settings for shallow-water blackouts of this type.

A blackout victim is in an extremely dangerous position at the point of unconsciousness. Seeing him underwater will fool his buddy: the unconscious diver often makes seemingly coordinated movements even after his faint comes on. He does not appear to be in difficulty. And irreversible physiological brain damage from lack of oxygen is only a few minutes away, even if he's saved from death.

Mouth-Pull Scuba Rescue

Suppose a blackout hits a diver on the bottom, in shallow water or at depth—what can you do? Here is a fast and easy technique that will get him to the surface where you can administer first aid for near-drowning.   Instructors of diving warn to make sure the diver's airway is open. They suggest the *bear hug method.* Then quickly rise with him by pulling him feetfirst. The bear hug won't entirely ensure an open airway, however. *The chin pull technique* also uses too much time, since you must reinsert the regulator mouthpiece before you start your ascent.

In areas where the water is cold and the unconscious diver is dressed warmly with a lot of gear on, pulling him to the surface is very difficult.   In southern California, where the Professional Diving Instructor College (PDIC) is located, the recommended procedure is to dump the victim's weight belt and simply swim with him toward the surface at the usual rate.

Since you have almost four minutes from the moment of a diver's unconsciousness to save his life and prevent irreversible brain damage, you might adopt the *mouth-pull scuba rescue.* Approach the unconscious diver and roll him to his back. Pull his weight-belt buckle to drop the lead, but don't bother to inflate his life vest. Remove the unused regulator mouthpiece from his face and insert your thumb in its place. Latch onto his lower jaw behind the teeth and wrap the fingers of the same hand under the chin. This action will open the airway. As you ascend with the victim in this mouth-pull scuba rescue, water will not enter his lungs; expanding gas will keep pushing it out exactly the way it would if he were making a free ascent on his own.

If the diver's body is considerably bulkier or heavier than you can manage, inflate your own life vest as an ascent assist. Keep your thumb in his mouth and your fingers tucked under his chin as you pull upward on his lower jaw. However, false teeth could cause an extra problem in that they might slip out and cause your grip to loosen. If that's the case, it's better to remove those expensive dentures rather than be defeated in your attempt to save his life. Upon reaching the surface inflate the victim's life vest and begin mouth-to-mouth resuscitation immediately, even in the water. In cold water the victim's wet suit may give sufficient buoyancy without inflating his life vest, unless he is still wearing the weight belt.

Resuscitation Techniques

Snorkel-to-Mouth Resuscitation

At this point, on the surface with an unconscious near-drowning victim, the diver's float or a life buoy will come in very handy. Use it to support the person whose life you're trying to save while other rescuers are on their way to assist. Slip the float under his chest to hold him up. Pull the quick-release buckles on his scuba harness to get rid of the air tank. Then turn him over on his back with the float as a support if it will stay in place.

You have a choice now, depending upon whether help is on its way or you must tow the unconscious diver to safety. In the latter case, snorkel-to-mouth resuscitation should be administered. That way, you can resuscitate and tow at the same time. This is how to do it:

Drain the water from the unconscious diver's mask and seal it back on his face to block the escape of air from his nose. Scoop your fingers into his mouth and pull his tongue forward to make sure he hasn't swallowed it. Slip his snorkel from its mask-strap fastening and drain it of water by blowing through the open end. Insert its mouthpiece into the diver's mouth and hold his lips shut with a cupping motion under his chin. Blow into the tube end and feel the victim's chest expand. Don't let the mask ride up or the airtight seal will be broken. If the face mask leaks, remove it, jettison it, and pinch the diver's nostrils together.

After each exhalation of yours into the unconscious diver's lungs, give him a chance to exhale the air too. He'll do this automatically if he's alive. As you wait for his exhalation you'll be able to inhale. Repeat this action about thirteen times per minute. It will take all your coordination as a swimmer to use your hands to manipulate the victim, systematically breathe the breath of life into his lungs, and use your fins for steady progress toward safety.

But even at shore or when the rescue boat has arrived, don't stop your life-saving actions. Perhaps the snorkel will be discarded as too cumbersome, but that's when the plastic Johnson & Johnson airway performs its function best. You may prefer to go directly to mouth-to-mouth resuscitation without using any devices.

Mouth-to-mouth Resuscitation

Mouth-to-mouth resuscitation is best applied on shore or on a boat deck. It can, however, be administered in the water without the use of a snorkel. With the victim on his back, hold his jaw in a

Mouth-to-mouth resuscitation can be administered effectively in the water without use of a snorkel. With the victim on his back, hold his jaw so that it is in a forward jutting position, the same as it was when you ascended with him from the bottom applying the Mouth-Pull Scuba Rescue. Pulling on his nose will tend to make his mouth stand ajar and his jaw jut out.

Photograph courtesy of the Professional Diving Instructor College.

forward-jutting position, the same as it was when you ascended with him from the bottom applying the mouth-pull scuba rescue.

With your other hand, close his nostrils. Put your mouth over the victim's, placed so as to produce a good seal. Breathe into his mouth with a smooth, steady flow so as to cause his chest to expand. Exhale all your breath, remove your mouth, and allow the unconscious person to exhale while you inhale. Put pressure

With one hand, close the nostrils of a near-drowning victim prior to applying inwater mouth-to-mouth resuscitation without use of a snorkel. Put your mouth over the victim's, producing a good seal. Breathe into his mouth with a smooth, steady air flow causing his chest to expand. Exhale all your breath, remove your mouth and allow the unconscious person to exhale while you inhale.

Photograph courtesy of the Professional Diving Instructor College.

on his chest if there is no response to your resuscitation effort.

In the water, you can make use of your own or the near-drowned diver's single-hose regulator for artificial respiration.

The purge valve can be pressed to create a systematic breathing rhythm. Be sure to seal the victim's nose. Administer the compressed air by pushing the valve button in the same way you might surge air into his lungs with a snorkel tube. You may, in fact, find this easier than snorkel-to-mouth resuscitation, since you can breathe regularly yourself without having to coordinate your exhalations with the victim's inhalations. On the other hand, you do have to count the thirteen air surges and time your button-pushing at four or five seconds. You must determine also that there is enough air pressure left in his tank and yours by reading the tank-pressure gauges.

An arrested heartbeat can sometimes be started again by a sharp blow to the drowning victim's chest. This is called the *precordial thump.*

11

Particular Diving Precautions

Exposure to Cold and Exhaustion

Jumping into cold water can cause an acute allergic response to a sudden lowering of environmental temperature. It can produce unconsciousness or an anaphylactic reaction. Either condition is a hazard to health, but both can be avoided by proper diving dress.

Cold water invariably has a numbing effect on a diver's limbs; this could immobilize even an expert swimmer. It can bring on earlier exhaustion, too, leaving a diver with insufficient strength to return to safety. Diving in Lake Winnipesaukee, New Hampshire, one day in August, I had an experience with allergy to cold. My water-skier's wet suit proved inadequate when I hit a thermocline at 35 feet. The temperature dropped at least twenty degrees, and I felt paralyzed by the severe cold. Only through force of will could I make my legs move sufficiently to kick me up a few feet out of the thermocline. Then I found that my strength had been completely drained by the exhausting cold. I used my BC to carry me to the surface.

Oversensitivity to cold and resultant allergic reaction is not an uncommon problem. Don't treat it lightly as if it were a sissy reaction. Potentially, anaphylaxis shows up within a few minutes, as giant hives, sneezing, cough, bronchial asthma, fainting, or even death. The allergic response depends on your level of sensitivity and on the coldness of the water. Nevertheless, consider overexposure to cold as a possible complication in every incidence of someone's near-drowning.

Treatment of cold-water allergy and of near-drowning includes the giving of antihistamine by mouth. If a doctor suspects anaphylaxis, he'll probably inject 1 cc. of 1:1000 epinephrine solution intramuscularly and use other pharmaceutical products beyond the scope of a diver's first aid. One thing you can make sure of is that the victim's airway is open. Do this by administering 100 percent oxygen to improve his ventilation.

Since water is an excellent conductor of heat—it dissipates heat twenty-five times faster than air—cold water can quickly produce immersion hypothermia in the submerged individual. This is rapid, excessive heat loss while he is in the water or under its surface. The loss of body heat can sneak up on a diver from his natural swimming motions and from his ordinary respirations. As his skin cools to the surrounding temperature, blood is shunted into the core tissues to heat his internal organs. The skin-tissue blood, which is already cool, drops the diver's body core temperature even more. Several dangerous physiological reactions can set in at this point.

Due to allergy to cold the blood can be shunted into the core tissues to heat the internal organs, and a diver can suffer from dangerous physiological and psychological reactions. Overexposure to cold is a possible complication in every incidence of near-drowning. For example, a diver can lose his sense of presence in the watery environment—forget where he is, what he's doing, even who he is. Sudden exhaustion hits muscles and paralysis won't let him command limbs to move.

Photograph courtesy of the Professional Diving Instructor College.

A cold-affected diver can lose his sense of presence in the watery environment—forget where he is, what he's doing, even who he is. Sudden exhaustion hits his muscles and paralysis won't let him command his limbs to move. Death might occur underwater, too, but not from drowning or lack of air—it can result from immersion hypothermia. When the usual body temperature drops from 98.6° F. to 94° F., amnesia hits. At a body temperature drop to 86° F., the muscles lose strength and become paralyzed. By the time the body's temperature approaches 77° F., it's likely that cardiac arrest has set in and it's all over—from a combination of accelerated body-heat loss and respiratory heat loss characteristic of any exercise.

Emergency treatment of a scuba diver suffering from overexposure to cold with subsequent exhaustion is this: leave his wet suit on him and let hot water circulate between the suit and the skin. Throw him under a hot shower and let the water run inside the suit so as to hold the heat in. Give him a hot, nonstimulating drink, such as hot chocolate. Don't give him coffee or the traditional shot of whiskey; these will increase the circulation to the skin and take it away from his vital organs, making his immersion hypothermia worse.

On shore, if a hospital isn't available, call a doctor and immediately appply hot water baths. A tub water temperature of 104° to 106° F. is called for. Immerse his body fully. Wrap him afterwards in blankets, towels, or warm clothing. The idea is to prevent the victim from lying around at home with nothing more than a blanket over him. Prevent what's known as *paradoxical cooling*. That is, as skin blood vessels dilate in response to warm air, the warm core blood flows outward. Then, since the body's outer surface is still as cold as the environment from which the victim has emerged, the blood returning to his body's core is cool and lowers his core temperature even further. The victim's condition deteriorates from that point.

Ear Squeeze and Sinus Squeeze

The source of at least 50 percent of all medical complaints in diving is "squeeze." The head sinuses and the middle ear are the

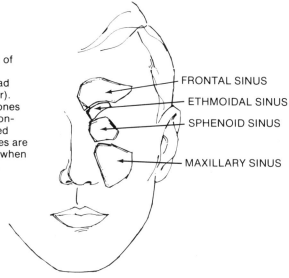

The source of at least 50 percent of medical complaints in diving is "squeeze" which involves the head sinuses (as well as the middle ear). The sinuses are cavities in the bones of the face and head. They are connected through the nose and lined with nasal membrane. The sinuses are affected by pressure on descent when air inside head spaces contracts.

FRONTAL SINUS

ETHMOIDAL SINUS

SPHENOID SINUS

MAXILLARY SINUS

sites of this unpleasantness. It occurs on descent when air inside head spaces contracts. This contraction on body-space walls causes an enclosure, such as an ear, to rupture, for two reasons: vacuum suction from within and ambient pressure from without. A diver doesn't have to descend very far to suffer the painful feeling of squeeze. He can develop sinus pain and ear pain at about ten feet from the surface, and experience dizziness and some hearing loss afterward.

William L. Orris, M.D., director of medical services at the Scripps Institution of Oceanography, University of California at San Diego, told me of some of the pathology and treatment of middle ear squeeze. When the injured diver's physician looks inside the middle ear with an instrument, the doctor can see an eardrum that appears red and retracted. The knobby portions of the ear bones protrude as bulges in the soft tissues. The eustachian tubes may be blocked by inflammation, infection, or enlarged adenoids or tonsils.

Ear squeeze symptoms the diver may experience, besides pain, are variable. He may hear ringing, buzzing, roaring or clicking inside his head. And these sounds are not imagined; they can sometimes even be heard by his companions. The noises result

Ear squeeze symptoms a diver may experience include pain; a noise that is ringing, buzzing, roaring or clicking inside his head; bloody sputum and tinnitis; and a temporary total hearing loss. The diver to the right in this photograph is performing the *Valsalva Manuever,* pinching off the nostrils by use of the fingers in order to stretch open the eustachian tubes. Other "no hands" squeeze treatment or ear clearing consists of yawning, swallowing, wiggling the jaw from side to side and forcefully "snorting" through the nose into the mask. *Photograph by Morton Walker.*

from a condition of catarrhal otitis media. Bloody sputum and tinnitus noises could be signs of eardrum rupture caused by an implosion upon descent, or by explosion caused by a spontaneous closure of the eustachian tube after the diver has taken a breath at depth and ascended. A ruptured eardrum can produce a temporary total hearing loss, too, with some mechanical damage of the ear ossicles or oval or round window membranes.

You can prevent squeeze of your sinuses and middle ear by taking Boyle's law into consideration. Remember that the greatest pressure changes take place within a few feet of the surface. You simply must not ignore sudden ear or sinus pain and continue to descend to make eardrum rupture inevitable. Realize that when your ear vent is blocked by an acute cold or chronic sinusitis you are fated for trouble. Blockage creates a negative pressure within the closed cavity as you descend. Air constricts inside the cavity and attempts to occupy less space. Or, as you ascend, the blocked cavity creates a positive pressure and the air within tries to expand

and blow out the membranes. Thus, bleeding from a rupture or mechanical damage can result.

To avoid squeeze trouble altogether, don't dive with any kind of nasal or ear congestion. But if you must chance it, take the precaution of using a spray decongestant beforehand. Oxymetazoline under Schering Corporation's brand name Afrin, or pseudoephedrine under Burroughs Wellcome's brand Sudafed, is good for decongesting blocked body vents.

Here is an anti-squeeze precaution: under the surface, as you go deeper, test your ability to hear by covering one ear and producing an outside noise near the other. Ascending from depth too fast increases the chance for eardrum explosion. If you have ear or nasal congestion, double the time you spend in your usual rate of rise to sixty feet in 120 seconds instead of sixty feet per minute. And if you experience an ear or sinus problem after a dive, get to an ear, nose, and throat physician right away.

Breathing Bad Air

Carbon monoxide poisoning is a possibility in any scuba diving accident, either as its initial cause or as one component. Consider that it does not take much carbon monoxide (CO) to poison and cause eventual death. That's because the gas combines with hemoglobin about two hundred times as readily as does oxygen. If CO is pumped into a tank over a compressor's engine exhaust it will contaminate the air you'll be inhaling below. When you buy air at a dive shop where the facilities are unfamiliar to you, ask to see the tank filling station. This is a perfectly reasonable request, and one that could ensure that you will be breathing from an uncontaminated air supply.

In all fairness, I must point out that dive shops make certain that their air is pure, for two very good reasons. One is monetary and connected with liability. Any shop whose compressor breaks down and leaks oil to contaminate air will soon lose business, especially if some diving accident should occur as a result. But there is a second more pertinent reason that keeps dive shop or dive resort air pure—the shops' instructors breathe that compressed air themselves while conducting dives. Consequently, self-preservation is an even better determining factor of good air being sold to you than any monetary one.

Air Embolisim

The sudden decrease in pressure a diver experiences when he returns to the surface is the primary perpetrator of diving problems. Decreased pressure can cause the bends or decompression sickness. It can also produce a cerebral air embolism—by far the worst diving danger—most often fatal by lung air expansion, rupturing of lung blood vessels, and forced air embolism first to the heart and then to the brain. As a potential provider of emergency first aid for either condition, you should watch for signs of the bends and you should watch for air embolism. And whereas you can't do much more for a diver suffering from decompression sickness than rush him to a recompression chamber, you can help him somewhat if he's been hit by an air embolism.

What do we mean by air embolism? Air embolism is a condition that comes on from the forcing of air through the alveoli walls into the bloodstream. The hazard is always present when a diver inhales from scuba and holds his breath while ascending, even as little as four feet. Boyle's Law applies here in reverse of its effect on squeeze. As you ascend and ambient pressure decreases, interior lung pressure increases. You can overexpand your alveoli sacs like thousands of bursting balloons. The result is leakage of air bubbles from the lung sacs into the bloodstream, where the air bubbles rush through and get stuck in a small blood vessel. This could be the area of the heart or the brain, causing instant death.

Eric P. Kindwall, M.D., director of the hyperbaric medicine department at Milwaukee's St. Luke's Hospital and author of *The Scuba Safety Report #3,* describes symptoms of embolism as unconsciousness, bleeding from the mouth due to ruptured lung vessels, convulsions, paralysis, mottled tongue, unequal pupils, change of voice quality, chest pain, possible pneumothorax (an accumulation of air or gas in the pleural cavity from the rupture of a lung), difficulty in breathing, and air under the skin. "The first thing I touch on a diver is the collarbone area," says Dr. Kindwall. "If it's crunchy with air under the skin, I know it's definitely embolism." Although both the bends and air embolism may lead to paralysis, if paralysis is vertical from face to toes it is probably caused by an air embolism. "Air embolism can hit a diver in eight feet of water," Dr. Kindwall warns, "and theoretically it can hit in less than four."

The condition requires recompression as quickly as possible. Never send a diver back into the water to recompress; this takes too long, and you might be complicating his symptoms by adding exposure.

For a first-aid measure while you're heading toward a recompression chamber with the victim, position him with his buttocks higher than his head. His body should be turned to the left at about 10 degrees and his air passages checked for blockage. Give oxygen if it's available since it decreases nitrogen back-pressure.

If the diver must be taken to the chamber in an aircraft, make sure the plane hops hedges really low. Indeed, a growing medical occurrence is the diver who lives far inland and flies his own plane. He might pack up his gear an hour after he leaves the water and jet on home—and what does not hit him in the water may well strike him in the air.

Ed Brawley, president of PDIC, suggests, "The technique called 'tilting' is quite effective to overcome air embolism. It pumps bubbles and blood clots through by placing the victim in a head-down position to increase head pressure and dilate the blood vessels. After ten to fifteen seconds tilt him up, then down again, to cause a pumping effect. Use a board in a type of teeter-totter." Once at the recompression chamber, embolism cases are preferably started at six times normal atmospheric pressure and brought to normal over a five- to six-hour period.

The United States Government supplies a national air embolism and bends watch. Call collect any time of the day or night for medical help with diving emergencies. The U.S. Naval Experimental Diving Unit encourages inquiry about any aspect of diving—especially for medical emergencies. The Panama City, Florida, telephone number is (904) 234-4355. In addition, the officers at the U.S. Naval Experimental Diving Unit maintain a current list of recompression diving chambers for every area of the world, about eight inches thick of computer printout pages. To learn in advance the location of the recompression chamber nearest to where you intend to dive, request this information from the United States Navy Experimental Diving Unit, Building 300, NCSL, Panama City, FL 32401.

For the most complete diving emergency information gathered together in one place, get the two-volume set of the current *U.S. Navy Diving Manual.* Send $16.70 per set with your request for stock number 0846-00072 to the Superintendent of Documents, U.S. Government Printing Office, Washington, DC 20402.

"No-Calculation" Dive Tables. Simplified Linear System for Repetitive Scuba Dives by S. Harold Reuter, M.D. *Tables courtesy of Dacor Corporation.*

NO-DECOMPRESSION LIMITS AND REPETITIVE GROUP DESIGNATION TABLE FOR NO-DECOMPRESSION AIR DIVES

Depth (feet)	No-decompression limits (min)	A	B	C	D	E	F	G	H	I	J	K	L	M	N	O
10	60	120	210	300												
15	35	70	110	160	225	350										
20	25	50	75	100	135	180	240	325								
25	20	35	55	75	100	125	160	195	245	315						
30	15	30	45	60	75	95	120	145	170	205	250	310				
35	310	5	15	25	40	50	60	80	100	120	140	160	190	220	270	310
40	200	5	15	25	30	40	50	70	80	100	110	130	150	170	200	
50	100		10	15	25	30	40	50	60	70	80	90	100			
60	60		10	15	20	25	30	40	50	55	60					
70	50		5	10	15	20	30	35	40	45	50					
80	40		5	10	15	20	25	30	35	40						
90	30		5	10	12	15	20	25	30							
100	25		5	7	10	15	20	22	25							
110	20			5	10	13	15	20								
120	15			5	10	12	15									
130	10			5	8	10										
140	10			5	7	10										
150	5			5												
160	5				5											
170	5				5											
180	5				5											
190	5				5											

U.S NAVY STANDARD AIR DECOMPRESSION TABLE

Depth (feet)	Bottom time (min)	Time first stop (min:sec)	50	40	30	20	10	Total ascent (min:sec)	Repetitive group
40	200						0	0:40	*
	210	0:30					2	2:40	N
	230	0:30					7	7:40	N
	250	0:30					11	11:40	O
	270	0:30					15	15:40	O
	300	0:30					19	19:40	Z
50	100						0	0:50	*
	110	0:40					3	3:50	L
	120	0:40					5	5:50	M
	140	0:40					10	10:50	M
	160	0:40					21	21:50	N
	180	0:40					29	29:50	O
	200	0:40					35	35:50	O
	220	0:40					40	40:50	Z
	240	0:40					47	47:50	Z
60	60						0	1:00	*
	70	0:50					2	3:00	K
	80	0:50					7	8:00	L
	100	0:50					14	15:00	M
	120	0:50					26	27:00	N
	140	0:50					39	40:00	O
	160	0:50					48	49:00	Z
	180	0:50					56	57:00	Z
	200	0:40				1	69	71:00	Z
70	50						0	1:10	*
	60	1:00					8	9:10	K
	70	1:00					14	15:10	L
	80	1:00					18	19:10	M
	90	1:00					23	24:10	N
	100	1:00					33	34:10	N
	110	0:50				2	41	44:10	O
	120	0:50				4	47	52:10	O
	130	0:50				6	52	59:10	O
	140	0:50				8	56	65:10	Z
	150	0:50				9	61	71:10	Z
	160	0:50				13	72	86:10	Z
	170	0:50				19	79	99:10	Z
80	40						0	1:20	*
	50	1:10					10	11:20	K
	60	1:10					17	18:20	L
	70	1:10					23	24:20	M
	80	1:00				2	31	34:20	N
	90	1:00				7	39	47:20	N
	100	1:00				11	46	58:20	O
	110	1:00				13	53	67:20	O
	120	1:00				17	56	74:20	Z
	130	1:00				19	63	83:20	Z
	140	1:00				26	69	96:20	Z
	150	1:00				32	77	110:20	Z
90	30						0	1:30	*
	40	1:20					7	8:30	J
	50	1:20					18	19:30	L
	60	1:20					25	26:30	M
	70	1:10				7	30	38:30	N
	80	1:10				13	40	54:30	N
	90	1:10				18	48	67:30	O
	100	1:10				21	54	76:30	Z
	110	1:10				24	61	86:30	Z
	120	1:10				32	68	101:30	Z
	130	1:00			5	36	74	116:30	Z

* SEE NO-DECOMPRESSION TABLE FOR REPETITIVE GROUPS

U.S NAVY STANDARD AIR DECOMPRESSION TABLE

Depth (feet)	Bottom time (min)	Time first stop (min:sec)	Decompression stops (feet) 50	40	30	20	10	Total ascent (min:sec)	Repetitive group
100	25						0	1:40	*
	30	1:30					3	4:40	I
	40	1:30					15	16:40	K
	50	1:20				2	24	27:40	L
	60	1:20				9	28	38:40	N
	70	1:20				17	39	57:40	O
	80	1:20				23	48	72:40	O
	90	1:10			3	23	57	84:40	Z
	100	1:10			7	23	66	97:40	Z
	110	1:10			10	34	72	117:40	Z
	120	1:10			12	41	78	132:40	Z
110	20						0	1:50	*
	25	1:40					3	4:50	H
	30	1:40					7	8:50	J
	40	1:30				2	21	24:50	L
	50	1:30				8	26	35:50	M
	60	1:30				18	36	55:50	N
	70	1:20			1	23	48	73:50	O
	80	1:20			7	23	57	88:50	Z
	90	1:20			12	30	84	107:50	Z
	100	1:20			15	37	72	125:50	Z

Depth (feet)	Bottom time (min)	Time to first stop (min:sec)	Decompression stops (feet) 50	40	30	20	10	Total ascent (min:sec)	Repetitive group
120	15						0	2:00	*
	20	1:50					2	4:00	H
	25	1:50					6	8:00	I
	30	1:50					14	16:00	J
	40	1:40				5	25	32:00	L
	50	1:40				15	31	48:00	N
	60	1:30			2	22	45	71:00	O
	70	1:30			9	23	55	89:00	O
	80	1:30			15	27	63	107:00	Z
	90	1:30			19	37	74	132:00	Z
	100	1:30			23	45	80	150:00	Z
130	10						0	2:10	*
	15	2:00					1	3:10	F
	20	2:00					4	6:10	H
	25	2:00					10	12:10	J
	30	1:50				3	18	23:10	M
	40	1:50				10	25	37:10	N
	50	1:40			3	21	37	63:10	O
	60	1:40			9	23	52	86:10	Z
	70	1:40			16	24	61	103:10	Z
	80	1:30		3	19	35	72	131:10	Z
	90	1:30		8	19	45	80	154:10	Z

Depth (feet)	Bottom time (min)	Time to first stop (min:sec)	Decompression stops (feet) 50	40	30	20	10	Total ascent (min:sec)	Repetitive group
140	10						0	2:20	*
	15	2:10					2	4:20	G
	20	2:10					6	8:20	I
	25	2:00				2	14	18:20	J
	30	2:00				5	21	28:20	K
	40	1:50			2	16	26	46:20	N
	50	1:50			6	24	44	76:20	O
	60	1:50			16	23	56	97:20	Z
	70	1:40		4	19	32	68	125:20	Z
	80	1:40			10	23	41	79	155:20	Z

* SEE NO-DECOMPRESSION TABLE FOR REPETITIVE GROUPS

RESIDUAL NITROGEN TIMETABLE FOR REPETITIVE AIR DIVES

*Dives following surface intervals of more than 12 hours are not repetitive dives. Use actual bottom times in the Standard Air Decompression Tables to compute decompression for such dives.

Repetitive group at the beginning of the surface interval

The upper table gives the surface interval time range (top value to bottom value) for each repetitive group. The starting repetitive group is in the left-most labeled column; the resulting new group designation is read from the column headings at the bottom.

Start	Z	O	N	M	L	K	J	I	H	G	F	E	D	C	B	A
A																0:10–12:00*
B															0:10–2:10	2:11–12:00*
C														0:10–1:39	1:40–2:49	2:50–12:00*
D													0:10–1:09	1:10–2:38	2:39–5:48	5:49–12:00*
E												0:10–0:54	0:55–1:57	1:58–3:22	3:23–6:32	6:33–12:00*
F											0:10–0:45	0:46–1:29	1:30–2:28	2:29–3:57	3:58–7:05	7:06–12:00*
G										0:10–0:40	0:41–1:15	1:16–1:59	2:00–2:58	2:59–4:25	4:26–7:35	7:36–12:00*
H									0:10–0:36	0:37–1:06	1:07–1:41	1:42–2:23	2:24–3:20	3:21–4:49	4:50–7:59	8:00–12:00*
I								0:10–0:33	0:34–0:59	1:00–1:29	1:30–2:02	2:03–2:44	2:45–3:43	3:44–5:12	5:13–8:21	8:22–12:00*
J							0:10–0:31	0:32–0:54	0:55–1:19	1:20–1:47	1:48–2:20	2:21–3:04	3:05–4:02	4:03–5:40	5:41–8:40	8:41–12:00*
K						0:10–0:28	0:29–0:49	0:50–1:11	1:12–1:35	1:36–2:03	2:04–2:38	2:39–3:21	3:22–4:19	4:20–5:48	5:49–8:58	8:59–12:00*
L					0:10–0:26	0:27–0:45	0:46–1:04	1:05–1:25	1:26–1:49	1:50–2:19	2:20–2:53	2:54–3:36	3:37–4:35	4:36–6:02	6:03–9:12	9:13–12:00*
M				0:10–0:25	0:26–0:42	0:43–0:59	1:00–1:18	1:19–1:39	1:40–2:05	2:06–2:34	2:35–3:08	3:09–3:52	3:53–4:49	4:50–6:18	6:19–9:28	9:29–12:00*
N			0:10–0:24	0:25–0:39	0:40–0:54	0:55–1:11	1:12–1:30	1:31–1:53	1:54–2:18	2:19–2:47	2:48–3:22	3:23–4:04	4:05–5:03	5:04–6:32	6:33–9:43	9:44–12:00*
O		0:10–0:23	0:24–0:36	0:37–0:51	0:52–1:07	1:08–1:24	1:25–1:43	1:44–2:04	2:05–2:29	2:30–2:59	3:00–3:33	3:34–4:17	4:18–5:16	5:17–6:44	6:45–9:54	9:55–12:00*
	0:10–0:22	0:23–0:34	0:35–0:48	0:49–1:02	1:03–1:18	1:19–1:36	1:37–1:55	1:56–2:17	2:18–2:42	2:43–3:10	3:11–3:45	3:46–4:29	4:30–5:27	5:28–6:56	6:57–10:05	10:06–12:00*

NEW → GROUP DESIGNATION

Z	O	N	M	L	K	J	I	H	G	F	E	D	C	B	A

RESIDUAL NITROGEN TIMES (MINUTES)

REPETITIVE DIVE DEPTH	Z	O	N	M	L	K	J	I	H	G	F	E	D	C	B	A
40	257	241	213	187	161	138	116	101	87	73	61	49	37	25	17	7
50	169	160	142	124	111	99	87	76	66	56	47	38	29	21	13	6
60	122	117	107	97	88	79	70	61	52	44	36	30	24	17	11	5
70	100	96	87	80	72	64	57	50	43	37	31	26	20	15	9	4
80	84	80	73	68	61	54	48	43	38	32	28	23	18	13	8	4
90	73	70	64	58	53	47	43	38	33	29	24	20	16	11	7	3
100	64	62	57	52	48	43	38	34	30	26	22	18	14	10	7	3
110	57	55	51	47	42	38	34	31	27	24	20	16	13	10	6	3
120	52	50	46	43	39	35	32	28	25	21	18	15	12	9	6	3
130	46	44	40	38	35	31	28	25	22	19	16	13	11	8	6	3
140	42	40	38	35	32	29	26	23	20	18	15	12	10	7	5	2
150	40	38	35	32	30	27	24	22	19	17	14	12	9	7	5	2
160	37	36	33	31	28	26	23	20	18	16	13	11	9	6	4	2
170	35	34	31	29	26	24	22	19	17	15	13	10	8	6	4	2
180	32	31	29	27	25	22	20	18	16	14	12	10	8	6	4	2
190	31	30	28	26	24	21	19	17	15	13	11	10	8	6	4	2

Dr. Kindwall also maintains a Midwestern 24-hour collect call service. It is a bends watch for advice in case of serious diving emergencies and for help in locating the recompression chamber nearest the accident. My telephone call immediately reached another hyperbaric specialist when Dr. Kindwall was off duty. A telephone call direct to Eric P. Kindwall, MD, Director of the Department of Hyperbaric Medicine, St. Luke's Hospital, 2900 Oklahoma Avenue, Milwaukee, WI 53215, can be made by dialing (414) 647-6577. For general information about the medical aspects of diving or for the location of the nearest recompression chamber, write his department in advance of your trip.

Reverse charges for telephone calls to these bends watch numbers only if you are in absolute need of emergency medical aid for a diving accident.

An Aquadoc for All Regions
In case your patient's difficulties don't fit into the limited realm of air embolism and you don't know what to do or where to turn, consult Appendix 1 for a directory of physicians with special expertise in handling aquatic emergencies. Note that some are truly specialized, restricting themselves to such areas as marine poisoning, while others will handle most any question—or patient—you put to them. The listing is revised annually with the help of aquadoc William L. Orris, M.D., of La Jolla, California; it is meant to be purely representative. It is published each year in *Emergency Medicine,* a journal published by Fischer-Murray, Inc., 280 Madison Avenue, New York, NY 10016. The listing is reprinted here from the June 1975 issue.

Chest and Pulmonary Barotrauma
Any time middle-ear squeeze or sinus squeeze strikes upon descent, *chest squeeze* is a possible problem too in the 100-foot-depth range. That's because during the descent blockage can hit the trachea either because the diver takes a deep breath as he enters the water and holds it or because he exhales steadily as he

Anytime middle-ear squeeze or sinus squeeze strikes upon descent, chest squeeze is a possible problem too in the 100-foot-depth range—especially if you hold your breath or merely expel it on the way down. Blockage can hit the trachea causing negative pressure pulling strongly on the alveoli from within, causing blood vessels to break and blood to flow into them. Consequently, as you drop over a coral wall as this picture illustrates divers doing, do not hold your breath or just exhale going down. Breathe normally and steadily and expel your bubbles. *Photograph by Bruce "Teacher" Bowker.*

goes down. In either event, the result is thoracic squeeze, with negative pressure pulling strongly on the alveoli from within. This causes the blood vessels to break and blood to flow into them.

Chest squeeze is manifested by chest pain and a bloody, frothy sputum flowing from the mouth. As a first-aider, your obligation is to quickly get the patient to a physician. His treatment will be aimed at neutralizing the internal swelling reaction by means of intravenous administration of high-molecular-weight fluids, accompanied by bed rest.

Spontaneous pneumothorax is a problem that can strike a submerged diver upon his ascent. But he will experience it only if he attempts a too-rapid rise to the surface, faster than the U.S. Navy's recommended ascent speed, and if he simultaneously does not exhale sufficiently. The diver sometimes compounds his error by taking an inhalation at depth and holding it as he rises. As the ambient pressure decreases with his ascent, the air in his lungs expands and tends to tear and burst the alveoli—spontaneous pneumothorax.

The resulting lung damage usually shows up almost immediately. However, a diver may emerge from the water and complain of chest pain, then ignore it, and twelve to twenty-four hours later fall into interstitial or subcutaneous emphysema or even air embolism. The symptoms are shortness of breath, dizziness, irregular pulse, a certain blueness to the diver's lips and fingernails, distention of neck veins, and chest pain. The discomfort is caused by air trapped in the space between the lungs and the chest wall. The lungs can collapse as the trapped air expands and increases pressure on them. The real danger is that enough internal pressure will cut off breathing and stop heart action.

Your emergency measure is to get that diver with spontaneous pneumothorax to a recompression chamber and call in a physician. His treatment will include a tap of the chest wall with needle and syringe to let out the trapped air. Of course, the true preventive measure for this kind of pulmonary barotrauma is a slow ascent—never faster than your bubbles, and never holding your breath. This particular diving precaution is the most important one.

A space located in the middle of the chest behind the sternum bone is called the mediastinum. It can trap air as you ascend, which produces pain within the chest cavity. The symptom is the result of *mediastinal emphysema.*

Sometimes air gets caught under the skin, causing a swelling to pop out. A cracking or crinkling sound may escape from the area of swelling, too, which indicates that *subcutaneous emphysema* is present. The problem is dangerous only insofar as it signals too fast an ascent, with or without breath-holding. That danger is, of course, a precursor to the more serious conditions of pneumothorax, air embolism, and the ever-present scuba hazard, decompression sickness—the bends.

Making emergency ascent fast is sometimes a necessity. Dangers connected with this requirement can be minimized if you ascend quickly below 30 feet and markedly slow your ascent thereafter. The primary danger is overexpansion of lung air and not speed of ascent from depth.

Decompression Sickness—the Bends

On the surface of the Earth the human body is in equilibrium with the ambient pressure, which is 1 atmosphere, and with the partial pressure of nitrogen in the air. When either or both change—and both do in underwater descending or ascending—there must be compensatory changes in tissues and body spaces. The tissues maintain their equilibrium with nitrogen by gas exchange. The problem of decompression sickness—the bends—is that the tissues normally maintain their saturation or equilibrium with nitrogen in the air by absorbing it from the bloodstream on descent and giving it back during ascent. This gas exchange is never instantaneous, however, and there is always a lag between the change in equilibrium and its restoration by the cell's absorption or loss of nitrogen.

As you relieve the pressure by ascending from the depths to the water's surface, the tissues liberate the nitrogen and allow it to slowly bubble out into the bloodstream and joint spaces. This is the same action that occurs when you take the pressure off a soda-water bottle by uncapping it.

The gas bubbles don't form within the body of an ascending diver quite as fast as in soda water—they may take a few hours to become big enough to cause pain. This is the bends characteristic, and what makes decompression sickness a sneaky hazard to safe scuba diving.

A diving enthusiast who hasn't felt the symptoms tends to think that making ascent stops at specific depths to decompress is foolish. That's fallacious thinking—and the particular diving hazard to guard against. If you ever experience the symptoms of decompression sickness, you'll soon understand the need to decompress.

What do the bends feel like? You may feel severe, deep, gnawing pain in an arm or leg, staggering dizziness, paralysis in a limb, choking shortness of breath, extreme fatigue, or collapse with unconsciousness. Occasionally a blotchy and mottled skin rash occurs, varying from a pinhead to the size of a dime. You might feel tingling, burning, or itching of the skin, as if ants were crawling over you.

The only really effective treatment of these symptoms is recompression. If you feel pain that might be a symptom of decompression sickness, you should be treated by recompression, even though the pain could turn out to be from a strain or sprain. Failure to treat doubtful cases is the most frequent cause of lasting injury. Before diving you should know the exact location of your nearest manned recompression chamber. It's as necessary a bit of knowledge as knowing how to use a regulator. Remember, if you need assistance or don't know where the nearest recompression chamber is, call, day or night, the duty officer at the Navy Experimental Diving Unit at Panama City, Florida: (904) 234-4355. Or call your local Coast Guard office, which not only knows where the nearest chamber is but will also transport the victim to it.

The recompression chamber is an airtight compartment whose pressure can be controlled. In any emergency, any diver who has rushed to the surface without taking his proper decompression must lose no time in getting to the recompression chamber, and must at once be put under the pressure at which he should have been held.

Recompression chamber locations change, but Appendix 2 contains a revised 1974 international listing of recompression chambers supplied by NAUI for possible use in diver treatment.

Emergency Care of the Bends

Internist William H. Spaur, senior medical research officer with the Navy's Experimental Diving Unit, points out that the bends are ordinarily divided into two categories. The first is the simpler, milder type—just pain. This pain usually begins in the region of a joint, such as an elbow, shoulder, or knee, and it starts within two hours after the dive has been completed. The other, more severe type involves the central nervous system or the organs of special sense—hearing, or the vestibular apparatus. It often starts before the diver surfaces.

But the victim should not reenter the water to go back down. Recompression takes a longer time than anyone's gas supply could last. In fact, redescending usually makes things worse.

Recompression in a chamber using recompression tables numbers 10 and 11 (formerly tables 5 and 6 of the 1963 U.S. Navy Diving Manual) call for 135 and 285 minutes, respectively. In air embolism, the standard time is 319 minutes. All chambers have oxygen treatment tables beside them. Without such treatment, the condition of sensory loss, paralysis, and other central nervous system complications is permanent. Even with treatment, residual impairment may occur.

If the recompression chamber is a long way off and pain is severe, give the victim aspirin or codeine or a combination of both. After years of research, it's still not known whether it's the nitrogen bubbles that really cause the pain, nor where the bubbles are at the time of pain. The assumption is that nitrogen is absorbed into the neutral fat tissues, that it bubbles as the diver ascends, and that the bubbles cause the pain by blocking small blood vessels.

The nitrogen bubbles can develop on the venous side of the blood vessels or in the tissues; medical science does not know. But they are disseminated in the general circulation, and through the use of Doppler devices they can be heard going into the arteries and veins. They are both within the circulation and within the tissues.

Divers with acute bends sometimes get the "chokes," a shortness of breath syndrome. This is caused by nitrogen bubbles clogging the capillaries or having some kind of effect on the lining of the respiratory membranes—like an acute bronchitis or inflammation. The immediate treatment is oxygenation. But this is a very serious condition, and if the diver isn't recompressed, he will probably go into paralysis or maybe unconsciousness very soon.

Contradictory to common belief about decompression sickness, you *can* get the bends even 33 feet down. At 35 feet, one can stay down for 310 minutes; at 60 feet, 60 minutes; at 100 feet, 25 minutes. The U.S. Navy diving tables in Appendix 3 assume an ascent of one foot per second. A faster ascent might possibly cause the bends.

Although decompression sickness can clear up spontaneously, doctors must be watchful and do a very careful neurological examination to make sure there is no sensory or central nervous system involvement. If a person has a residual bends injury—say to a knee—he might tend to get hit by the condition in that area again with repeated diving.

Nitrogen Narcosis

At depths beyond 100 feet, a euphoria effect takes command of reactive thinking. This euphoria is a symptom of a condition known medically as nitrogen narcosis, and commonly as the rapture of the deep. It is very common at 200 feet and becomes disabling at 250 feet except among the most experienced individuals. As a descriptive term for its symptoms, *Martini's Law* has been developed: the effect of nitrogen narcosis is like imbibing martinis on an empty stomach; it makes you feel tipsy. The farther you go beyond 100 feet, the drunker you will feel. Martini's Law suggests that the alteration in reactive thinking is equivalent to the effects of imbibing one martini for each fifty feet of descent; below 100 feet, alteration occurs at the rate of one martini for each additional twenty-five feet of descent.

Nitrogen narcosis is typical of the intoxicating effect of inhaling any of the inert gases under multiples of atmospheric pressure. For example, hydrogen, helium, argon, neon, xenon, and krypton are other inert gases present as traces in air—compared to nitrogen, which makes up 78 percent. Yet if the partial pressures of any of these trace gases were increased to sufficient levels, a narcotic effect similar to nitrogen's would develop. You can also get helium narcosis or neon narcosis.

The inert gases seem to impair the nervous system by concentrating in any of its fatty tissues. Nitrogen is among those that are dissolved more easily. Helium is four and a half times less soluble in fatty neural tissue than nitrogen, and therefore makes a more effective breathing gas to accompany oxygen for deeper diving.

The nitrogen of compressed air does affect people. Under its influence some divers do strange things—they spit out their mouthpieces at depth, or swim down instead of up. At what depth nitrogen narcosis will strike a diver varies with the individual and with his emotional or physical makeup. Some investigators say that hard drinkers who can hold their liquor well can withstand nitrogen narcosis at deeper depths than others. It is known that more corpulent divers can *not* hold off the effects of narcosis as well as thinner ones—perhaps because fat absorbs pressurized nitrogen like a sponge. Novice divers experience the raptures of depth sooner than experienced divers because emotionalism and uncertainty do play a part. But advanced divers doing underwater work, as in marine archaeology, also sense a nonclarity about their thinking when deep and have to concentrate, making an effort of the will to continue.

Physical activity underwater at depth causes increased inspiration of pressurized gases and can bring on nitrogen narcosis sooner. Carbon dioxide accumulation from exercise can cause increased breathing, too, and create the quicker intoxicating effects from intake of nitrogen.

As you ascend and exhale accumulated nitrogen out of the tissues where it has stored, the effects dissipate. Recompression seems to begin at 50 feet and the ascent time from that depth upward should be much slower than rising from anywhere below that. If you are coming up from a bounce dive to 200 feet and you have allotted 200 seconds to ascend in, it is better to give half your time to the last fifty feet of ascent.

Descending to depths beyond 100 feet, nitrogen narcosis, a kind of euphoria, can take over the mind of a diver. It is very common at 200 feet and becomes disabling at 250 feet except among the most experienced divers or exceptional individuals. Shown here is diving instructor Geri Murphy of Philadelphia who is striking a pose on the wreck of the *Windjammer* at 200 feet in the waters of Bonaire, N.A. Dropping the mouthpiece and smiling happily at the pleasant blue surroundings is typical of the narcosed diver.   *Photograph by Jo Furman.*

12

Putting Your Diving Skill into Action

Now, nearing the end of this instructional guide to scuba and skin diving, you know that your underwater fun and adventure have only begun. There are fabulous experiences waiting for you: diving on a coral reef, admiring a passing school of amberjacks, peeping inside a sunken wreck, exploring the twists and turns of a river cave, bringing home seafood you speared yourself, and many more adventures. All of this lies before you under the seven-tenths of the Earth not occupied by land. The only thing you need is to put your diving skill into action.

Wreck Diving

Wrecks hold the key to a large number of underwater activities. They furnish archaeological footnotes to history and sometimes hand up sunken treasure long thought lost. They provide backdrops of mystery for underwater photography; they are home to many species of strange and exotic fish. They offer a mixture of awesomeness, peace, and danger.

There are wrecks in all the waters of the world. The United States Naval Oceanographic Office has estimated that more than two thousand commercial vessels are lost each year, and have been lost at this rate for at least a century.

There is possible treasure to be found in wrecks of all kinds, such as this sunken LST (military landing craft) near Athol Island, Bahamas. Ship's hardware and fittings are collector's items that can bring a good price or a pride of ownership for your own collection. *Photograph courtesy of Dacor Corporation.*

The exploration of a sunken vessel, with its passageways, hatchways, portholes, staterooms, wheelhouse, and other chambers, has to be among the most exciting of pastimes. However, a little danger does accompany this recreation, so training and practice in scuba diving skills are mandatory before you attempt to dive on a wreck.

Entry into a wreck's interior, intriguing though it may be, holds certain unpredictable hazards that can entrap you. The simple mazelike quality of a large wreck's passageways could keep you scurrying like a rat in a watery cage. That's why a plan of the wreck dive is necessary—anticipate what you're going to get yourself into. *Never dive on a wreck alone, and always bring a lifeline and underwater lights.* Use these for the wreck penetration. And before attempting a wreck dive, learn how it's done.

Treasure Hunting

When you think of wrecks, the quest for gold, silver, and precious

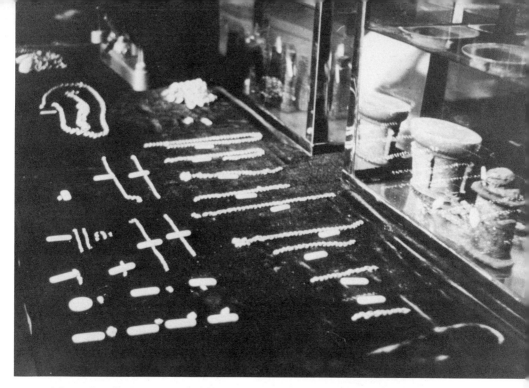

A form of underwater paradise for some is treasure trove—actual riches such as gold coins, silver bars, emerald and amethyst stones, jewelry, small chains of precious metal, and valuable artifacts such as plates, bowls, cups, pitchers, spoons, forks, knives, and more that can be sold to collectors and museums for millions of dollars. *Photograph courtesy of Dennis L. English, Salvage & Exploration Field Agent, Division of Archives, History, and Records Management, State of Florida.*

stones naturally pops into your head. Many an item of flotsam and jetsam has led to discoveries of riches. Underwater, nothing is lost—the liquid environment is a great storage house where untold treasures await discovery. With scuba fastened to your back, you need only to look for a treasure's location. Of all the gold that has ever been mined, officials of the British Admiralty have estimated that one-quarter lies at the bottom of the sea, a result of maritime accidents. Scuba can help you carry that treasure back to the bank.

Treasure fever invariably affects the most robust of underwater enthusiasts, because hunting for sunken riches is decidedly hard work. It takes stamina, patience, and lots of capital investment. Treasure-hunting equipment, the more efficient kind, costs a lot and isn't easy to come by. But even the ordinary diver, newly educated to going underwater, can take the opportunity to hunt for jewels, coins, gold bars, and religious articles. This doesn't have to require expensive and elaborate equipment. You just have to know where to look.

Treasure seekers research old records in archives that are usually stored overseas. They pick through insurance records, ships' logs, and eyewitness reports printed in old newspapers. That's where research begins when the treasure hunt is put together by design. But accident is another way of coming up with riches. Often an amphora or a tool is uncovered on the ocean floor and recognized unexpectedly, as the hallmark of a wreck. Then the outfitting starts for the salvage.

The *Andrea Doria* went down after being struck amidship by the Swedish ship *Stockholm* at 11:09 p.m. on July 25, 1956. Photographer John Clark in July, 1973, hangs onto the port-side boat davot of the sunken ship at 160 feet. Port-side lifeboats could not be used due to the great list of the stricken ship. This is why the davot is still in the folded position.

Photograph by Jack McKenny, Oceanic Films/Skin Diver Magazine.

Archaeological Search

Other riches than jewels await you, too. The treasures of antiquity
include cooking pots, jugs, cups, and sauceboats, the remains of a
vanished time.   Underwater archaeological searches have discovered many such hoards. On September 19, 1975, in the small
bay of Dokos, the islet between Hydra and the mainland of
Greece in the eastern Mediterranean Sea, a Bronze Age ship was
found by a team led by Peter Throckmorton of New York City. It
dates from about 2500 B.C., the earliest known shipwreck ever.
The wreckage was discovered by chance while the team dived in
sixty-five to seventy feet of water.

   This shipwreck is typical of how an archaeological search
underwater is accomplished. Throckmorton describes the seabed
at the wreck site: two heaps of broken pottery and "a lot of things

Shown here are ballast stones—a primary clue to the presence of an ancient
ship under the surface of an unmarked bottom. They are comprised of magnetite, a very heavy stone that acted as a stabilizer in old sailing vessels. Old
Spanish galleons almost always carried ballast stone of this type, so a reading
on an underwater metal detector—compact and hand-held—may be a strong
indication that the Spanish treasure galleon you are seeking needs only to be
dug up.   *Photograph courtesy of Dennis L. English, the State of Florida.*

in between" on the sand. "Shipwrecks are mostly a bunch of broken pots on a reef; there is usually nothing left of the ship. The good, beautiful shipwrecks where we have wood and treasure are one in a thousand."

This ship, says Throckmorton, apparently hit a rock at the entrance of the harbor. The ballast fell out, and the ship broke in two and sank. A pile of stones that must have been the ballast was found by the divers in about twenty-five feet of water. Until the discovery of this wreck, the earliest shipwreck found, off the southern coast of Turkey, was dated from 1300 B.C. Throckmorton discovered that one in 1960.

It is the scuba diver's destiny to photographically record underwater sights for land-based buddies to enjoy vicariously. Excellent underwater photographic equipment and special effort to perfect technique allows you the freedom to record and interpret what lies below the sea's surface. Underwater photography is a diving activity worthy of your unparalleled enthusiasm.

Photograph by Bruce "Teacher" Bowker.

Underwater Photography

Diving skill and topside camera techniques are easily combined into one all-encompassing activity. The result is another kind of treasure useful for archive storage and enjoyment: pictures of the creatures of the deep, and of your diving buddies among them. All kinds of camera equipment for the divers have been developed—still pictures and movies, in salt water or fresh.

It doesn't matter whether you're a skilled land photographer and an amateur diver or a skilled diver and an amateur underwater photographer: total immersion in your new hobby will give you hours of thrills, not only when you take the photographs but also when you view them. Underwater photography adds a new dimension to such other diving interests as shell collecting, archaeological search, and wreck diving.

To photograph successfully underwater, you need a basic understanding of the characteristics of underwater light. Other factors must be considered, too—limited visibility, the constant movement of sea life, adverse surface conditions, unusual reflections, loss of color at depth, and a myriad of changing circumstances. But there are photographs to be made underwater, some of them really gorgeous ones—and they will let the whole world glory in your underwater experiences. The technique required is application of skin diving and photographic skills simultaneously.

Night Diving

Underwater photographs can also be taken at night during excursions into the subsea blackness. Light beams at night slash paths through the water, and everywhere they touch color flashes in red, blue, yellow, and orange. Night dives are also the best time to find the "diver's bug," the lobster, supreme for good eating. Lobsters leave their lairs at night and go foraging on the sea floor. You will do best in your night forage for them, too.

There is nothing to fear in night diving. Diving in darkness, if you follow the rules, is almost as safe as diving in daylight. One thing is certain: night diving is beautiful, electrifying, inspiring, and educational. On night dives you learn how creatures underwater, large and small, sleep and eat and make love. Night dives will be treasured as among the most memorable of your experiences.

Of course, that first night dive for a novice is frightening. Anyone would feel tense—an intermix of fright and excitement—dropping into the inky blackness under the surface. Like anyone else, you could be filled with foreboding at the confrontation of stark reality in the form of some dangerous creature of the deep.

Photograph by Morton Walker.

Deep Diving

Deep diving underwater drop-offs at any of a thousand locations around the world is a marvelous experience, too. You'll see marine creatures of peculiar shapes and a variety of colors, which magically appear under your artificial light beam. It's almost as important to carry an underwater lamp with you to the deeper depths during the day as it is on a night dive. A succession of images appears as you move vertically or horizontally along a cliff face. Of course, you must be quite skilled in the use of scuba and accessory equipment before attempting deep dives. That comes with practice. When you're ready, visions that exist mainly in dreams await your exploration and study in the world of deep diving.

Dropping into deeper depths necessitates techniques somewhat different than going down a few dozen feet. For instance, the proficiency of your diving buddy is a factor. Your buddy can spell the difference between a safe dive and diving at risk.

Never dive alone. Take responsibility for the safety of your buddy, and stay within close and continuous visual contact. But having a buddy is no substitute for expert training and complete diver competency.

Photograph by Bruce "Teacher" Bowker.

Deep diving frequently entails decompression at stated depths for a specific interval. Ordinarily, the rule to follow is *avoid decompression dives.* If you must make a decompression dive, know the U.S. Navy Decompression Dive Tables or use a decompression meter. The record of your rate of nitrogen intake into the bloodstream is determined by these two methods. The decompression meter can accurately calculate repetitive dives; it has a six-hour memory zone and shows this information on a dial. Proper control of buoyancy is a must, too. In short, deep diving, like cave diving, demands very special skill.

Cave Diving

Of all the various diving activities you may enjoy, cave diving is probably the most dangerous. But caves have a certain magnetic

Dedicated cave divers continue to pursue the sport because they are anxious to explore an alien environment where no other person has gone before. They work with scientists and state agencies to study and map the hydraulogy, geology, stratigraphy and archaeology of the subterranean caverns. Shown here are divers exploring a blue hole in the warm waters of the Bahamas.

Photograph courtesy of Parkway Fabricators.

quality that draws divers to explore their mazes of tunnels. As an underwater caver, you will find yourself entering an underwater hole that will take the form of a straight or twisting shaft. It may curve or bend through total darkness until it terminates finally in a blind abutment or opens into a massive vault.

For cave diving, special equipment is an absolute must. And your life depends too on your cave-diving knowledge. At first, until you have become very skilled as an underwater spelunker, you shouldn't attempt cave entry without a well-experienced cave-diving group. Trust in your buddies is mandatory.

Lifelines and lights, as in wreck diving, are also important for cave diving. Two lights are necessary for the caver. One is the primary light, a large and powerful one, and the smaller is a spare for backup purposes. Surprising as it may sound, the use of a personal flotation device is taboo in cave diving, because accidental inflation can float you away from your buddies. Many well-versed divers avoid cave diving as too dangerous, but it does have an appeal for some and could be an attraction for you.

Spearfishing

Underwater hunting with a speargun has acquired an undeservedly bad reputation. A poor press in the past was earned by a very small number of skin divers who abused the environment. Divers are more educated now, and peer group pressure too has improved the situation. Now divers hunt without wearing scuba; snorkeling gear is the only permissible item for assistance in spearfishing. The ethical hunter chooses the fish he wants to kill, hunts it exclusively, stalks it, and takes his chances with that one species. He doesn't select a very easy prey, either.

Usually fish for hunting are of the special food variety common in a certain underwater area. Divers don't kill indiscriminately merely for "sport." The final motivation is to bring the freshest of fish to the family dining table. True sport divers with spearguns follow the ethical rules of the hunt. These self-imposed regulations are needed not only to conserve undersea resources but to preserve your buddies' health: the penetration power of a spear-

The author and his young son, Jules, go spearfishing. Jules is using the simplest kind of underwater hunting weapon, a wooden pole with multibarbs on the end like a small pitchfork that he jabs at the fish. It is useful for catching flounder, fluke, ray, and other flat fish that lie on the bottom and depend on camouflage for protection.
Photograph by Harold Weitzberg.

gun is great. Correctly applied rules ensure that other divers won't become victims of your cocked weapon.

Spearfishing is a wonderful sport. It should never be carried out while you wear scuba or in very populated areas. But skin diving to fetch a meal, where the country's law permits, is perfectly proper.

Traveling to Dive

Your scuba and skin diving explorations are bound to fire your wanderlust. You'll want to go to where the action is—wreck diving in the Bahamas, specimen gathering in the Florida Keys, artifact viewing in the Ionian Sea, and various other places in the world for unique adventure and fun. The total spectrum of salt- and fresh-water diving can be found only if you travel to it. The Caribbean, for example, with its remote tropical beaches, unhurried way of life, and friendly people, makes your diving visit a pleasant and satisfying experience.

Diving travel is one of the great attractions of the sport. It affords all kinds of conditions to test your mettle and arouse your enthusiasm. The Earth is a watery planet, 70 percent covered with the diving environment. You can explore it and enjoy it with the diving skills you've acquired. The world is your personal oyster, a means to a more meaningful way of life.

It can all be done in comfort, too. Even in the remotest areas, diving resorts and special diving excursion boats are in operation; diving professionals recognize that this is the fastest-growing form of outdoor recreation. And anyone in fairly good health can venture with ease into this new underwater world.

Appendix 1

Glossary

Absolute pressure: True pressure, the total pressure of atmosphere and water including the addition of 14.7 psi to the indicated gauge pressure, referred to in absolute atmospheres (ATA).

Abyss: A vast depth; usually designated as more than 1,000 feet deep.

Air embolism: Blockage of blood vessels by gas bubbles; usually reserved for the arteries leading to the brain. Generally this occurs in diving from overinflation of the lungs during a breath-holding ascent from depth. Bubbles of gas are forced from the alveoli into the blood vessels and travel through the circulation until they lodge in one of the brain arteries, causing obstruction and oxygen starvation. Death commonly occurs.

Alveolar exchange: An interchange of oxygen into the blood and carbon dioxide into the alveoli for expiration.

Ambient pressure: Surrounding pressure of the water at any depth; also called *liquid pressure*.

Apparatus: The combined parts and materials that create a breathing device.

Artificial respiration: The alternate increase and decrease in chest volume created in a near-drowning victim (or other nonbreathing person) in order to start his respiratory system working again. Mouth-to-mouth and mouth-to-nose resuscitation methods are currently used.

Bar: A ridge above the bottom formed into an offshore bank or shoal.

Barotrauma: Pressure effects producing injury.

Boyle's Law: The volume of a given quantity of gas whose temperature remains constant varies inversely as its pressure.

Breathing air: Compressed air inhaled by divers that is free of contaminants.

Breathing device: Mechanical parts and materials that, when assembled, permit a person to breathe compressed air.

Buddy breathing: An emergency breathing technique achieved through the sharing by two or more divers of air from the same air cylinder.

Bug: A lobster or crayfish.

Buoyancy: The conformation to Archimedes' principle that an immersed or floating body is buoyed up by a force equal to the weight of the liquid displaced.

Charles's Law or **Gay-Lussac's Law:** If the pressure of a gas remains unchanged, the volume is directly proportional to the absolute temperature.

Compressed-air demand regulator: A breathing device originally invented by Emile Gagnan and Jacques-Yves Cousteau to deliver air whenever the diver inhales.

Cylinder: A compressed-gas container with a narrow neck; also called a bottle or tank.

Dalton's Law: When a mixture of gases comes into contact with a liquid, each gas dissolves separately into the liquid, as if it were not part of the mixture. Each gas in a mixture of gases exerts a partial pressure proportionate to the percentage it represents of the total gases.

Debris: Wreckage, the flotsam and jetsam of an abandoned ship.

Decompression: The procedure in diving that releases internal pressure caused by a gathering of gases in the human body.

Decompression sickness: The symptoms of illness that result from using incorrect diving procedure; the formation of nitrogen and other gas bubbles in the tissues from increased pressure.

Density: The mass of any substance per unit volume.

Diaphragm: A partitioning membrane of two types recognized in diving: the muscle dividing the chest cavity from the abdominal cavity and the thin rubber material separating the regulator demand chamber from the surrounding water.

Ebb tide: The flow of current out from shore.

Eddy: A circular movement of water formed at one side of a main current, created where the mainstream meets an opposite current or passes a projection.

Exposure suit: An insulated covering for the diver to preserve body heat.

Fins: Effective devices attached to the swimmer's feet for faster propulsion; also appendages of fish.

Flood tide: The highest tide.

Flotation device: A piece of equipment worn by a diver to produce required buoyancy when desired.

Gauge pressure: The difference between the tank pressure being measured and the surrounding atmospheric pressure. Gauge pressure equals depth in feet times .445 psi.

Henry's Law: The amount of gas that will go into solution at a given temperature is directly proportional to the partial pressure of that gas.

Hookah: A diving apparatus that delivers air to a regulator from a compressor on the surface.

Inhale: To breathe in; to inspire.

Knot: The unit of speed at which boats, currents, or winds travel; 1.689 feet per second or 6,080.2 feet per hour.

Martini's Law: An idiomatic term that compares the nitrogen narcotic effect of each fifty feet of descent, breathing air, to the effect of drinking one dry martini.

Mask: A diver's window for underwater vision that provides an air space between the eyes and the water and usually covers only the diver's eyes and nose.

Nitrogen narcosis: A state of altered mental function that resembles alcoholic intoxication and is caused from exposure to the increased partial pressure of nitrogen and other gases.

Partial pressure: The effect of gas that is exerting a share of the total pressure in a given volume, such as oxygen in air (20.94 percent).

Recompression: Treatment of a diver suffering decompression sickness by use of a recompression chamber, following the U.S. Navy treatment tables.

Rip tide: A dangerously strong current flowing outward from the shore, caused by water escaping through a narrow gap in a bar or reef.

Runout: An undertow derived from water piled on the shore by breaking waves to create an outward current.

Safety buckle: A one-hand-operated release mechanism for fastening straps.

Scuba: Self-contained underwater breathing apparatus that holds breathable gas and is not attached to the surface.

Shoal: A shallow place in the water caused by a bank or bar.

Skin diving: A catchall term that refers to swimming on the surface and under the surface of the water while making use of certain advantageous swimming equipment including scuba or snorkel gear.

Snorkel diving: Swimming with the use of a rubber or plastic breathing tube.

Speargun: An underwater hunting tool that ejects a projectile powered by rubber bands, springs, gas, or gunpowder.

Sport diver: An enthusiast engaged in underwater swimming for recreational purposes.

Valve: A regulating device that permits air flow in one direction.

Yoke: A leakproof sealing device that attaches regulators to cylinders or cylinders to cylinders.

Appendix 2

Aquadoc Listings for All Regions

Used with permission of *Emergency Medicine* 7, no. 6 (June 1975). Irving Cohen, Editor, Fischer-Murray, Inc.

BAHAMAS

Graham Barry, M.D.
Lucayan Medical Group
Box F827
Grand Bahama Island
(809) 352-7288

R. J. Clement, M.R.C.S.
Antoni Clinic
P.O. Box F2575
Grand Bahama Island
(809) 373-3333

CALIFORNIA

Colton

Bruce W. Halstead, M.D.
World Life Research Institute
2300 Grand Terrace Rd. (92324)
(714) 825-4773
825-5368 (home)
marine venoms

Corona

Norman H. Mellor, M.D.
C3720 Old Magnolia Ave. (91720)
(714) 737-1454
737-1360 (home)

El Cajon

Gaylord B. Parkinson, M.D.
312 Highland, Suite A (92020)
(714) 444-1101

Fresno

Marvin C. Beil, M.D.
1616 West Shaw, Suite A-5 (93705)
(209) 224-3116

Glendale

Michael D. Rosco, M.D.
Roberts Medical Group
1808 Verdugo Blvd. (91208)
(213) 790-4188
244-3341 (home)

La Jolla

William L. Orris, M.D.
University of California at San Diego
Box 109 (92037)
(714) 239-0193
453-3794 (home)

255

Long Beach

George B. Hart, Capt., MC, USN
Director, Hyperbaric Clinical Medical
  Research Center
Naval Regional Medical Center
7500 E. Carson (90801)
(213) 420-5402
decompression sickness

Los Angeles

Murray Grossan, M.D.
8930 S. Sepulveda Blvd. (90045)
(213) 670-1777
ear, nose, throat

Eugene Nagel, M.D.
Department of Anesthesiology
Harbor General Hospital
1000 W. Carson St. (90509)
(213) 328-2380, ext. 1831

Thomas T. Noguchi, M.D.
Chief Medical Examiner-Coroner
County of Los Angeles
1104 North Mission Rd. (90033)
(213) 223-3231
drowning; scuba diving accidents

Findlay E. Russell, M.D.
Director, Laboratory of Neurological
  Research
Los Angeles County-University of
  Southern California Medical Center
Box 323, 1200 N. State St. (90033)
(213) 226-4906 (24 hrs.)
        226-4741; 226-4742
marine venoms

Jack Wainschel, M.D.
San Marino Medical Center
1427 San Marino Ave., Suite 4 (91108)
(213) 796-4460
marine poisoning

James J. Woodruff, M.D.
1711 West Temple (90026)
(213) 413-1313

Pacific Grove

Takashi Mattori, M.D.
Medical Diving Officer
City Marine Rescue Patrol
(408) 624-5311, ext. 364 (office)
        375-3146 (rescue patrol)

Riverside

Charles V. Brown, M.D.
4795 Somerset Drive (92507)
(714) 686-8058 (home)

San Diego

Paul G. Linaweaver, Capt., MC, USN
Submarine Development
Group 1
F.S.P.O. (92132)
(714) 225-7485

Patrick Mullaney, M.D.
Doctors Hospital
3475 Kenyon St. (92110)
(714) 222-0411

Stephen P. Murphy, M.D.
Anesthesia Service Medical Group, In
P.O. Box 400 (92138)
(714) 565-9666
drowning

Heston L. Wilson, M.D.
239 Laurel St. (92101)
(714) 239-3043

Frank B. Wisner, M.D.
1977 Sunset Cliffs Blvd. (92107)
(714) 224-3641

San Francisco

Albert R. Behnke, M.D.
2241 Sacramento St. (94115)
(415) 346-7421 (home)
*decompression sickness; diving
   accidents*

Santa Barbara

R. John Rutten, M.D.
Santa Barbara Medical Clinic
P.O. Box 1200 (91343)
(805) 964-6211

Sepulveda

John Alexander, M.D.
Pulmonary Division
Sepulveda Veterans Hospital
16111 Plummer St. (91343)
(213) 894-8271

West Covina

Russell A. Rhode, M.D.
Queen of the Valley Hospital
1535 W. Merced St. (91790)
(213) 962-4045, ext. 46

CANADA

Montreal

F. Limongelli, M.D.
5655 St. Zotique
(514) 254-1844

Toronto

David Elcombe, M.D.
Director, Civil Aviation Medical
   Unit, Defense and Civil
   Institute of Environmental
   Medicine
1133 Shepherd Ave (M3M3B9)
(416) 633-4240, ext. 263
      483-3231 (home)
hyperbaric medicine

Joe MacInnis, M.D.
21 McMaster Ave. (M4V1A8)
(416) 921-1652
industrial diving physician

CONNECTICUT

Essex

Edward S. Tucker, M.D.
64A N. Main St. (06426)
(203) 767-1411
      245-1608 (home)

Norwalk

Sreedhar Nair, M.D.
Norwalk Hospital (06856)
(203) 838-3611
      853-1919 (office)

Stamford

Morton Walker, D.P.M.
Freelance Communications
484 High Ridge Rd. (06905)
(203) 322-1551
      322-1506

DISTRICT OF COLUMBIA

Arthur J. Anderson, M.D.
2520 L St. N.W., No. 204 (20037)
(202) 337-1150 (office)

FLORIDA

Bradenton

David D. Fulghum, M.D.
1416 59th St., W. (33505)
(813) 474-2112
aquatic dermatologic specialist

Miami

Joseph H. Davis, M.D.
Office of the Medical Examiner
Dade County
1700 N.W. 10th Ave. (33136)
(305) 325-7337
*forensic pathology; circumstances of
deaths due to drowning*

Fred Furgang, M.D.
Department of Anesthesiology
Jackson Memorial Hospital
1700 N.W. 10th Ave. (33136)
(305) 325-6970
        251-2067 (home)

Miami Beach

Edwin Boyle, Jr., M.D.
Research Director
Miami Heart Institute
4701 N. Meridian Ave. (33140)
(305) 672-1113
hyperbaric research

Arthur J. Gosselin, M.D.
Miami Heart Institute
4701 N. Meridian Ave. (33140)
(305) 672-1113

Ronald Lee Samson, M.D.
Department of Anesthesiology
Mt. Sinai Medical Center (33140)
(305) 674-2720
*drowning; extra alveolar air syndrome;
decompression sickness*

HAWAII

Honolulu

Henry Street, M.D.
Pearl Harbor Navy Clinic (96818)
(808) 474-1224
        472-5955 (decompression center)

Alan Pavel, M.D.
Suite 403
1441 Kapiolani Blvd. (96814)
(808) 949-0067

Jon Pegg, M.D.
Box 1384 (96807)
(808) 259-7448
        595-6283 (home)
consultant

Jack H. Scaff, M.D.
The Honolulu Medical Group
550 S. Beretania St. (96813)
(808) 537-2211

ILLINOIS

Chicago

Edwin R. Levine, M.D.
Hyperbaric Unit
Edgewater Hospital
5700 N. Ashland Ave. (60660)
(312) 878-6000
        728-3556 (home)

Chicago Heights

Richard J. Wallyn, M.D.
St. James Hospital (60411)
(312) 756-1000, ext. 515

Evanston

Sheldon H. Steiner, M.D.
1325 Howard St.
Suite 300 (60202)
(312) 675-2448 (24 hrs.)

INDIANA

Indianapolis

Sherman Minton, M.D.
Department of Microbiology
Indiana University
School of Medicine
1100 W. Michigan St. (46202)
(317) 264-7671 (office)
    849-2596 (home)
marine animal injuries

IOWA

Des Moines

Daniel A. Glomset, M.D.
2932 Ingersoll (50312)
(515) 288-2291
    255-4272 (home)

KANSAS

Kansas City

Richard A. Gruendel, M.D.
1029 North 32nd St. (66102)
(913) 281-5252

LOUISIANA

New Orleans

Hewitte A. Thian, M.D.
4637 S. Carrolton Ave. (70119)
(504) 488-3751 (office)
    288-5434 (home)
    288-4858 (home)

MARYLAND

Annapolis

H. Logan Holtgrewe, M.D.
16 Murray Ave. (21401)
(301) 268-3821
    647-2693 (home)

MICHIGAN

Carson City

Charles J. Crosby, M.D.
Carson City Hospital (48811)
(517) 584-3131

MINNESOTA

Minneapolis

John J. Haglin, M.D.
Hennepin County General Hospital
5th St. and Portland S. (55415)
(612) 348-2370
    348-2276

Ernest Ruiz, M.D.
Hennepin County General Hospital
5th St. and Portland S. (55415)
(612) 348-2370
    348-3930 (office)

NEW YORK

Buffalo

Harry J. Alvis, M.D.
Millard Fillmore Hospital
3 Gates Circle (14209)
(716) 845-4600 (hospital)
    845-4663 (office)
    876-6974 (home)
hyperbaric medicine

Rockaway Beach

I. G. Frohman, M.D.
91-01 Rockaway Beach Blvd. (11693)
(212) 474-3884

NORTH CAROLINA

Mebane

Giles Y. Mebane, M.D.
Mebane Medical Arts Bldg.
202 S. 5th (27302)
(919) 563-9341

Morehead City

Charles P. Nicholson, Jr., M.D.
Carteret Medical Center
3108 Arendell St. (28557)
(919) 726-2101 (office)
marine poisoning

Wilmington

H. William Gillen, M.D.
Institue of Marine Bio-Medical Research
7205 Wrightsville Ave. (28401)
(919) 256-3721
        762-8501 (service)

OHIO

Toledo

Donald Woodson, M.D.
Medical College of Ohio (43614)
(419) 385-4661
hyperbaric medicine

OREGON

Portland

James L. McMillan, M.D.
5013 S.E. Hawthorne Blvd. (97215)
(503) 234-0863 (office)
        223-3181 (service)

PENNSYLVANIA

Emmaus

Ralph E. Stolz, D.O.
Doctors Clinic
555 Harrison St. (18049)
(215) 967-3115
        439-4000 (24 hrs.)
hyperbaric medicine
aquatic medicine

Philadelphia

Kristopher M. Greene, M.D.
Institute for Environmental Medicine
University of Pennsylvania (19174)
(215) 243-8692 (24 hrs.)
hyperbaric medicine

SOUTH DAKOTA

Aberdeen

Carson B. Murdy, M.D.
Clinic Building
423 S. Lincoln St. (57401)
(605) 225-7964
        225-0358 (home)

TENNESSEE

Morristown

Donald C. Thompson, M.D.
Doctors Hospital
726 McFarland St. (37814)
(615) 586-2302 (24 hrs.)

TEXAS

Galveston

William H. Hulet, M.D.
Chief, Marine Medicine
Marine Biomedical Institute
Univ. of Texas Medical Branch (7755
(713) 765-2101
hyperbaric medicine

H. G. Love, Jr., M.D.
University Burn Center
Univ. of Texas Medical Branch (7755
(713) 765-1011
hyperbaric medicine

Houston

S. Harold Reuter, M.D.
637 Hermann Professional Building
(77025)
(713) 524-1831
    668-4366 (home)

UTAH

Salt Lake City

Henry P. Plenk, M.D.
Radiation Center
Latter-Day Saints Hospital
325 8th Ave. (84143)
(801) 322-5105 (office)
    322-5761, ext. 2785 (hospital)
hyperbaric medicine

VIRGINIA

Centreville

Oscar D. Yarbrough, M.D.
14315 Compton Rd. (22020)
(703) 631-9000

Falls Church

John E. Alexander, M.D.
7 Corners Medical Building (22042)
(703) 534-3095

Staunton

Jon R. Hammersberg, M.D.
King's Daughters' Hospital
1410 N. Augusta St.
Box 2007 (24401)
(703) 885-6848 (ER)
    885-6367 (home)

WASHINGTON

Seattle

Alan Carson, M.D.
Providence Hospital
500 17th Ave. (98122)
(206) 323-6129 (hospital)

Frank Henry, M.D.
1120 Cherry St. (98104)
Room 320
(206) 622-3555

Leon Sealey, M.D.
Virginia Mason Hospital
1111 Terry Ave. (98101)
(206) 624-1144 (24 hrs.)
    682-3343 (office)

Merrill P. Spencer, M.D.
Providence Hospital
500 17th Ave. (98122)
(206) 322-5700 (24 hrs.)
    322-3140 (day)
    442-7330 (Institute of Applied
            Physiology)

WISCONSIN

Milwaukee

Eric Kindwall, M.D.
Department of Hyperbaric Medicine
St. Luke's Hospital
2900 W. Oklahoma Ave. (53215)
(414) 647-6423 (24 hrs.)

Appendix 3

International Listing of Recompression Chambers for Possible Use in Diver Treatment

Prepared by the National Association of Underwater Instructors, revised 1974. States with no chambers deleted from listing.

UNITED STATES

ALABAMA

Huntsville

Marshall Space Flight Center
Bldg. 4706, Redstone Arsenal (35821)
(205) 453-0121
881-4888

ALASKA

Adak

U.S. Naval Station,
Box 5, FPO Seattle, WA (98791)
(907) 579-2224/2225

CALIFORNIA

Avalon

Avalon Municipal Hospital
100 Falls Canyon Rd.
P.O. Box 1563 (90704)

Chino

California Institute for Men
14901 Central Ave.
P.O. Box 128 (91710)
(714) 597-1821, ext. 374

Coronado

Underwater Demolition Team Eleve
NAVINSWAR/PHIBGRUEASTPA
U.S. Naval Amphibious Base (9215
(714) 437-2574/2576

Edwards

Edwards Air Force Base (93523)
(805) 277-1110, ext. 73443 or 7233

Goleta

Associated Divers, Inc.
154 Norman Firestone Rd. (93017)
(805) 967-8118

Delco Electronics
6767 Hollister Ave.

Long Beach

Long Beach Naval Shipyard (90801)
(213) 547-6524/6226/7567

U.S. Naval Hospital
7500 E. Carson St. (90801)

Merced

USAF Hospital (SGT)
Physiological Training Unit
Castle Air Force Base (95342)
(209) 726-2861/2789/2686

Oakland

Coastal Diving Company
320 29th Avenue (94601)
(415) 532-4211
      254-2647

Pacific Grove

Pacific Grove Fire Department
Pacific Grove Fire House (93950)
(408) 375-3146

Pasadena

Morris Dam, Pasadena Laboratory
3202 East Foothill Blvd. (91107)
(213) 547-7254

San Clemente Island,
Pasadena Laboratory
3202 East Foothill Blvd. (91107)
(213) 547-7254

Port Hueneme

Call Naval Range
Duty Officer
(805) 982-8841

San Diego

U.S. Navy Second Class Diving School
Box DT6, U.S. Naval Station (92136)
(714) 235-1478/1230

San Francisco

Transit Compressed Air Medical Center
56 Julian Ave. (94103)
(415) 621-5472
      454-7521

Zellerbach Saroni Tumor Institute
Mt. Zion Hospital and Medical Center
1600 Divisadero (94115)

Santa Ana

U.S. Divers Company
3323 West Warner Ave. (92702)
(714) 540-8010
      539-8575

Santa Barbara

Oceaneering International
Stearn's Warf
P.O. Box 4488 (93103)
(805) 963-1414

Ocean Systems, Inc.
108 Los Aguajes Ave.
P.O. Box 1331 (93102)
(805) 965-3321

Santa Barbara City College
Marine Technology Program
312 North Nopal Street (93103)
(805) 962-7519, 965-0581, ext. 201

Wilmington

Commercial Diving Center
272 So. Fries Ave. (90744)
(213) 834-2501

COLORADO
Fort Collins

Colorado State University
Department of Physiology and Biophysics (80521)
(303) 491-6106

CONNECTICUT
New London

U.S. Naval Submarine Medical Center
Bldg. 141, U.S. Naval Submarine Base (06320)
(203) 449-3263

Norwalk

Norwalk Hospital (06856)

DISTRICT OF COLUMBIA
Washington

U.S. Navy Experimental Diving Unit
Bldg. 214, Washington Navy Yard (20390)
(202) 433-2790/3716

U.S. Naval Medical Research Institute
National Naval Medical Center (20014)
(202) 295-0540

U.S. Naval Oceanographic Office
Diving Officer, Code 3421 (20373)
(202) 433-2531

U.S. Naval School of Diving and Salvage
Washington Navy Yard (20374)
(202) 433-3008

FLORIDA
Fort Lauderdale

U.S. Naval Ordnance Laboratory Test Facility
1651 Southwest 40th Street (33315)
(305) 524-8467

Fort Pierce

Divers Training Academy, IN.
Linkport, RFD 1, Box 193 C (33450)

Gainesville

Shands Teaching Hospital
University of Florida, College of Medicine (32601)
(904) 392-3441

Kennedy Space Center

John F. Kennedy Space Center
National Aeronautics & Space Agency (32899)
(305) 867-2121

Key West

U.S. Navy Underwater Swimmers School
U.S. Naval Station (33040)
(305) 296-3511, ext. 563 or 564

Lake Park

InterCity First Aid Squad
640 Old Dixie Hwy. (33403)
(305) 844-6577

Miami

Rosenstiel School of Marine & Atmospheric Science
University of Miami
10 Rickenbacker Causeway (33149)
(305) 350-7259
      446-7071
      445-8926

Panama City

Naval Coastal Systems Laboratory (32401)
(904) 234-4278

Pensacola

Naval Aerospace Medical Institute
Physiological Training Division
Naval Aerospace Medical Center (32512)

GEORGIA

Decatur

Dixie Divers
2546 Mellville Ave. (30032)
(404) 289-3483

HAWAII

Honolulu

Explosive Ordnance Disposal Group
West Loch, U.S. Naval Base, Pearl Harbor (96818)
EODGRUPAC, FPO San Francisco, CA 96611
(808) 431-8384/8385

Naval Submarine Training Center Pacific
Escape Training Tank, Submarine Base, Pearl Harbor (96818)
FPO San Francisco, CA 96610
(808) 422-5955

University of Hawaii
Department of Ocean Engineering
J.K.K. Look Laboratory of Oceanographic Engineering (96813)
(808) 533-6412

Pearl Harbor

Escape Training Tank
Naval Submarine Training Center Pacific (96818)
(808) 422-5955

Waimanalo

Makai Range
Makapuu Point (96795)
(808) 259-9911

ILLINOIS

Chicago

Edgewater Hospital
Hyperbaric Unit, 5700 N. Ashland Ave. (Heliport Facilities) (60660)
(312) 878-6000, ext. 580 or 584

Chicago Heights

St. James Hospital
1423 Chicago Rd. and 14th St. (60411)
(312) 756-1000

Park Ridge

Lutheran General Hospital
1775 Dempster St. (60068)
(312) 696-2210, ext. 1353 or 1357

LOUISIANA

Belle Chasse

Action Divers
Belle Chasse Hwy. & Melvin Dr. (70037)
(504) 366-0285/5686

Taylor Diving & Salvage Co., Inc.
795 Engineers Rd. (70037)
(504) 368-2000

Berwick

Fluor Ocean Services, Inc.
Underseas Projects (70342)
(504) 458-8371

Grand Isle

Action Divers (70358)
(504) 366-5686/0285

Harvey

McDermott Diving Division
J. Ray McDermott & Co., Inc.
P. O. Drawer 38 (70058)
(504) 366-8111

Pelican Marine Divers, Inc.
P.O. Box 751 (70058)
(504) 362-7367
    366-3720

Morgan City

Divcon, Inc.
1601 Frank Street
P.O. Box 1730 (70380)
(504) 459-6448

Hydrotech Service, Inc.
Highway 90E (70380)
(504) 384-5126

Oceans Systems, Inc.
Highway 90E (70380)
(504) 384-2860

S&H Services Corp.
P.O. Box 1136 (70380)
(504) 631-2156/2157

World Wide Divers, Inc.
P.O. Box 2624 (70380)
(504) 395-5247
    458-8672

MAINE

Kittery
Portsmouth Naval Shipyard
Kittery (03804)
(207) 439-1000, ext. 1900

MARYLAND

Annapolis

Westinghouse Ocean Research & Engineering Center
P.O. Box 1488 (21404)
(301) 765-5667/5661

Baltimore

Maryland Institute for Emergency Medicine
22 S. Greene St. (21201)
(301) 528-6020/6844/6846
        752-5326

Indian Head (Stump Neck)

U.S. Naval Explosive Ordnance Disposal Facility (20640)
(301) 743-4535/4545 (after 4 PM)

Indian Head

U.S. Naval Ordnance Station
Naval School, Explosive Ordnance Disposal (20640)
(301) 743-4817/4476

Solomons

U.S. Naval Ordnance Laboratory (20688)
(301) 326-3466

MASSACHUSETTS

Boston

Boston Children's Hospital Medical Center
300 Longwood Ave. (02115)
(617) 734-6000, ext. 3261

Boston Naval Shipyard (02129)
(617) 242-1400, ext. 188

MICHIGAN

Ann Arbor

1038 G. G. Brown Building North Campus,
University of Michigan
(313) 332-2521, ext. 201

Eloise

Wayne County General Hospital (48132)
(313) 274-3000

MINNESOTA

Minneapolis

Hennepin County General Hospital
Minneapolis Medical Research Foundation, Inc.
619 So. 5th St. (55415)
(612) 348-2276/2370/2522/3965

MISSOURI

Kansas City

St. Luke's Hospital
Wornall Rd. and 44th Street (64111)

St. Louis

McDonnell Douglas Corp.
P.O. Box 516 (63166)

MONTANA

Fort Peck

U.S. Army Corps of Engineers Headquarters
Fort Peck, Montana (59223)
(3-5 days to operate. No operators or Med. Personnel)
(406) 526-3411

NEW HAMPSHIRE

Kittery, Maine

Portsmouth Naval Shipyard (03804)
(207) 439-1000

NEW JERSEY

Hackensack

Hackensack Hospital
22 Hospital Pl., (07601)

Livingston

Saint Barnabas Medical Center
Old Short Hills Rd. (07039)
(201) 992-5500, ext. 575, 576, 577, or 578
        992-5161 after 3:30 PM

Toms River

Ocean County Diving, Ltd.
P.O. Box 401, 910 Boyd Street (08753)
(For their own use only)
(201) 244-0747

NEW MEXICO

Albuquerque

Presbyterian Hospital Center
1100 Central SE (87106)
(505) 243-9411

NEW YORK

Buffalo

Millard Fillmore Hospital
3 Gates Circle (14209)
(716) 845-4600/4698

State University of New York at Buffalo
Dept. of Physiology, Sherman Hall, The Circle (14214)

Veterans Administration Hospital
3495 Bailey Avenue (14215)
(716) 834-9200, ext. 261

New York City

Cornell Medical Center
1300 York Avenue (10021)
(212) 249-4350

Institute of Rehabilitation Medicine
New York University Medical Center
400 East 34th Street (10016)
(212) 679-3200, ext. 3803

Presbyterian Hospital
622 W. 168th Street

Vascular Surgical Service, Mt. Sinai Hospital
100th Street and 5th Ave. (10029)
(212) 876-1000, ext. 372
At night call TR 6-1000 and ask for Director of Nursing

NORTH CAROLINA

Durham
Duke University Medical Center
F.G. Hall Laboratory for Environmental Research
P.O. Box 2904 (27710)
(919) 684-4149/8111

OHIO

Cleveland

Cleveland Clinic Hospital
Division of Anesthesiology
9500 Euclid Ave. (44106)

St. Vincent's Charity Hospital
2351 22nd Street (44115)

Columbus

Battelle-Columbus Laboratories
Battelle Memorial Institute, 505 King Avenue (43201)
(Primarily used for equipment studies)
(614) 299-3151, ext. 2683

Ohio State University College of Medicine
Wiseman Hall, 400 West 12th Avenue (43210)
(Inoperable at this time)
(614) 422-8736

Fairborn

U.S. Air Force Medical Center
Physiological Training Division, Wright-Patterson AFB (45433)
(513) 257-2968

Toledo

Medical College of Ohio Hospital
Arlington & S. Detroit (43614)
(419) 385-4661

OREGON

McNary

McNary Dam (97858)
(503) 922-3211/3214

Oxbow

Oxbow Dam (97840)
(503) 785-3365

Portland

Commercial Divers, Inc.
1220 Southwest Morrison Street (97205)
P.O. Box 144 (97043)
(503) 223-6393
        285-5660

Fred Devine Diving & Salvage, Inc.
6211 N. Ensign (97217)
(503) 283-2488

PENNSYLVANIA

Philadelphia

Institute for Environmental Medicine
University of Pennsylvania Medical Center (19174)
(215) 594-8692
Hospital - 662-2500

Philadelphia Naval Shipyard (19112)
(215) 755-3350
        443-3350

U.S. Naval Base
Building 538 (19112)
(215) 755-3891/3506/2676

RHODE ISLAND

Newport

U.S. Naval Base, Newport Laboratory
U.S. Naval Underwater Systems Center (02840)
(401) 841-3018

SOUTH CAROLINA

Beaufort

Marine Corps., Air Station Medical Dept.
Aerospace Physiology Trn. Div.

SOUTH DAKOTA

Ellsworth

Ellsworth Air Force Base
Physiological Training Unit/Compression Therapy Team
Ellsworth AFB (57706)
(605) 399-2554/2273

Pierre

U.S. Army Corps of Engineers Headquarters
Oahe Area, Box 997 (57501)
(605) 224-5252/5862

TEXAS

Corpus Christi

Blue Water Industries (78401)
(512) 883-7207
        945-1285

Galveston

University of Texas Medical Branch
The Marine Biomedical Institute,
200 University Blvd. (77550)
(713) 765-2101/1856 (Sundays, Holidays, Nights)

Houston

Lyndon B. Johnson Space Center (NASA),
J.S.C. Clinic (77058)
(713) 483-4111

Ocean Corporation
2120 Peckham Street (77019)
(713) 526-8957

Pasadena

J & J Marine Diving Co., Inc.
P.O. Box 4117 (77502)
(713) 487-0990

San Antonio

Southwest Research Institute
8500 Culebra Road (78228)
(512) 684-2000, ext. 435

U.S. Air Force School of Aerospace Medicine,
EDP, Brooks Air Force Base (78235)
(512) 536-3278

UTAH

Salt Lake City

St. Marks Hospital
1200 East 3900 South (84117)

VIRGINIA

Fort Belvoir

U.S. Army 77th Engineer Company (PC) (22060)
(703) 664-1814/6990

Fort Eustis

U.S. Army Transportation School
497 Engineer Co (PC), Diving Section (23604)
(804) 878-2390/2139, (804) 878-3793 after 1700

Norfolk

U.S. Naval Amphibious Base
Harbor Clearance Unit Two (23521)
(703) 464-7433

WASHINGTON

Chelan

Wells Hydroelectric Project,
Public Utility District #1 of Douglas County
P.O. Box 827 (98816)
(509) 923-2226

Fairchild

Fairchild Air Force Base
USAF Regional Hospital/SGT
Compression Therapy Team
(509) 247-5269/5887
        247-5661 after hours

Keyport

U.S. Naval Torpedo Station (98345)
(206) 396-2522/2563
(2551 during nonworking hours)

Midway

Highline Community College
Redondo Pier (98031)

Seattle

Borton Divers
1107 Northeast 45th Street (98105)
(206) 632-6111/3138

Divers Institute of Technology, Inc.
P.O. Box 70312, 1133 Northwest 45th Street (98107)
(206) 783-5543
        784-6681

Garrison 8 Divers Corporation
119 Southwest Peninsula Place (98106)
(206) 767-3180, 937-5541, 226-2253

National Marine Fisheries Service
Biological Laboratory, 2725 Montlake Blvd. E. (98102)
(206) 583-5327

Providence Hospital
Institute of Environmental Medicine & Physiology
500 17th Avenue (98122)
(206) 322-3140, ext. 330 or 332

University Hospital
1959 N.E. Pacific Street (98105)

Virginia Mason Research Center
1000 Seneca Street (98101)
(206) 624-1144, exts. 421, 422

WISCONSIN

Milwaukee

St. Luke's Hospital Hyperbaric Unit
2900 West Oklahoma Ave. (53215)
(414) 647-6577/6423

Milwaukee County Hyperbaric Unit
2430 West Wisconsin Avenue (53233)
(414) 342-3605, 289-6024

CANADA

ALBERTA

Edmonton

Divers Den
10550 109th Street
(403) 426-3483, 488-1409

BRITISH COLUMBIA

Nanaimo

Fisheries Research Board of Canada
Biological Station
(604) 758-5202/5828

Pitt Meadows

Seaboard Marine Divers & Consultants, Ltd.
13554 Reichenback Rd.
(604) 465-4006

Vancouver

Vancouver General Hospital
Hyperbaric Research Unit, University of British Columbia
(604) 879-5355
        876-3211/2739/3335

Videospection Engineering Co., Ltd.
1661 West 8th Avenue
(604) 736-7361
        922-1943

North Vancouver

International Hydrodynamics Co., Ltd.
145 Riverside Drive
(604) 929-2391

Can-Dive Services, Ltd.
250 East Esplanade
(604) 988-3029
        987-4913

Victoria

Fleet Diving Unit (Pacific)
F.M.O.
(604) 388-2379

NEWFOUNDLAND

St. John's

Marine Sciences Research Laboratory
Memorial University of Newfoundland
(709) 726-6687
        368-0475

NOVA SCOTIA

Dartmouth

Bedford Institute of Oceanography,
Department of Mines, Energy, and Resources
(902) 426-3870

Fleet Diving Unit (Atlantic)
Grove Street
(902) 426-4120/4269/4271/4273

ONTARIO

Downsview

Defence and Civil Institute of Environmental Medicine
P.O. Box 2000, 1133 Sheppard Avenue West
(416) 633-4240, ext. 261 or 258

Port Alma

Consolidated West Petroleum
No. 3 Highway
(416) 689-4203/4480

Thunder Bay

Deep Diving Systems Ltd.
Lakeshore Drive, Box 717
(807) 344-7621

Toronto

Toronto General Hospital
Hyperbaric Department
101 College Street
(416) 595-4131/4132/3155

QUEBEC

Montreal

Royal Victoria Hospital
687 Pine Street West
(514) 842-1251/1660/1500, ext. 544

BAHAMA ISLANDS

Andros Island

Atlantic Undersea Test & Evaluation Center
Andros Ranges, Andros Island, Fresh Creek, Bahamas
Officer in Charge, Atlantic Undersea Test & Evaluation Center
Andros Ranges, FPO NY 09559
Call Nassau, Bahamas and ask for the
    Atlantic Undersea Test & Evaluation Center

Freeport, Grand Bahama

Underwater Explorer Club
P. O. Box F2433
3-1244

JAPAN

HOKKAIDO

Otaru City

Asari Hospital
(0134) 4-6543

Sapporo

Sapporo Medical College
Department of Cardiothoracic Surgery
(011) 611-2111, ext. 380

HONSHU

Hiroshima

Japanese Maritime Self Defense Forces
1st Service School
Nakago
Etajima-cho
(08234) 2-1211

Kyoto

The Hyperbaric Therapy Unit
Medical School Hospital, Kyoto University
53 Kawahara-cho
Syagoin Sokyoku
771-8111, Intercom 5931 or 701-4482

Yokosuka

Japanese Maritime Self Defense Forces
Underwater Medical Laboratory
2-7-1 Nagase
Yokosuka-shi
Kanagawa-ken
(0468) 41-7560, Ext. 283/7653

Ship Repair Facility
U.S. Fleet Activity
Diving Officer, Code 338, Box 8, Ship Repair Facility
FPO Seattle, WA 98762
234-5652/5488

KYUSHU

Sasebo

Ship Repair Office
Sasebo, Kyushu, Japan
Ship Repair Officer, Box 11, U.S. Fleet Activity
FPO Seattle, WA 98766

MEXICO

Acapulco

Primera Compania del Comando Submarino
Base Naval Militar
4-00-34

Divers de Mexico
Miguel Aleman 100

Mexico City

Centro Hospitalario
Av. Coyoacan y Felix Cuevas (12)

Equipos y Tecnicas, S.A.
Y/O Organizacion Submarina Mexicana, S.A.
Gutenberg 47-803 (5)
531-6439/6440
598-0926/0939

Hospital Emergencias de Coyoacan (Xoco)
Avenida Churubusco y Calzada Coyoacan (2P19)
5-24-25-39/22-16

GERMANY

Berlin

German Lifesaving Society (D.L.R.G.) House 1
Berlin 20
AM Pichelssee 20
368-9966
369-1001

Wiesbaden

USAFE Central Aeromedical Services
Wiesbaden Air Base, Germany
Bldg. 26
Wiesbaden Military 5730 or 5231

U.S. TERRITORIES AND POSSESSIONS

Guantanamo Bay

Ship Repair Department, U.S. Naval Station
Guantanamo Bay, Cuba
Commanding Officer, U.S. Naval Station, Box 13
FPO New York, NY 09593

GUAM

Diving Officer
U.S. Naval Ship Repair Facility, Guam
FPO San Francisco, CA 96630

PANAMA CANAL ZONE

Gatun

Salvage Depot
Panama Canal Company
43-5189/5431/2196

PUERTO RICO

San German

Hospital de la Concepcion
San German (00753)
892-1860

Mayaguez

University of Puerto Rico
Mayaguez (00708)

VIRGIN ISLANDS

St. John

Virgin Islands Ecological Research Station
Lameshur Bay
774-0001/6013/6196/5990

Appendix 4

Self-Grading System for Scuba Divers

A reef competence grading system has been devised by Captain Don Stewart to assist his skin-diving guests in selecting a suitable reef program at Aquaventure, Bonaire, Netherlands Antilles. Each diver grades himself in relation to certain diving areas and their topographies. The grades range from AAA, the easiest and least hazardous, to EEE, the roughest and most hazardous. The only differences between an AAA diver and an EEE diver are individual diving experience, knowledge, and application of diving techniques. The self-grading system follows:

AAA   You are a student diver; this is your first salt-water or open-water dive or you have logged only one or two dives. This is an area good for checking scuba gear or diver competence. It has an easy beach entry and exit, no surf, and safety floats handy. The diving area is small and easy to watch.

BBB   You are certified and somewhat experienced as a diver. You could descend underwater to 60 feet and remain there for as long as forty minutes. This is a medium-sized diving area of semirough terrain with a coral and sand beach and small surf. A short surface swim is required because entry and exit are by boat.

CCC   You are well experienced and physically fit; can descend to 60 feet and remain there for fifty minutes; can do a snorkel surface swim of 600 feet wearing full scuba gear as well as a 2,500-foot U/W swim. You can work the repetitive diving tables. This diving site has rough terrain with a moderately difficult entry and exit and a moderately long surface swim. There is some current and the possible need to make a twelve-foot jump into the water.

DDD   You are so well experienced that you could work alone if you had to. You have been deep diving and find no problem with long surface swims. You have air-conserving capability of remaining at 60 feet for sixty minutes and have a full knowledge of how to use all scuba gear, including decompression meters. This diving area has quite a difficult entry and exit, with strong currents and a required 4,000-foot underwater swim.

EEE   You are the ultimate in experienced divers, even to having tried some hard-hat diving. Certainly you have been decompression diving many times. This dive site is only for the advanced diver because it offers extremely difficult and hazardous diving conditions. There is rough water, the need to descend to extreme depths and use decompression tables and meters, and the presence of predatory activity (sharks).

Appendix 5

Equipment Suppliers

Full Line of Diving Products

AMF Voit	3801 South Harbor Blvd., Santa Ana, CA 92704
Dacor Corp.	161 Northfield Rd., Northfield, IL 60093
Healthways	5340 West 102nd St., Los Angeles, CA 90045
Scubapro	3105 East Harcourt, Compton, CA 90221
Seatec Systems	425 West Palmyra, Orange, CA 92666
Sportsways	2050 Laura Ave., Huntington Park, CA 90255
White Stag Water Sports	1046 Princetown Dr., Marina Del Rey, CA 90291
U.S. Divers Co.	3323 West Warner Ave., Santa Ana, CA 92702
U.S. Nemrod, Inc.	2315 Whitney Ave., Hamden, CT 06518

Specialized Diving Accessories

Aqua-Craft	3280 Kurtz St., San Diego, CA 92110
Bayfront Industries, Inc.	4225 Ponce de Leon Rd., Coral Gables, FL 33146
EZ Divers Accessories	1575 Magnolia, Long Beach, CA

Global Manufacturing Corp.	P.O. Box 4714, Milwaukee, WI 53215
Farallon Industries, Inc.	1333 Old County Rd., Belmont, CA 94002
Marine Specialties	P.O. Box 61, Mastic Beach, NY
Nautical Enterprises	1 Waterman Ave., East Providence, RI
Sea Research & Development, Inc.	P.O. Box 589, Bartow, FL 33830
Trident U/W Products	10048 Oso Ave., Chatsworth, CA 91311
Farallon Industries, Inc.	1333 Old County Rd., Belmont, CA 94002
Marine Specialties	P.O. Box 61, Mastic Beach, NY
Nautical Enterprises	1 Waterman Ave., East Providence, RI
Sea Research & Development, Inc.	P.O. Box 589, Bartow, FL 33830
Trident U/W Products	10048 Oso Ave., Chatsworth, CA 91311

Buoyancy Compensators

Sea Quest	11525 Sorrento Valley Rd., San Diego, CA
Seatec Systems	425 West Palmyra, Orange, CA 92666
U.S. Nemrod, Inc.	2315 Whitney Ave., Hamden, CT 06518
U.S. Divers Co.	3323 West Warner Ave., Santa Ana, CA 92702
Prospect Dive	506 East Northwest Hwy., Mt. Prospect, IL
Stebco Industries	1020 West 40th St., Chicago, IL
Watergill, Inc.	18100 South Euclid, Fountain Valley, CA
Sportsways	2050 Laura Ave., Huntington Park, CA 90255
Healthways	5340 West 102nd St., Los Angeles, CA 90045
AMF Voit	3801 South Harbor Blvd., Santa Ana, CA 92704
Scubapro	3105 East Harcourt, Compton, CA 90221
La Spirotechnique	114 rue Marius Aufan, 92306 Levallois, France
Dacor Corp.	161 Northfield Rd., Northfield, IL 60093
White Stag Water Sports	1046 Princeton Dr., Marina Del Rey, CA 90291

Compasses and Binoculars

Supermarine Products, Inc.	1 Johnson Dr., Raritan, NJ

Communication Systems Underwater

Helle Engineering, Inc.	7198 Convoy Court, San Diego, CA 92111
Metro-Tech Electronics	3338 Olive St., St. Louis, MO
Sub-Aquatics, Inc.	8855 East Broadway, RR1, Reynoldsburg, OH 43068

Compressors, Parts, and Accessories

Haskel Engineering and Supply Co.	100 East Graham Pl., Burbank, CA 91502
Deltech Engineering, Inc.	Century Park, New Castle, DE 19720
Air Associated	6115 South Richmond St., Chicago, IL 60629
American Bristol Industries	25032 Broadwell Ave., Harbor City, CA
Innerspace Research	4780 East 11th Ave., Hialeah, FL
Mako Engineering	3131 Northeast 188th St., North Miami, FL
McWhorter Engineering	P.O. Box 9014, Birmingham, AL
Pressure Systems, Inc.	1712 Spring Garden, Greensboro, NC 27403
Rix Industries	6460 Hollis, Emeryville, CA
Supreme Divers	168 King St. East, Toronto, Ontario, Canada
Trident Systems, Inc.	325 Hickory Ave., Merritt Island, FL

Defogging Compound

Albert Industries, Inc.	140 West 36th St., New York, NY

Decompression Diving Tables

Aquatic Recreational Enterprises	Delsea Dr., Tr. 47 Hurffville, NJ
Asking Diving Schools	591 Simbury St., Columbus, OH

Divers' Game Bags

Payne's Demersal Divers Supply	117 South H St., Lompoc, CA 94436

Diving Equipment Carrying Bags

Logan, Inc.	16952 Milliken Ave., Irvine, CA
Sports Leather Products	3430 Macon Rd., Memphis, TN

Exposure Suits

BayleySuit, Inc. (Wet and Dry)	900 South Fortuna Blvd., Fortuna, CA 95540
Dacor Corp. (Wet only)	161 Northfield Rd., Northfield, IL 60093
Del Mar Supplies, Inc. (Wet only)	472 West Palmyra St., Orange, CA 92666
Harvey's (Wet and Dry)	2505 South 252, Kent, WA 98301
Henderson Aquatics, Inc. (Wet only)	Buck and Sassafras Sts., Millville, NJ 08332
Imperial Manufacturing Co. (Wet and Dry)	P.O. Box 4119, Bremerton, WA 98310
O'Neill, Inc. (Wet and Dry)	1071 41st Ave., Santa Cruz, CA 95060
Parkway Fabricators (Wet and Dry); Poseidon Systems, U.S.A. (Dry)	241 Raritan St., South Amboy, NJ 08879
Sea Suits (Wet and Dry)	837 West 18th St., Costa Mesa, CA 92627
Seatec (Dry only)	425 West Palmyra St., Orange, CA 92666
Sub-Aquatic Systems (Dry only)	530 6th St., Hermosa Beach, CA 90254
U.S. Divers Co. (Wet and Dry)	3323 West Warner Ave., Santa Ana, CA 92702
U.S. Nemrod, Inc. (Wet only)	2351 Whitney Ave., Hamden, CT 06518
White Stag Water Sports (Wet and Dry)	1046 Princeton Dr., Marina del Rey, CA 90291

Hydrostatic Testing Equipment

Trans World Industries, Inc.	P.O. Box 635, Sandersville, GA 31082

Knives and Accessories

Bicco, Inc.	P.O. Box 5332, New Orleans, LA
Buck Knives, Inc.	P.O. Box 1267, El Cajon, CA
W. R. Case & Sons	20 Russell Blvd., Bradford, PA

Metal Detectors

White's Electronics	1012 Pleasant Valley, Sweet Home, OR
Relco, Inc.	P.O. Box 10839, Houston, TX
Research Products	P.O. Box 13441, Tampa, FL 33611
J. W. Fishers Manufacturing Co.	Anthony St., Taunton MA 02780

Recompression Chambers

Dive-Med International   1101 North Calvert, Baltimore, MD 21202

Scuba Parts and Repair

Underwater Innovators   18100 South Euclid, Fountain Valley, CA
Pennform Plastic
   Products, Inc.   365 Mulberry, Wyandotte, MI 48192
WD-40 Co.   1061 Cudahy St., San Diego, CA
Aqua-Kinetics   P.O. Box 38, Allen Park, MI
ECR Enterprises   16704 Elgar Ave., Torrance, CA
National Scuba Repair   16442 Gothard St. B, Huntington Beach, CA
   92647

Slurp Guns

Bayfront Industries, Inc.   4225 Ponce de Leon Blvd., Coral Gables, FL
   33146

Underwater Lights

AMF Voit   3801 South Harbor Blvd., Santa Ana, CA
   92704
Dacor Corp.   161 Northfield Rd., Northfield, IL 60093
G/F Industries, Inc.   144 Paul Dr., San Rafael, CA 94903
Ikelite U/W Systems   3303 N. Illinois St., Indianapolis, IN 46208
U.S. Nemrod, Inc.   2315 Whitney Ave., Hamden, CT 06518
U.S. Divers Co.   3323 West Warner Ave., Santa Ana, CA
   92702
Scubapro   3105 Harcourt St., Compton, CA 90221
Darrell-Allan Corp.   110 West North St., Healdsburg, CA 95448
Oceanic Products, Inc.   814 Castro St., San Leandro, CA 94544
Farallon Industries   1333 Old County Rd., Belmont, CA 94002
Sea Research &
   Development, Inc.   P.O. Box 589, Bartow, FL 33830
Subsea Products   P.O. Box 9532, San Diego, CA
AMF Mares   29 Essex St., Maywood, NJ
F. L. Diamond Co.   12445 Woodley Ave., Granada Hills, CA
National Divers
   Manufacturing Co.   217 West Julian St., San Jose, CA

Underwater Optical Lenses

Scuba Spec Co.	P.O. Box 3356, Savannah, GA 31403
Leonard Maggiore	1702 Gates Ave., Brooklyn, NY 11227
A. S. Newton, O.D.	575 6th St., San Pedro, CA 90731
Benson Optical Co.	1812 Park Ave., Minneapolis, MN
Underwater Vision	950 Cooper St., Venice, FL
Underwater Optics	P.O. Box 933, Temple City, CA 91780

Underwater Photographic Equipment

Harry Gocho Enterprises, Inc.	56-01 Queens Blvd., Woodside, NY
Image Devices, Inc.	811 NW 111 St., Miami, FL 33168
Scuba Specialties	10956 El Nopal, Lakeside, CA
Hydro-Photo	3909 13 Ave. South, Seattle, WA
Hydrotech	P.O. Box 1444, Long Beach, CA
Sea Research & Development, Inc.	P.O. Box 589, Bartow, FL 33830
Fiberbilt Photo Products Division	601 West 26 St., New York, NY
Hawaii Camera	1415 Kapiolani, Honolulu, HI
Ikelite U/W Systems	3303 North Illinois St., Indianapolis, IN 46208
Oceanic Products, Inc.	814 Castro St., San Leandro, CA 94544
Ehrenreich Photo Optical, Inc. (Nikon)	623 Stewart Ave., Garden City, NY 11533
Honeywell Denver	4800 E. Dry Creek Rd., Denver, CO 80210
Astro Nautical Research, Inc.	103 Erie St., Cambridge, MA 02139

Underwater Vehicles

Perry Oceanographic, Inc.	Perry Bldg., 100 East 17th St., Riviera Beach, FL 33404
Pan Western Research Corp.	19531 Airport Way South, Santa Ana, CA
Farallon Industries, Inc.	1333 Old County Rd., Belmont, CA 94002

Underwater Watches

Aquadive	3600 Wilshire Blvd., Los Angeles, CA 90010

Chronosport	135 Rowayton Ave., Rowayton, CT
Novelty House	1217 Ave. L, Brooklyn, NY
Ollech & Wajs Watch Co.	Stockerstra 55 8039, Zurich, Switzerland
Rolex	665 5th Ave., New York, NY
Zodiac	1212 Ave. of the Americas, New York, NY
B-J Enterprises	P.O. Box 245, Costa Mesa, CA
House of Clocks, Inc.	707 South Hill, Los Angeles, CA 90014
Norman M. Morris Corp. (Omega)	Omega Bldg., 301 East 57th St., New York, NY 10022

Appendix 6

Scuba Certification Programs

National Association of Underwater Instructors (NAUI)
    22809 Barton Rd., Grand Terrace, CA 92324
YMCA National Scuba Headquarters
    1611 Candler Bldg., Atlanta, GA 30303
Professional Association of Diving Instructors
    1297 Logan, Costa Mesa, CA
National Association of Skin Diving Schools
    1757 Long Beach Blvd., Long Beach, CA 90813
Scuba Schools International
    1634 South College, Fort Collins, CO
Los Angeles County Parks and Recreation
    155 West Washington Blvd., Los Angeles, CA
British Sub Aqua Club
    160 Great Portland St., London W1N 5TB
Professional Diving Instructor College
    598 Foam St., Monterey, CA 93940
International Underwater Explorers Society
    P. O. Box F-2433, Freeport, Bahamas

Appendix 7

Questions Diving Instructors Often Ask and Answer

General Questions

1. Give the exact psia at 85 feet of seawater.
2. Give the breathing media and the percentage of each gas at sea level used by sport divers.
3. Give the partial pressures of these gases and prove your answer.
4. Explain what an air embolism is, telling the cause, symptoms, treatment, and prevention.
5. Explain what decompression sickness is, telling the cause, symptoms, treatment, and prevention.
6. Explain Boyle's Law and provide at least one diving hazard example.
7. Why may you feel pain in your ears on descent? What is happening? What should be your course of action?
8. If your air supply failed while you were descended to 74 feet, what would you do?
9. Name all the *essential* equipment you must take on a sport dive.
10. Explain just the basic principles of Haldane's Law. Could it be a danger to a diver?
11. What is hyperventilation? Explain how it could be dangerous.
12. What is the type of regulator a sport diver should use?
13. What is the most important rule to follow when breathing with scuba?

293

14. How often should your scuba tank be tested? Who says so?
15. Why should no other gas besides compressed air be used by a sport diver?
16. Why is sport diving limited to less than 300 feet?

Water Safety and First Aid

17. What water temperature range is ideal?
18. How would you go about selecting a suitable swimming area?
19. Explain the proper procedure for adjusting to the water.
20. Define panic.
21. How should you swim in a current?
22. What areas of the body are affected most frequently by cramps?
23. Give at least three causes for drownings.
24. Describe two types of drownings.
25. Name three kinds of rescues.
26. List five types of extensions.
27. What are three things to consider before attempting a swimming rescue?
28. Explain how to give mouth-to-mouth resuscitation.
29. Explain how to give closed heart massage.
30. What takes place in the body of a victim in shock?
31. How would you position a person with a chest injury, shortness of breath, or respiratory obstruction?

Scuba Diving History

32. In what year and by whom was the first satisfactory demand regulator for open-circuit scuba patented?
33. Who was responsible for the development of stage decompression, and what are the advantages of it?
34. What is the purpose of the Navy Experimental Diving Unit?

Basic Scuba Equipment

35. Draw a J-valve and explain its operation.
36. Draw a single-stage two-hose regulator and explain its operation.
37. Draw a two-stage double-hose regulator.
38. Draw a balanced piston first stage with a downstream second stage and explain its operation.

39. What is the advantage of a downstream second stage over an upstream second stage?

Underwater Physics

40. What is the composition of air?
41. Define pressure, kinetic theory of gases, atmospheric pressure, psia, and psig.
42. What is the density of salt water? Of fresh water?
43. Define the following gas laws and explain a diving hazard and condition to which each is most closely related.
    a. Charles's Law
    b. Dalton's Law
    c. Henry's Law
    d. Archimedes' Principle
44. A tank is charged to 2985 psig at a temperature of 100° C. When the tank is used the air has cooled to 60° F. If a diver breathes .5 ft³ per minute, what is the maximum dive time he has at a depth of 67 feet, assuming the tank he is using is rated at 100 ft³ at a pressure of 2800 psig?
45. A diver weighs 177 pounds and needs ten pounds of weight for neutral buoyancy in salt water. How much salt water does he displace?
46. What effect does distortion of light have on the diver's vision?
47. What are the three basic requirements for sound?
48. List three ways that heat is transmitted.
49. Explain why a diver isn't crushed by the increased pressures he encounters.

Diving Physiology

50. Define physiology.
51. Define oxidation.
52. Define metabolism.
53. Define respiration of the internal and external types.
54. List six important steps in the process of respiration.
55. What comprises the anatomy of the circulatory system?
56. Describe where the heart is located and explain how its chambers function.
57. Make a schematic drawing of the circulatory system and trace the path of a drop of blood.

58. How many liters of blood does the body contain?
59. In what form is oxygen carried in the blood?
60. How does hemoglobin combine with oxygen?
61. What are the lungs constructed of?
62. Define the following:
    a. Respiratory cycle
    b. Respiratory rate
    c. Total lung capacity
    d. Vital capacity
    e. Tidal volume
    f. Inspiratory reserve volume
    g. Expiratory reserve volume
    h. Residual volume
    i. Respiratory minute volume
    j. Maximum breathing capacity
    k. Respiratory dead space
    l. Net alveolar ventilation
63. What are the gas partial pressures in the lungs?
64. What are the partial pressures of the gases dissolved in arterial and venous blood?
65. Tell of the primary stimuli to respiration and the mechanical action that follows.
66. What is an oxygen debt and what does it enable a diver to do?
67. Define respiratory quotient.
68. Expired air contains what percentage more CO_2 and what percentage less O_2 than inspired air?
69. Why does open-circuit scuba provide less breathing time at depth than at the surface?
70. What happens to CO_2 as depth increases?
71. Define hypoxia and explain how it can occur in a diving situation.
72. What determines whether the amount of oxygen in a breathing medium is adequate?
73. What are the effects on respiration if inspired air contains 5 percent CO_2?
74. What effect can skip breathing have on a diver?
75. List several causes of "self-poisoning" with CO_2.
76. What role does excess CO_2 play in decompression illness, narcosis, and O_2 toxicity?
77. How is narcosis prevented?

Decompression Illness

78. If a victim has symptoms of staggering, dizziness, and joint pain, what treatment run would you make on him?
79. How would you treat a diver who experiences joint pain in the shoulder one hour after surfacing?
80. What treatment table would you advise for "bends" that take place at the 20-foot stop?
81. Give at least five contributing factors of decompression illness.
82. Define bottom time, equivalent bottom time, residual N_2, surface interval, repetitive dive.
83. Plan two dives in one day:

    8 A.M. dive—120 feet—ten minutes.

    10 A.M. dive— 60 feet—thirty minutes.
84. A diver accidentally surfaces from a dive to 90 feet for forty-five minutes; what emergency procedure should he follow?

Equipment

85. If a regulator free-flows immediately upon turning it on, which stage is the trouble most likely in?
86. How should one pack equipment when transporting it in a car?·
87. What maintenance should be made on equipment after each dive?

Environment

88. List three causes of currents.
89. Define rip current.
90. How should one enter the water in heavy surf?
91. What three marine organisms are responsible for the most agony to divers?
92. How should a diver react when sharks are in the area?
93. Why is cave diving considered hazardous?
94. Describe the technique of finger walking.
95. List the minimum cave-diving equipment.
96. You are the dive master for a dive in 100 feet of water and you suspect a strong current may be running; what precautions should you take?
97. How would you swim in kelp?

Navigation

98. What is the primary method of navigation for divers?
99. When making a compass run, what special things should you pay attention to in order to avoid deviation?
100. Explain how you would swim a circular search pattern.
101. Explain a grid search pattern.

General

102. Explain how to operate a high-pressure air cascade system.
103. If using oxygen for treatment, what special fire precautions should be taken?
104. What three things should be done when making an ascent?
105. If diving out of a boat, how many people should be in the water if three divers are together? Why?
106. Give cause, precautions, symptoms and treatment of each of the following:
    a. Air embolism
    b. Pneumothorax
    c. Medidstinal emphysema
    d. Subconscious emphysema
107. What are the hand signals underwater for "Go back," "Is everything OK?", "I need help," "Help me (on the surface)"?
108. What is a remedy for being stabbed with sea-urchin spines?
109. What is the lens technology for improving underwater vision?
110. To get informational assistance for a diving accident or to learn the location of the nearest recompression chamber, call—day or night—the duty officer at the U.S. Navy Experimental Diving Unit at Panama City, Florida. What is that phone number?

Appendix 8

Bibliography

Diving Medicine and Physiology

Dueker, Christopher W. *Medical Aspects of Sport Diving.* South Brunswick, New Jersey: A. S. Barnes & Company, Inc., 1970.

McAniff, Schenck, and Kindwall. *Non-Fatal, Pressure-Related Scuba Accidents, Identification and Emergency Treatment:* Scuba Safety Report Series, Report No. 3. Kingston, Rhode Island: Dept. of Ocean Engineering, University of Rhode Island, 1970.

Miles, Stanley. *Underwater Medicine* (Third Edition). Philadelphia, Pennsylvania: J. B. Lipincott Company, 1969.

Modell, Jerome H., M.D. *Drowning and Near Drowning.* Springfield, Illinois: Charles C. Thomas, Inc., 1972.

First Aid, Life-Saving, Scuba Rescue, and Water Safety

Cross, E. R. *Underwater Safety.* Los Angeles, California: Healthways 1912, 1956.

Eastman, Peter F., M.D. *Advanced First Aid Afloat.* Cambridge, Maryland: Cornell Maritime Press, 1972.

Henderson, John. *The Complete Book of First Aid.* New York, New York: Bantam Books, Inc., 1957.

Red Cross. *Swimming and Water Safety.* Washington, D.C.: The American National Red Cross, 1952.

Silvia, Charles E.   *Lifesaving and Water Safety Today for Students and Instructors.* New York, New York: Association Press, 1971.

Sport Diving and Underwater Education

Bergaust, Erik, and Foss, William J.   *Skin Divers in Action.* New York, New York: G. P. Putnam's Sons, 1965.

Bird, Peter.   *Skin Diving.* New Rochelle, New York: Soccer Associates, 1963.

Bortstein, Larry, and Berkowitz, Henry.   *Scuba, Spear and Snorkel.* Chicago, Illinois: Cowles Book Company, Inc., 1971.

Bridges, Lloyd.   *Mask and Flippers—The Story of Skin Diving.* New York, New York: Affiliated Publishers, Inc., 1961.

Craig, John D., and Degn, Morgan.   *Invitation to Skin and Scuba Diving.* New York, New York: Simon & Schuster, 1965.

Cross, E. R.   *Advanced Skin and Scuba Diving.* Honolulu, Hawaii: Marine Research Publishing Co., 1969.

Dresner, Simon.   *Skin and Scuba Diving.* New York, New York: Collier Books, 1963.

Ellman, Van.   *Scuba Diving.* Fort Lee, New Jersey: Publishers Service Company, 1968.

Frey, Hank and Shaney.   *Diver Below!* New York, New York: Collier Books, 1969.

Frey, Shaney.   *The Complete Beginner's Guide to Skin Diving.* Garden City, New York: Doubleday & Company, Inc., 1965.

Lee, Owen S.   *The Skin Diver's Bible.* Garden City, New York: Doubleday & Company, Inc., 1968.

Parker, Eugene K.   *Complete Handbook of Skin Diving.* New York, New York: Avon Books, Div. of Hearst Corp., 1965.

Sand, George X.   *Skin and Scuba Diving.* New York, New York: Hawthorn Books, 1964.

Strykowski, Joe G.   *Diving for Fun.* Northfield, Illinois: Dacor Corporation, 1970.

Sullivan, George D.   *The Complete Book of Skin and Scuba Diving.* New York, New York: Coward-McCann, Inc., 1969.

Tinker, Gene.   *The Skin Diving Travel Guide.* Garden City, New York: Doubleday & Company, Inc., 1967.

Underwater Instruction: Swimming, Skin, and Scuba Diving

Barada, Bill.   *Let's Go Diving.* Santa Ana, California: U.S. Divers Company, 1962.

Zanelli, Leo. *Underwater Swimming.* South Brunswick, New Jersey: A. S. Barnes & Company, Inc., 1969.

Underwater Navigation and Search Procedure

Erickson, Ralph D. *A Guide to Underwater Navigation.* Chicago, Illinois: Dives, Inc., 1971.

Glatt, Jack E. *Diver's Navigation Manual.* Northfield, Illinois: Dacor Corporation, 1970.

Diving and Marine Publications

NAUI News. NAUI Headquarters, 22809 Barton Road, Grand Terrace (Colton), CA 92324.

Oceans. The Oceanic Society, 240 Fort Mason, San Francisco, CA 94123.

Sea Frontiers. The International Oceanographic Foundation, 1 Rickenbacker Causeway, Virginia Key, Miami, FL 33149.

Sea Secrets. The International Oceanographic Foundation, 1 Rickenbacker Causeway, Virginia Key, Miami, FL 33149.

Skin Diver magazine. Petersen Publishing Company, 5050 Hollywood Boulevard, Los Angeles, CA 90069.

Undercurrent. P.O. Box 1658, Sausalito, CA 94965.

The Undersea Journal. Professional Association of Diving Instructors, P.O. Box 177 Mesa Center Station, Costa Mesa, CA 92627.

Index

A

Abrasions, 206
    foot, 49
Absolute pressure, 162
    gauge pressure and, 171-172
Accidents, 175. *See also* Death; Hazards; Injuries; Safety measures
    aquadocs, 256, 257
Acidosis, 211
Adhesive bandage and tape, 206
Adjustments, equipment, xvi, 195
Age, 3. *See also* Older people
    children, 7: snorkel fit, 48
    youth, 8: watermanship, 16-18
Air, impure, 90, 92, 94, 223-224
Air bottle, 56
Air compressor, 90-94
    suppliers, 287
Air embolism, 149, 163, 224-230
    flotation devices, 54
    recompression time, 235
Air filling station, 90-94, 223-224
Air tank. *See* Compressed-air tank
Air travel, hazard to divers, 225
Airway, plastic, 205
Alabama, 262
Alaska, 262
Alberta, Canada, 276
Alcohol, 8
    liquor drinking harmful, 157
    nitrogen narcosis compared, 167;
        holding one's liquor, 237; Martini's law, 236
Allergic reactions, 205
    cold, 218-220
Alone, diving, 137-140, 175, 240, 247
Alveoli, of lungs, 149
    air embolism, 224
    barotrauma, 231, 232
Ama, Japanese divers, 6-7
Ambient pressure, 162, 167, 168, 171, 172
Amnesia, 220
Anaphylaxis, 218-219

Anchor line, submerging, 129, 131
Andrea Dorea, x, 242
Andros Island, 16-18, 279
Anspach, Gayle, ix, 138-139
Antibiotic ointment, 205, 208
Antidote, food poisoning, 206
Antifreeze, 75
Antihistamine, 219
Antilles, 44-45. *See also* Bonaire
Antiseptics, 205, 206
Aqua Bell helmet, 40
Aquadoc, 203, 230
    listings, 255-61
Archaeology, 243-244
    Central American venture, 60, 61
    fatal jump, 125
    ice ax advised, 109-110
    nitrogen narcosis, 237
Archimedes' principle, 20, 170-171
Arm strokes, 27, 28, 31
Artery, injury to, 207
Ascent, 21
    air embolism, 54, 163, 224
    barotrauma, 231-232, 233
    bends, the, 168, 233-234, 236
    breath-holding, a hazard, 163
    buddy breathing, 137, 139
    decompression table, 227-228
    emergency swimming, 199-201
    flotation devices, 53, 54, 57
    free, 143-144
    hyperventilation, 19-20, 211-212
    Israeli divers, 174
    losing contact with buddy, 180
    mouth-pull scuba rescue, 213-214
    nitrogen narcosis, 237
Asphyxia, 209
Aspirin, 157
Assembling, signal for, 187
Astigmatism, 191, 192
Athol Island, sunken LST, 240
Atmospheric pressure, 161-162
Attention, signal for, 186

B

Backpack, 94-99, 119
    ditch and don, 141, 142

Back roll, tank first, 126-127
Back step, feetfirst entry, 126
Back strokes, elementary, 28
Bahamas, 10, 16-18, 250, 255, 279
   Athol Island, sunken LST, 240
   cave diving, 248
Baja California, 136-137
Ballast stones, 243, 244
Ball-like bladder, 59
Bandage, 206, 208
Barbados, grandmother diver, 3
Barotrauma, 230-233
Bart, Paul, 168
Bear hug method, of rescue, 213
Belt, weight. *See* Weight belt
Bends, the, decompression sickness,
   167-168, 233-236
   aquadocs, 256, 257, 258
   questions about, 297
Bicycling, 30
Blackout, shallow-water, 211-212
Blood, 149
   cold and, 219, 220: medicines, 157
   loss, in wounds, 207
   oxygen and, 148
"Blow and go", 199-200
Boat, xii, 3, 60-65
   air compressor, 94
   anchor line, submerging, 129, 131
   diver's flag, 189
   in, out of water from, 125-128
   Israeli divers, 174-175
   signal for, 182
   signaling to and from, 179-180
Bob-diving, 32
Bonaire, Netherlands Antilles, ix-x, 7,
   95-97, 107, 123, 238
   dive shop, 68, 93, 104
   reef competence grading, 283-284
   song, diving, v
Books, listing of, 299-301
Boots, 51, 103, 121
Bowker, Bruce, ix, x, 107
Boyle's Law, 162-165, 222, 224
Brawley, Ed, ix, xiii, 22
   air embolism, 225
   buddy breathing, 137

buoyancy, 5
   emergency ascent, 200-201
   watermanship, 14, 16
Breast stroke, 28
Breath holding, 18-19, 41
   dangers of, 163, 167
Breathing, hyperventilated, 19-20, 149-
   150, 179, 211-212
Breathing tube, 4, 5, 41, 46-49
British Columbia, Canada, 276-277
British West Indies, 3. *See also* Grand
   Cayman
Bronze Age shipwreck, 243-244
Buddy breathing, 137-140, 201
   neck strap hinders, 120
   octopus rig replaces, 78-79, 125
Buddy system, 175-179
   deep diving, 247
   losing contact, 180
Buoyancy, 5, 20-21, 120, 170
   Archimedes' principle, 20, 170-171
   deep diving, 248
   inflatable craft, 61, 62
   personal flotation devices. *See* Per-
     sonal flotation devices
   weights, adjustable by, 106-107
   wet-suit, 21, 22
Buoyancy compensator, 36, 38, 54, 55-
   58
   emergency use, 195-196
   foreign countries, 173, 174
   inflating during descent, 21, 22
   preparing to submerge, 130
   rescue use, 189
   suppliers of, 286
Burst-disc assembly, 69
Buying equipment, 35-38

C

Caisson disease, 168. *See also* Bends,
   the
California, 155, 171, 213, 230, 255-257,
   262-263
   diving schools, ix, 5, 22, 25
   Los Angeles County ordinance, 202
Camera, 3, 245
   entering the water, 127

slipping strap around neck, 135
suppliers, 290
Canada, 257, 276-278
Canal Zone, Panama, 282
Cannonball tuck, 32
Carbon dioxide, 161, 166-167
  air mixture contains, 149, 161
  breath holding, 18-19, 167
  emergency ascent, 200
  flotation devices, 52-53, 54: compensator, 55, 57, 58
  hyperventilation, 18-19, 211-212
  nitrogen narcosis, 237
  panic caused by, 179
  removed by hemoglobin, 148
Carbon monoxide, 90, 92, 223
Cardiopulmonary resuscitation, 203
Care, of equipment, 59-60
  air delivery system, 79, 81, 87-88, 90
  compressed-air tank, 73-74
  flotation devices, 54
  gauges, 111, 113
  hookah, unit, 39
  knife, 109
  regulator, 118
  weights and weight belt, 106
  wet suit, 104-105, 120
Caribbean Sea, 250
Cave diving, 248-249
  octopus regulator, 197
Central America, 60, 61
Certification, 1-2, 8
  courses, 22-24
  programs, 292
Charles's Law, 165-166
Chest, 144
  pneumothorax, 150, 224-225; spontaneous, 231-232
  squeeze, 230-231
Children, 7
  snorkels, right size needed, 48
Chin pull technique, rescue, 213
Chokes, 235
Cigarette smoking, 8
Circulatory system, 147-149
Clamp-on backpack, 95-97

Clark, John, 242
Clearing
  ear and sinus, 132-133: failure, signal, 185; nose grabber, 46
  mask, 133-135: purge valve, 45
  mouthpiece, 135-137
  snorkel, valve, 47, 48
Closed-circuit scuba, 114
Clothing, 99-105. *See also* Dry Suit; Wet Suit
Cold, infection, 151
  ear and sinus squeeze, 151, 222
Cold water diving, 99-100
  antifreeze, 75
  exposure, 218-220: rescue, 16-18
  signal for cold, 184
Colorado, 264
Color changes, underwater, 153
Comfort, 8, 36, 103
  backpack and harness, 94-95
  cold water diving, 99
  food and drink affects, 157
  foot, 49-50
Communication, 153-155
  in-water signal system, 179-188
  suppliers of devices, 287
Compass, 113
  magnetic wrist, 144-145
  supplier of, 286
Compressed-air tank, 66-68
  air capacity, 164
  backpack and, 95-97
  backstroke and, 28
  buddy breathing, 137-138
  buoyancy compensator and, 57
  composition of air, 161
  ditch and don exercise, 140-143
  ditching: free ascent, 143-144; class, 24; shifting and, 123
  dive, safety in, 125
  donning, 118-120, 124
  filler valve, 69-74
  impure air, 90, 92, 94, 223-224
  Israeli divers, 175
  regulator and, 76-77, 116-118
  signaling air supply low, 185

slippage danger, 199-200
tank/reserve valve, 70-71
Compressor, air, 90-94
suppliers of, 287
Confidence, water, 22
Connecticut, 257, 264
Contact lenses, 191
Corrective lenses, 191-195
Cotton, first-aid supply, 206
Council for National Cooperation in Aquatics, 14, 157
Counting, signals for, 188
Cousteau, Jacques-Yves, 75, 153
Cramps, 178, 179
personal flotation device, 52
signal for, 184
Cuba, Guantanamo Bay, 281
Curacao, eye squeeze, 44-45
Cuts, minor, treatment, 205-206
Cut-throat gesture, 138, 184
Cylinder. *See* Compressed-air tank

D

Dalton's Law, 166-167, 168
Darkness, diving in, 245-246
Death, 159-161, 175, 177-178
air embolism, 224: vests, 54
bends, the, 168
carbon monoxide, 223
drowning, 179, 203, 209, 212: aqua-doc, 258
epilepsy, 25
heat loss, 155, 156, 219, 220
holding breath, 163
jumping into water, 125
panic, 179
Decompression meter, 248
Decompression sickness. *See* Bends, the
Decompression tables, 168, 169, 227-228
no-decompression dives, 226
suppliers of, 287
Decongestant, 206, 223
Deep diving, 247-248

Demand-type scuba, 114-116
Depth gauge, 111, 112-113, 171-172
Descent, 132-137
Aqua Bell helmet, 40
buoyancy compensator, 56
buoyancy during, 20, 21, 22
chest squeeze, 230-231
ear squeeze, 151-152: sinus squeeze and, 220-223
Japanese Ama, 6-7
nitrogen narcosis, 236, 238
preparing to submerge, 129-131
weight belt, 106
Detonator cord, 53
Direction, finding, 144-145
Direction, signaling, 181-182
Disabilities, diving with, 11
correcting visual flaws, 190-195
Diseases. *See also* Air embolism; Bends, the; Injuries; Nitrogen narcosis
barotrauma, 230-233
diving and, 25-26, 157-158
oxygen toxicity, 116
respiratory, 25-26, 150, 151
Distortion, in water, 153
Ditch and don, 140-143
Ditching, of air tank, 24
free ascent, 143-144
shifting and, 123
Diver's down flag, 58-59
modified, 189-190
Dive shops. *See* Shops, dive
Dog paddles, 28
Dolphin kick, 31
Double-hose regulator, 76, 78
accident, 136-137
care of, 88, 90
ditch and don, 142
draining air tank, 120
octopus type, 197
Drink, 157, 220
Drowning, 179, 203, 209, 212, 258. *See also* Near-drowning
Drugs, first-aid, 205
Dry suit, 99-100, 101
suppliers of, 288

E

Earplugs, hazard, 133
Ears, 153-155
 clearing, 132-133: failure, signal, 185;
  nose grabber, 46
 squeeze, 151-152: sinus squeeze and,
  220-223
Efficiency, human, in water, 9
Elementary back stroke, 28
Embolism, air. *See* Air embolism
Emergencies, 195-199
 air embolism, 224-226, 230
 aquadocs, 230: listing, 255-261
 ascent, 233: free, 143-144; mouth-pull
  rescue, 213-214; swimming, 199-
  201
 back-up scuba system, 78-79
 bends, the, 234-236
 flotation devices, 52-53, 54-55
 government agencies, 225-226
 overexposure, 220
 panic, danger of, 179
 resuscitation, 203, 209-211, 214-217
 signals, 184-186
 spontaneous pneumothorax, 232
Emergency Medicine, x, 230
 aquadoc listings, 255-261
Emphysema, 150, 232
Entanglement, 175, 176
 ditch and don, 140-143
 signal for, 184
Entering the water, 125-127
Epilepsy, 25
Equipment, 2, 3, 35-65
 ditching and donning, 140-143
 donning sequence, 123-124
 failure, 160
 fixing, xvi, 195, 289
 questions about, 294-295, 297
 securing: backpack, 95-98; octopus
  regulator, 197, 198, 199
 suppliers, listing of, 285-291
Euphoria, 236, 238
Eustachian tubes, 132, 133, 162
 ear squeeze, 151-152, 221, 222
Examination, medical, 24-26, 157-158

Examiner, air tanks, 66-68
Exhaustion, 55. *See also* Fatigue
 cold, 155, 218, 219, 220
Exiting the water, 125, 127-128
Explosion, danger of, 116
Exposure, 155, 156, 218-220
 Bahamas incident, 16-18
Exposure suit, 99-105. *See also* Wet suit
 buoyancy, 22
 suppliers, 288
Eyeglasses, 191-195
Eyes, in water, 4-5, 152-153. *See also* Vi-
 sion
 squeeze, 44-45

F

Faceplate, 5, 40, 153
 correcting visual flaws, 191-195
 purge valve, 45
Fainting, underwater, 211-212
Farallon Fara-Fin, 51-52
Fatigue, 16
 before entering water, 125
 cold, exhaustion from, 218, 219, 220:
  Bahamas incident, 17-18
 fatal result of panic, 179
 personal flotation device, 52
 signal for, 184
 wet suit prevents, 104
Feetfirst dives, 33-34, 125-127
 avoiding injuries, 45-46, 125
Filler valves, 69-74
Fins, 5, 38, 49-52
 comfort, 36, 103
 ditch and don, 140, 141, 143
 inspection, 121-122
 kicks, 27, 28-31, 49
First aid, 204-209
 books on, 299-300
 questions, 294
Fish, poisoning antidote, 206
Fish, signal for, 186
Fishing, underwater, 249-250
Fit, proper, importance of, 8, 49
 exposure suit, 100, 103
 oversized snorkel, 48

Fitness, 10, 18-19, 20, 156-158
  panic and, 179
Fixing equipment, xvi, 195, 289
Flag, diver's down, 58-59
  modified, 189-190
Flippers, 5, 49-52
Float, diver's, 58-59, 189, 214
Floatability. *See* Buoyancy
Florida, 147-148, 155, 226, 234, 250, 257-258, 264-265
  coral reef park incident, 177
Flotation, laws of, 20, 170-171
Flotation devices, personal. *See* Personal flotation devices
Flutter kick, 29-30
Food, 157
  lobster: hunt, 245: signal, 187
  poisoning, antidote, 206
  spearfishing for, 249-250
Foot comfort, 49-50, 121
Foreign countries, 173-175
Free ascent, 143-144
Free diving, 5-7
Front step, feetfirst, 125-126
Frying pan, used underwater, 154
Furman, Aaron, 109-110

G

Gagnan, Emile, 74-75
Galleon, Spanish, 243
Gastrointestinal functioning, 156-158
Gauge pressure, 171-172
Gauges, 110-113, 123, 171-172
  problems in reading, 190-191
  tank-pressure, 77, 116-117, 217
Gauze pad, 206, 207, 208
Gay-Lussac's Law, 165-166
Georgia, 266
Germany, 281
Germs, 207
Glasses, 191-195
Glossary, 251-254
Gloves, 103, 121, 124
Goggles, 7, 190
  hazardous, 44
Gold, treasure hunting, 241

Grand Cayman, ix, xv, 178
  buddy-breathing check, 138-139
Grand Bahamas, 10, 255
Greece, ship find, 243-244
Guam, recompression chamber, 281
Guantanamo Bay, Cuba, 281

H

Handicapped persons, 11
Hand signals, 179-188
  cut-throat, 138, 184
Harness, 94-99, 138, 214
  ditch and don, 140, 141, 142-143
  free ascent, 143-144
Hawaii, 258, 266
Hazards. *See also* Air embolism; Bends, the; Emergencies; Injuries; Leaks
  averting, 203-217. *See also* Safety measures
  barotrauma, 230-233
  drownings, 179, 203, 209, 212. *See also* Near-drownings
  earplugs and headgear, 133
  epilepsy, 25
  food and drink, wrong kinds, 157
  goggles, 44
  heat loss, 155-156, 157, 218-220
  hyperventilation, 19-20, 149-150, 211-212
  impure air, 90, 92, 94, 223-224
  nitrogen narcosis, 137, 161, 167, 168, 236-238
  oxygen toxicity, 116
  pollution, 207
  pressure gradients, 132-33: sinus cavities, 150-151
  signals for, 184-186
  stress, 146, 147: hyperventilation, 19-20
  tourniquets, 207
  wreck diving, 240
Headfirst diving, 45-46, 125
Health problems, 25-26
Hearing, underwater, 153-155
Heart, diving and, 25-26
Heat loss, 155-156, 157, 218-220
Helium, 236, 237

Hellephone, 154-155
Helmets, 40
Help, signals for needing, 184-185
Hemoglobin, 148, 223
Henry's Law, 167-169
Holding breath, 18-19, 41
    dangers of, 163, 167
Hookah diving, 39-40
Hospitalization, 211, 220
Hunting, underwater
    lobster, 245: signal for, 187
    spearfishing, 249-250
Hydrogen peroxide, 205-206, 208
Hydrostatic testing, 66-67
    equipment, suppliers of, 288
Hyperbaric medicine, 224, 230
    aquadocs, 257, 258, 259, 260, 261
Hyperventilation, 19-20, 149-150, 179,
    211-212
Hypothermia, 219, 220
Hypoxia, 209-210, 211, 212

I

Ice, descent under, suit, 99-100
Ice ax, 109-110
Identification, underwater, 122, 198
Illinois, 258, 266-267
Income, of divers, 3
Indiana, 44, 62, 211-212, 259
Inert gases, 236-237
Infection, 207, 208-209
Inflatable craft, 60-62
    Israeli divers, 174, 175
Inflatable suit, 99-100, 101
Inflator valve, 123, 124
Inhalation, 148-149. *See also* Breath
    holding; Hyperventilation
Injuries, 121, 124. *See also* Diseases;
    Hazards avoidance. *See* Safety
    measures
    ear squeeze, 151-152: sinus squeeze
        and, 220-223
    eye squeeze, 44-45
    first-aid treatment, 204-207
    headfirst diving, 45-46, 125

Inspection. *See also* Testing
    air filling station, 92
    compressed-air tank, 66, 68
    flotation devices, 54, 120
    pre- and postdive tips, 120-123
Instructor, xi-xii, xvi, 2, 35, 38, 93, 97,
    138-139
    air supply, 223-224
    associations, 15
    certification courses, 22, 24
    ditch and don test, 140-143
    gear, scuba, 79, 81, 83, 85
    near-drowning, rescue from, 213
    nitrogen narcosis, 238
    nonswimmers taught, 15
    octopus regulator use, 196-197
    older people, 10
    questions, listing of, 293-298
    watermanship, 15, 16
    women, 9
Insulation, exposure suit, 99-100, 102,
    104
International Underwater Society,
    Ltd., 9-10
Iowa, aquadoc, 259
Israel, scuba divers, 173-175

J

Jackknife pike, 32-33
Japan, 6-7, 279-280
J-valve, 72, 73

K

Kansas, aquadoc, 259
Kayak-paddleboard, 63-65
Kicks, fin, 27, 28-31, 49
Kindwall, Eric P., 224-225, 230
Knife, 107-109
    signaling use, 154, 180
    suppliers, 288
K-valve, 72, 73

L

Ladder, 127, 128, 175
    pontoon boat, 63

Leaks, 116-117, 136-137
  flotation devices, 54
  mask, 133-135: purge valve, 45
Lenses, 191-195, 290
Life buoy, 214
Lifeline, 240, 249
Life-saving, books on, 299-300
Life vest, 52, 53-55
  buoyancy compensator replaces, 38
  emergency ascent: mouth-pull res-
    cue, 213-214; swimming, 200
  foreign countries, 173, 174
  inflator valve, 123, 124
  inspection, 120
Light refraction, 5, 152, 153
Lights, 240, 245, 247, 249
  suppliers of, 289
List of terms, 251-254
Lobster, 245
  signal for, 187
Logging, of dives, 201-202
Losing contact, with buddy, 180
Lost, getting, 144-145
Louisiana, 259, 267
Lungs, physiology of, 149-150
  air embolism, 149, 163, 224-230
  breath holding, 18-19, 41: danger,
    163, 167
  buoyancy and, 21
  carbon dioxide, 167
  hyperventilation, 19-20, 149-150,
    211-212
  near-drowning, 210, 211-212: rescue,
    213; resuscitation, 214-217
  spontaneous pneumothorax, 232

M

Mae West life vest, 53
Magazines, x, 301. *See also Skin Diver*
Magnetic wrist compass, 144-45
Magnetite, 242
Maine, recompression chamber, 268
Maintenance, equipment. *See* Care
Martini's Law, 236
Maryland, 259, 268

Mask, 4-5, 38, 41-46, 122, 124
  clearing, 133-135: valve, 45
  correcting visual flaws, 191-195
  ditch and don, 142
  Israeli divers, 175
  resuscitation, 214
  safety measures, 45-46, 125, 127
  vision through, 41-43, 152, 153
Massachusetts, 268
Median age, of divers, 3
Medical examination, 24-26, 157-158
Medical training, 203-212
Medications, first-aid, 205-206
Medicine, books about, 299
Medicines to avoid, diving, 157
Mediterranean Sea, 243-244
Mental outlook, 11-12
Michigan, 259, 269
Middle-aged people, 3
Minnesota, 259, 269
Missouri, 269
Mittens, 103
Montana, recompression unit, 269
Monterey, California
  diving shops, ix, 5, 22, 25
Mouthpiece, 74, 116, 199-200
  buddy-breathing, 138-139
  buoyancy compensator, 55, 58
  clearing, 135-137
  ditch and don, 142
  octopus regulator, 198
  resuscitation, 214
  signal, 185
  snorkel tube, 47-48
  speech, 153
  washing, 88
Mouth-pull scuba rescue, 213-214
Mouth-to-mouth resuscitation, 209-
  211, 215-217

N

National Association of Underwater Instructors, x, 1, 123
  diver certification program, 15
  recompression chamber listings, 234,
    262-282

National Safety Council, 160, 203
National Scuba Advisory Committee, 159, 160
Nausea, 205
    signal for, 184
Navigation, 145
    books about, 301
    questions about, 298
Near-drowning, 209-212, 214-217
    mouth-pull scuba rescue, 213-214
    overexposure and, 219
Needles, sewing, 204, 208
Negative buoyancy, 5, 20-21, 170
Netherlands Antilles, 44-45. *See also* Bonaire
Neutral buoyancy, 21, 22, 120
Nevada, 171
Newfoundland, Canada, 277
New Hampshire, 218, 269
New Jersey, 73, 270
New York, state, 259, 270-271
New York City, 230, 243, 270-271
Night diving, 245-246
Nitrogen, 166
    air mixture contains, 149, 161
    bends, the, 167-168, 233, 235
    residual, timetable, 229
Nitrogen narcosis, 137, 161, 167, 168, 236-238
No-decompression dives, 168-169, 174, 226
North Carolina, 259-260, 271
Nose, emergency trick, 132, 133
Nose grabber, 45, 46
Nova Scotia, Canada, 278
Numbers, signals for, 188

O

Obesity, 21, 156, 170
    nitrogen narcosis and, 167, 237
Octopus rig, 78-79, 125, 196-199
Ohio, 199, 260, 271-272
Older people, 3, 9-11
    correcting visual flaws, 190-191
Ontario, Canada, 278
    aquadoc, Toronto, 257

Open-circuit scuba, 114-116
Optical lenses, 191-195
    suppliers of, 290
Optometrist, 191
Oral inflator, 52, 54, 190
    buoyancy compensator, 56, 57, 58
Oregon, 260, 272
O-ring, 117-118
Orris, William L., x, 221, 230
Outlook, mental, 11-12
Overexposure, 155, 218-220
    Bahamas incident, 16-18
Oxygen, 148, 149, 161
    air embolism, 225
    bends, the, 235
    breath holding, 18-19
    capacity, diving increases, 10-11
    dangers, 116
    deficiency, in near-drowning, 209-212
    exposure to cold, 219
    first-aid supply, 206
    hyperventilation, 19-20, 212

P

Pain, 162, 195
    bends, the, 168, 233, 234-235
    chest, 144, 231, 232
    ears, 129, 133: squeeze, 151-152, 221, 222
    first-aid treatment, 205
    sinus, 150-151: squeeze, 221
    wounds, 208, 209
Panama, 60
    Canal Zone, 282
Panic, 140, 179, 198
    free ascent, 143-144
    incidents, 17-18, 136, 178
    octopus regulator, 198, 199
Paradoxical cooling, 220
Paralysis, 163
    air embolism, 225
    cold, 218, 219, 220
Partial pressure, of gas, 166, 167
    shallow-water blackout, 211
Pennsylvania, 260, 272

Personal flotation devices, 38, 52-59.
See also Buoyancy Compensator;
Life Vest
cave diving, taboo in, 249
foreign countries, 173
inspection, 120
Phoenicians, 39
Photography, underwater, 244, 245
acknowledgements, ix, x
buddies, 177
equipment, suppliers of, 290
wreck diving, 242
Physical activity, dangers of, 237
Physical capacity, 24-26
Physical fitness. *See* Fitness
Physical laws, 159-172
Archimedes' principle, 20, 170-171
questions about, 295
Physicians, 208, 209
aquadocs, 203, 230: listings, 255-261
bends, the, 236
chest squeeze, 231
ear and sinus squeeze, 221, 223
examination by, 24-26, 157-158
overexposure, 220
spontaneous pneumothorax, 232
Physiology, underwater, 146-158
books about, 299
questions about 295-296
Pinocchio nose grabber, 45, 46
Plasma, 148, 149, 210
Pneumothorax, 150, 224-225. *See also*
Air embolism; Bends, the
spontaneous, 231-232
Poisoning
aquadocs, marine venoms and poi-
sons, 255, 256, 260
carbon dioxide, 167
carbon monoxide, 223
food, antidote, 206
oxygen, 116
Pollution, 207
Pontoon boats, 62-63, 65
Pony bottle, 198-199
Positions, for victims, 207, 210
air embolism, 225

Positive buoyancy, 5, 20-21, 170
Precordial thump, 217
Pressure, 161-162
gauge and absolute, 171-172
gradient, hazard, 132-133: sinus cavities, 150-151
laws regarding, 162-169
Pressure gauge, 72, 73, 112, 113
hoses, 198
Prices
backpack and harness, 99
boats, 62, 63, 65
compressed-air tank, 73
exposure suit, 100, 103
fins, 52
flotation devices, 54-55, 57-58
gauges, 113
helmet, 40
hookah unit, 39
knife and sheaf, 108
mask, 43
regulator, 78-79
snorkel, 48
vision correction, 193, 194-195
Professional Association of Diving Instructors, x, 15
Publications, 301. *See also Emergency
Medicine; Skin Diver*
Puerto Rico, 282
Pulmonary barotrauma, 232
Puncture wounds, 207, 209
Purchasing equipment, 35-38
Purge devices, 45
buoyancy compensator, 56
mask, 135
regulator, 88, 118: artificial respiration, 217

Q

Quebec, province, Canada, 278
aquadoc, Montreal, 257
Question, signal for, 182
Questions, listing of, 293-298
Quick release harness, 95, 97, 98, 141,
143-144, 214

R

Rapture of deep, nitrogen narcosis, 137,
    161, 167, 168, 236, 238
Razor blade, first-aid tool, 204
Recompression, 225
    bends, the, 234, 235
    chambers, 226, 232, 234: listing of,
        262-282; supplier, 289
    nitrogen narcosis, 237
Red Sea, scuba divers, 173-175
Reef competence grading, 283-284
Refraction of light, 5, 152, 153
Regulator, 74-94
    alternatives to use, 69, 72
    artificial respiration, 216-217
    buoyancy compensator, 57
    ditch and don, 142
    donning equipment, 124: air tank,
        120
    failure, 72, 160
    mounting instructions, 116-118
    mouthpiece. See Mouthpiece
    octopus, 78-79, 125, 196-199
Repairing equipment, xvi, 195, 289
Residual nitrogen timetable, 229
Resort, diving, xii, 2
    instructors, 24
Respiratory system, 149-150
    ailments, 25-26, 150, 151
Resuscitation, 203, 214-217
    mouth-to-mouth, 209-211, 215-217
Retailers, number of, 2
Rhode Island, 160, 273
Royak, 63-64
Rust, problem of, 108, 109

S

Safety, degree of, 159-161
Safety aids, 52-59. See also Personal
    flotation devices
Safety measures. See also Buddy brea-
    thing; Buddy system; First aid; Fit-
    ness; Personal flotation devices;
    Resuscitation
    books on, 299-300

correcting visual flaws, 190-195
descent, 132-137
ditch and don, 140-143
entering and leaving water, 125-128:
    feetfirst diving, 45-46, 125
fixing equipment, 195
free ascent, 143-144
mouth-pull scuba rescue, 213-214
octopus rig, 78-79, 125, 196-199
preparing to submerge, 129-131
questions, listing of, 294
securing units: backpack, 95-98; oc-
    topus rig, 197, 198, 199
signaling, 179-180
Safety pins, first-aid tool, 205
Safety vest. See Life vest
Salvage, 242
San Diego, 155, 221, 256, 263
Schirra, Wally, 10
Scissors, first-aid tool, 204
Scuba, xvi, 1, 2, 35, 66-113
    books on, 299-301
    certification, 22-24, 292
    hunting forbidden, 249
    older people, 9-11
    parts and repair, firms, 289
    physical capacity, 24-26
    preparations, 114-128
    questions about, 294-295
    swim strokes, 27-34
    teenagers, 8
    watermanship guidelines, 15, 16
Sculling, 31
Seasickness, 205
Seawater, near-drowning in, 210
Securing, of equipment
    backpack, 95-98
    octopus regulator, 197, 198, 199
Self-confidence, 22
Self-inflating personal flotation devi-
    ces, 53-54
Sewing needles, 204, 208
Shallow-water blackout, 211-212
Shamlian, Ralph, 159, 160
Shark, signal for, 186
Ships, wreck diving, 239-242

archaeological search, 243-244
Shops, dive, xii, 35, 36
    air filling station, 90-91, 92, 93-94,
        223-224
    compressed-air tanks, 68
    instructors, 24
    wet suits: 100; care of, 104
Side roll technique, 126-127
Sight. *See* Vision
Signals, diving, 153-154, 179-188
Single-hose regulator, 75-76, 77-78, 88,
        90, 120
    artificial respiration, 216-217
    buoyancy compensator, 57
    ditch and don, 142
    octopus type, 197
Sinus cavities, 150-152, 162
    squeeze, 220-223
Size, apparent, water, 152-153
Sizes, signaling, 185
Skin breaks, treating, 207-209
    minor, 206
Skin Diver, magazine, x, 3
    diving suits, 100
    fitness, importance of, 156-157
    octopus scuba system, 78
    safety of sport, 159-160
Skin diving, xvi, xvii, 1, 2-3, 3-4, 35-65
    books about, 300-301
    surface dives, 31-34
Smoking, 8
Snively, W. D., 211-212
Snorkel diving, 1, 4-5, 38, 41-59
    spearfishing, 249-250
    swim strokes, 27-34
    youngsters, 7
Snorkel-to-mouth resuscitation, 214-215
Song, scuba diving, v
Sound barrier, underwater, 153
South Carolina, 273
South Dakota, 260, 273
Spasm, 207
Spaur, William H., 234-235
Spearfishing, 249-250
    breath holding, 41
Spectacles, 191-195

Speech, 153, 180
    Hellephone, 154-155
Spontaneous pneumothorax, 231-232
Spray decongestants, 223
Squeeze
    chest, 230-231
    ear, 151-152: sinus and, 220-223
    eye, 44-45
Standing clothes tree, 105
Statistics, diving, 1-3
Stewart, Don, x, 68, 93, 123-124
    overweighting, 107
    reef competence grading, 283-284
    underwater tools, 109
Storage
    air delivery system, 79, 90
    hookah unit, 39
    knife, 109
    snorkel tubes, 49
    wet suits, 104-105
Strap
    air tank, 118, 119-120
    camera, slipping round neck, 135
    fastening, dangers, 120, 124
    fins, 51, 52, 121, 122
    flotation devices, 53, 54, 55
    harness, 95, 97, 98, 138: ditch and
        don, 142-143
    mask, 41, 43, 122
Stress, 146, 147
    hyperventilation, 19-20
Submerging, preparation, 129-131
Suntan lotions, 206
Suppliers, listing of, 285-291
Surface air supply diving, 39-40
Surface dives, 31-34
Surface float, 38
Surface observations, 129, 130
Surgical tools, 204-205
Swimming requirements, 14-15
Swim strokes, 27-34

T

Tank-pressure gauge, 77, 116-117
    artificial respiration, 217
Tank/reserve valve, 70-71

Tank. *See* Compressed-air Tank
Tank valve, 117-118, 142
Teenagers, 8, 16-18
Temperature
    hazard, 155-156, 218-220: medicines, 157; signal, cold, 184
    pressure related to, 165-166
    wet suit and, 102, 104
Tennessee, 260
Terms, list of, 251-254
Testing. *See also* Inspection
    air supply, 92, 94
    hydrostatic, 66-67: equipment suppliers, 288
    leaks, checking for, 54, 116-117
Tetanus injection, 209
Texas, 260-261, 273-274
Therapy, diving as, 10-11
Thoracic squeeze, 231
Thread, surgical, 204, 208
Throckmorton, Peter, 243-244
Tilt valve, 197
Tire inner tubes, 59
Tongue depressor, 205
Tools, 107-110
Tourniquet, avoiding use of, 207
Toxicity, oxygen, 116
Trauma, 207
    barotrauma, 230-233
Traveling to dive, 250
    air travel hazardous, 225
    boat trips, xii
    vacation diving, 2-3
Treading water, 31
Treasure hunting, 240-242
Trendelenburg position, 210
Tripling, buddy system, 176-177
Tube, snorkel, 4, 5, 41, 46-49
Tweezers, first-aid tool, 204
Tympanic membrane, 132
Tzimoulis, Paul
    fitness, 156-157
    octopus regulator, 78

U

Unconsciousness, 211-212, 213-214
    carbon dioxide causes, 167
    cold temperatures, 155, 156, 218
    resuscitation, 214-217
Underwater dog paddle, 28
Underwater Explorers Club
    disabled persons, 11
    training older persons, 9-10
United States Naval Experimental Diving Unit, 225-226, 234
United States Naval Institute, heat loss effects, 155-156
United States Naval Oceanographic Office, 239
United States Navy, 114, 226
    inflatable suit, 99-100
    standard air decompression tables, 168, 169, 227-228
Utah, 261, 274

V

Vacation diving, 2-3
Valsalva Maneuver, 132, 222
Valves, 101, 197
    air-pressure reduction. *See* Regulator
    buoyancy compensator, 55, 56, 57, 58
    inflator, 123, 124
    purge, 56, 217
    snorkel, clearing, 47, 48
    tank, 68, 77: ditch and don, 142; filler, 69-74; O-ring, 117-118; tank/reserve, 70-71
Vein, injury to, 207
Vertigo, 195
Virginia, 261, 274-275
Virgin Islands, 282
Vision, 4-5, 41-43, 76, 152-153
    clearing mask, 133-135
    correcting visual flaws, 190-195
    eye squeeze, 44-45
Visual inspection, tank, 66, 68

W

Washington, state, 261, 275-276
Watch, 110-111, 113
  orientation, use for, 145
  suppliers of, 290-291
Watermanship, 13-14
  guidelines, 15-22
Water transportation, 60-65. *See also*
  Boats; Ships
Weather, importance of, 129, 130
Weight belt, 5, 106-107, 170, 195
  ascent, 200, 201: free, 143-144
  checkup, 120
  ditch and don, 140, 141, 142, 143
  frying pan attached, 154
Weightlessness, 21, 25
Weights, 106-107, 195
Wet suit, 99, 100, 102-105, 198
  buoyancy, 21, 22
  cold and, 16, 156, 220
  donning equipment, 123, 124
  inspection, 120
  suppliers, 288

Wisconsin, 261, 276
Women, 8-9
  eye squeeze, 44-45
  Japanese, 7
  snorkels, right size needed, 48
Word list, 251-254
Wounds, 205-206, 207-209
Wreck diving, 239-242
  archaeological search, 243-244
Writing, logging dives, 201-202
Writing, underwater, 180

Y

Yawning, 132, 133
YMCA, 8, 15, 23
Youngsters, 7
  snorkels, right size needed, 48
Youth, 8, 16-18

Z

Zipper, 105